Remembering a Vanished World

Remembering a Vanished World

A Jewish Childhood in Interwar Poland

Theodore S. Hamerow

Berghahn Books
NEW YORK • OXFORD

First published in 2001 by
Berghahn Books

www.berghahnbooks.com

© 2001 Theodore S. Hamerow

Library of Congress Cataloging-in-Publication Data

Hamerow, Theodore S.
    Remembering a vanished world : a Jewish childhood in interwar
Poland / Theodore S. Hamerow.
        p. cm.
    Includes bibliographical references (p.) and index.
    ISBN 1-57181-281-4 (alk. paper)
        1. Hamerow, Theodore S.–Childhood and youth. 2. Jews–
Poland–Warsaw–Biography. 3. Warsaw (Poland)–Biography.
4. Jews–Poland–Social conditions–20th century. 5. Warsaw
(Poland)–Ethnic relations. I. Title.

DS135.P63 H3564 2001
943.8'4–dc21
[B]   2001025782

British Library Cataloguing in Publication Data
A catalogue record for this book is available from
the British Library.

Printed in the United States on acid-free paper.

To the memory of Sterling Fishman

Contents

Preface

Most people in the twilight of life see the years of their childhood and adolescence through a warm, shimmering haze of nostalgia. Things were so different in the old days, they feel, so different and so much better. The world was simpler, gentler, kinder. Living conditions may have been more primitive, but they bred loyalties and values that are now being eroded or abandoned. As they look back at their youth, the elderly like to tell heartwarming stories about events in the distant past, they exchange anecdotes and reminiscences, they remember with affection relatives and friends who are no longer among the living, and sometimes they wonder when they will be joining those departed companions of their early years. Old age is a period of remembrance and reflection, of fond memories and gentle regrets.

The people who write memoirs and autobiographies frequently express in a more systematic or sophisticated way that same longing to recapture a bygone age, to recreate a vanished world. They may in general believe that they are simply describing what happened, that they are providing posterity with a factual, accurate account of its background and history. But more often than not, the passage of time distorts their recollection of events. Without realizing it, they too yield to the spell of nostalgia. Successes and rewards achieved fifty years before seem a little sweeter, disappointments and defeats a little less bitter. Relatives appear in retrospect more lovable, sweethearts more attractive, friends more devoted, and supporters more loyal. For that matter, even the rivals and adversaries of the past are now remembered as perhaps not quite so wicked or hateful. In short, the memoirist must always be on guard against the distortions that come with advancing years.

In writing about my own childhood in Poland during the 1920s, I have tried to keep in mind these dangers confronting the autobiographer. I have made a conscious effort not to allow the passage of time to prettify or idealize or heroize the past. I cannot of course be sure that I have always succeeded in escaping the risks of memoir writing. Here and there I may in fact have underestimated or even succumbed to them. But I can say that I have been aware of them, that I have taken them seriously, and that I have tried to the best of my ability to overcome them. What more can a memoirist do?

Although the problems I faced in writing this account of my early years are similar to those with which every autobiographer must grapple, there is an important respect in which my memoirs are different from most. While all of them try to recreate a vanished world, in the great majority of cases that world has vanished gradually and slowly with the passage of time. An older generation dies off, a younger one takes its place, customs change, values alter, loyalties shift, and in fifty years or so a new order replaces the old. That is the normal and unalterable process of social transformation. But the world about which I am writing, the world of Polish Jewry and indeed of East European Jewry as a whole, vanished not as the result of a gradual historical evolution but within the space of a few years, amid an outburst of genocidal fury exceeding in intensity anything previously experienced. The organized, systematic extermination of millions of people because of their cultural identity or ethnic origin was until then not only unprecedented but almost inconceivable. The society in which I grew up and of which I was part stood unawares on the brink of an unspeakable tragedy.

That tragedy lies not only in the physical extermination of the Jews of Eastern Europe. The ideological world in which they lived, their hopes and beliefs, their struggles and aspirations, these have sometimes been forgotten as well. The excitement of their formative intellectual experiences, when an old traditional order was slowly dying and a new challenging era of cultural and social reconstruction was emerging, has for many of us become a dim memory. Not only has the material existence of the Jewish community been destroyed by the Holocaust, but its historical image has often become distorted and obscured. The passage of time has too frequently had the effect of sugarcoating, of sentimentalizing a way of life that was harsh and demanding yet full of promise and excitement.

To be sure, there is a large and growing body of historical scholarship, centered in the United States and Israel, which deals with the collective experience of the East European Jewish community. Yet there is still a widespread popular perception of that community as essentially not much more than the touching, sentimental story portrayed in a popular

Broadway musical. There are those quaint little men in caftans and black hats, the women in shawls and kerchiefs, singing about sunrise and sunset, about the flow of years, and about happiness and tears. All this amid the faint aroma of grandma's chicken soup and chopped liver, cheese blintzes and gefilte fish. It seems a little saccharine, a little syrupy. Those who perished in the Holocaust deserve a deeper and more sophisticated understanding of the rich diversity of their vanished way of life.

And that brings me back to my reason for deciding to write these recollections of a childhood in interwar Poland. I cannot deny that I too felt an urge to look back at my early years, to remember amusing incidents, to tell interesting stories, to recall the world in which I grew up. Yet I do not believe that I would have succumbed to that urge if it had merely reflected the longing felt by so many people in the twilight of life to recapture the experiences of their youth. What persuaded me to embark on this autobiographical account was the hope that it might in a small way help broaden the common perception of the way of life of East European Jewry.

Admittedly, I cannot claim that I have always resisted the temptation to digress a little, to dwell occasionally on events or incidents that have a purely personal meaning for me. But in general I have tried to emphasize those recollections that might to some extent throw light on the vanished world in which I grew up. I have done so almost out of a sense of obligation, as a sort of moral debt to those among whom I once lived, whom I left only a few years before a great catastrophe overwhelmed them, and whose tragic fate I narrowly escaped. I rarely thought about them in the past, excluding them, deliberately perhaps, from my consciousness. But now, with the passage of time, I have strangely come to feel closer to them than ever before. I remember them more clearly, I think about them more frequently. These reminiscences represent in a sense a loving farewell embrace of those long-ago departed companions of my childhood.

Finally, I should add that in writing about the vanished world of East European Jewry, I received advice and encouragement from a number of friends and colleagues whose assistance I should acknowledge. John Milton Cooper, Jr., Richard Leffler, and Irving S. Saposnick read the manuscript in its entirety and gave me valuable suggestions for its improvement. David Wetzel helped me find a suitable publisher. And my wife Diane offered support and reassurance whenever the going got rough, which was fairly often. My heartfelt thanks to all of them.

Introduction: *Ancestral Faith and Modernist Rebellion*

The half-century preceding the Holocaust was a period of exciting change and promising renewal in the history of the Jews of Eastern Europe. The traditional foundation of their community, the religious faith that shaped their sense of identity for more than a thousand years, had begun to give way to new ideas, beliefs, and allegiances. There was a spreading conviction among them that protection against the persecutions of a hostile world should no longer be left to divine mercy and intervention. They began to believe more and more that only some process of adaptation, secularization, and modernization could achieve for them a position of equality within a Christian society that had traditionally regarded them as inherently and dangerously alien. This is not to deny that orthodox religion remained a powerful force in the life of East European Jewry. But it was a force increasingly on the defensive against its modernist and secularist critics. The bitter struggle within the Jewish community between the supporters of an old order and the advocates of a new one continued unabated until the Holocaust destroyed them both.

The ideological divisions among the Jews of Eastern Europe, however, did not simply separate traditionalists from modernizers. Among the modernizers themselves there were sharp differences regarding the form that secularization should take. A small but influential minority favored the strategy that the German Jews had adopted about a hundred years earlier, the strategy of total cultural assimilation. They shaved off their beards and cut their earlocks; they exchanged the black coats and skullcaps of their fathers for the modern dress of their Christian neighbors; they became indistinguishable in style and manner from their gentile compatriots. More than that, they sought to identify with the dominant national culture by speaking only Russian in Russia, Polish in

Poland, Hungarian in Hungary, and Romanian in Romania. By their unremitting efforts at adaptation they hoped to refute the age-old charge that the Jews were incurably clannish and cliquish.

Some of them even converted to Christianity to prove their loyalty to the country of their birth. They became Catholic in Poland and Hungary or Orthodox in Russia and Romania. But those were exceptions. Most of the assimilated Jews of Eastern Europe remained faithful, at least nominally, to their ancestral religion. Nevertheless, they insisted that they were just as loyal to the nation, just as patriotic, as their non-Jewish neighbors. They were Russians or Poles or Hungarians or Romanians of the "Mosaic persuasion," indistinguishable except in religious belief from those of their countrymen who happened to be of the "Christian persuasion." The fact that the latter generally refused to acknowledge this indistinguishability failed to shake the faith of the assimilationists that some day they would. They continued to believe to the tragic end that their strenuous, untiring efforts at adaptation would ultimately be rewarded with complete social and cultural acceptance.

Most of the secularized Jews of Eastern Europe did not follow this strategy, however. They found it not only economically too demanding but psychologically too demeaning. To adopt the styles and customs of well-to-do Christian society required financial resources that few of them possessed. Worse still, it demanded a suppression of beliefs and loyalties in which they had grown up and to which they still remained in some measure attached. Nor did the dominant culture really encourage assimilation. Those Jews who sought to become like their gentile neighbors soon discovered that their efforts were largely futile, that they continued to be regarded as incorrigibly foreign. There was always something about them that was not quite right: their appearance, their speech, their dress, their manner, their mentality, or some other ineffable, indefinable quality that stamped them as eternal aliens. Acceptance seemed to remain just beyond their grasp, however long or hard they tried.

The rebellion against traditional forms of Jewish life in Eastern Europe was thus forced into a direction different from that followed in Western or Central Europe. Its supporters began to advocate the establishment of a culturally and socially autonomous secular community within the framework of existing national boundaries. After all, Poland, to take an example, had large Ukrainian, German, and White Russian minorities inside its frontiers, each seeking to retain a separate identity under Polish rule. A similar diversity of nationalities existed elsewhere in the region, in Russia, for instance, or Romania. Why then should not the Jews seek a similar status, that of a distinct, officially recognized ethnic community established on a nonreligious foundation of language, history, and culture? The goal seemed not only reasonable but attainable.

Yet what ought to be the guiding ideology of this new Jewish community? What should replace the bond of faith that had been the unifying force of the old community? On that point there was sharp disagreement. The opening decades of the twentieth century were a period of endless fierce debate among the Jews of Eastern Europe regarding the fundamental nature of their community, its purpose, its direction, and its ultimate destiny. Not since the Roman occupation of Palestine some two thousand years before had there been a disputation of such scope and intensity regarding the essential character of Judaism. The orthodox argued with the secularists, the assimilationists with the separatists, the Zionists with the anti-Zionists, the liberals with the socialists, and the socialists with the communists. East European Jewry was in a ferment of heated argumentation. Nothing seemed more important than the outcome of this struggle of ideologies, neither the First World War nor the fall of the old imperial order nor the establishment of the succession states nor the domestic politics of the postwar years nor even the onset of the Great Depression. The crucial issue was the nature of the new Jewish community that was in the process of being born. Only the Second World War put an end to the debate by putting an end to those who were debating.

I was born on August 24, 1920, in Warsaw, during that great, fierce debate, at what was also a critical moment in the history of the newly established Polish Republic. That spring a bitter boundary dispute with Russia had led to the outbreak of hostilities between the two countries in which neither was able to gain a decisive victory. First the Poles, led by Joseph Pilsudski, hero of the national struggle for independence, advanced deep into the Ukraine and captured Kiev. Then the Russians under the most gifted of the Bolshevik generals, Mikhail Tukhachevsky, whom Stalin later rewarded for his services with a death sentence, launched a successful counterattack. By late summer they stood on the outskirts of Warsaw. What was at stake now was no longer merely Poland's eastern frontier. It was Poland's survival. But then the Poles initiated a counterattack of their own, forcing the Russian troops into retreat. The seesaw struggle finally came to an end in October, when a peace treaty established the fiercely contested boundary roughly midway between the points of farthest advance by the opposing armies.

My mother who, like many accomplished raconteurs, refused to let mere facts stand in the way of a good story, used to tell me when I was young that I had been born during that "miracle on the Vistula," the successful Polish offensive which drove the Bolsheviks back from the gates of the capital. That was something of an exaggeration. The decisive battle had actually taken place more than a week earlier, and by the time I appeared the Russian forces were already in retreat. But no matter. The early 1920s were indeed a crucial period for the new Poland, a period of privation, danger, struggle, and ultimate triumph.

They were also a crucial period for the Jewish community of Poland, but for different reasons. To the Poles the overriding issue was the establishment of an independent national state after more than a century of partition and oppression. The Jews, on the other hand, though not indifferent to the military and political struggles raging around them, were more concerned with a conflict of their own, an ideological conflict regarding the nature and destiny of their community. That conflict had begun much earlier, during the 1880s, and had then continued with increasing vehemence until 1939. It was a result of the gradual decline of the religious faith that had served as the unifying cultural force of East European Jewry. And that decline in turn led to a quest for some alternate central principle or belief that could serve as the foundation for a new sense of community. This quest continued to preoccupy the Jews of Poland with growing intensity throughout the half century preceding the Second World War.

Essentially, what accounted for the decline of the traditional beliefs and loyalties that had provided the cohesive force in Jewish life for almost two millennia was what accounted for the transformation of European society as a whole. A great social revolution resulting from industrialization and urbanization had profound consequences for Jews and non-Jews alike. It led to the displacement of small artisan shops and neighborhood stores by large factories and commercial establishments. That in turn had the effect of rigidifying economic differences and class distinctions. It became increasingly difficult for the skilled workingman to rise from apprentice to journeyman and then to master craftsman. The gulf between employer and employee, between mill owner and mill hand, began to widen until it was almost impassable. Jewish workers in Poland were generally not employed in large industrial enterprises. They were more likely to be found in small and middle-sized shops or factories. But they too were becoming increasingly segregated, isolated, and stratified. For the first time a permanent industrial proletariat began to emerge among the Jews of Eastern Europe.

The position of Jewish storeowners and shopkeepers was also changing. The smaller ones were growing increasingly dependent on the larger ones, serving as their subcontractors, suppliers, or auxiliaries. They were still able to retain a measure of independence and even prosper under the new economic order. But their freedom of action, their ability to make decisions regarding output, marketing, and distribution, was shrinking. They too were experiencing the effects of economic and social rigidification. The relative class fluidity of East European Jewry, a result in part of the common experience of prejudice and oppression, was congealing under the pressure of industrialization. A new age was beginning for the Jewish bourgeoisie of Poland as well.

Underlying this economic transformation, partly its cause, partly its effect, was the growing shift of the Jewish population from towns and villages to the large cities. This was a process taking place throughout Europe, among non-Jews as well as Jews. The Jewish migration from Ozorkov, Berdichev, Ostrov, and Chelm to Warsaw, Lodz, Vilna, and Lublin was similar to the migration of Englishmen to Manchester, Frenchmen to Lille, Germans to Essen, and Italians to Turin. The motives were essentially the same and the consequences were the same as well. Most of the Jewish migrants to the big city settled in dreary slums, where they lived generally in a state of permanent privation. In their new, unfamiliar environment, the bonds of faith and piety that had shaped life in the small town began to unravel. A spirit of rebelliousness started to emerge, leading to a bitter generational struggle. This struggle was manifested in a rejection of the values and morals of the old order. It engendered a spreading demand for some new ideal on which to build the Jewish community. The years around the turn of the century thus became a period of ferment and excitement for East European Jewry.

This profound cultural transformation can be seen or at least sensed in the works of the first generation of major Yiddish writers, writers like Mendele Moykher Sforim, Sholem Aleichem, and Isaac Leib Peretz. They still portrayed by and large the old familiar world of Jewish tradition, belief, and morality. But here and there could be caught glimpses, sometimes more than glimpses, of changing attitudes and values, of a quest for some new definition of communal purpose and destiny. Sholem Aleichem's Tevye the dairyman remains loyal to the customs and teachings of the ancestral faith. He represents the older generation, still obedient to the commandments of Jewish orthodoxy.

But his daughters display the new spirit of rebelliousness that is growing among the young people. One of them refuses to accept the suitor chosen for her by her father, deciding instead to marry the man she loves. Another marries a political revolutionary, joining him in his exile to Siberia to which he had been condemned for opposing czarism. And still another breaks her father's heart by marrying a gentile, thereby accepting permanent exclusion from the Jewish community. Tevye can only watch in anguish as the world in which he had grown up starts to fall apart.

The disintegration of the old order can be seen even more clearly in Peretz's writings. Most of them still deal with the familiar themes of Jewish literature. *The Golden Chain*, for example, one of his best-known works, portrays the conflict between religious idealism and economic exigency. But occasionally, especially in his short stories, there are disturbing portrayals of the unraveling of the moral fabric of East European Jewry.

Peretz's *Four Generations, Four Wills* is a good example. Here he presents the fictional testaments of four members of successive generations in a well-to-do Jewish family. The first testament, that of a pious, prosperous merchant, urges his heirs to remain in the lumber business, to repair the roof of the synagogue, and to provide a gate for the cemetery. The second, his son's, is much more detailed. He exhorts his heirs to continue to observe Jewish customs and traditions, revealing his inner doubts about their religious steadfastness. The third will, this one written in Polish, is that of "Moritz Benditsohn," the son of Reb Benjamin-Chaikils and grandson of Reb Eliezer-Chaikils. It requests that his funeral service be delayed until his son, who resides in Paris, can be summoned home, and that a "learned scholar" instead of his returning heir be asked to recite the traditional prayer for the dead. The last will is that of the errant son of Moritz Benditsohn. Having tasted all the pleasures and temptations of life, sated, alienated, and spiritually empty, he is now preparing to commit suicide. Peretz presents in five or six pages a frightening portrayal of the disintegration of traditional values in the Jewish community of Poland.

Most members of that community faced problems of a different sort, however. Their impoverishment was not only spiritual but material. In the small towns and villages of their birth, the prescriptions of custom and religion had effectively controlled private conduct. There were strong social pressures inhibiting delinquent forms of behavior. But in the slums of the big city, in which more and more Jews now lived, those restraints rapidly weakened. The uprooted, alienated dweller of the urban ghetto became indifferent to what relatives, friends, and neighbors might think or say. He was less concerned about rabbinical censure or even divine displeasure. He became more independent, more assertive, more unscrupulous, more ruthless. He began to resemble the inhabitants of the slums of London, Paris, or Berlin. The big cities of Eastern Europe became a breeding ground for Jewish pickpockets, burglars, extortionists, prostitutes, and pimps. The pious and respectable preferred to look the other way, to pretend that the problem of mass demoralization did not really exist. But it was proving increasingly difficult for even the most otherworldly members of the community to go on ignoring the erosion of traditional values and beliefs among big-city Jews.

The first generation of Yiddish writers generally shared this reluctance to dwell on the moral unraveling of their society. They preferred to depict the vanishing world of small-town loyalties and pieties in which they had grown up. But shortly before the First World War the Jewish community was scandalized by a dramatic work that graphically portrayed the seamy underside of life in the ghetto. In his *God of Vengeance* the young Sholem Asch, still in his twenties, depicted unsparingly the moral corruption behind a facade of religious conformity that had become part of life in the urban slums. What outraged public opinion was not only the play's cautious but unmistakable suggestion of lesbianism, not only its portrayal of a Jew who is the proprietor of a bawdyhouse. It was also the presentation of two pillars of Jewish respectability, a scribe and a broker, who know what business the protagonist of the play is in, and yet encourage him to assume the considerable expense of preparing a handwritten copy of the Torah with which he hopes to bribe God into granting him forgiveness. This implicit condemnation of religious hypocrisy appeared to many Jews of the older generation shockingly impious.

Their outcry was loud enough to delay the production of the play for three years. It finally appeared on the stage in 1910, but not in Poland or anywhere else in Eastern Europe, for that matter. The first performance was given in German at the Deutches Theater in Berlin under the direction of Max Reinhardt. To that extent the sensibilities of the old order were spared. But to members of the younger generation Asch became the spokesman for a growing cultural rebellion against the orthodox tradition. They saw in him the Jewish Gerhart Hauptmann or Maxim Gorky. He was stripping away the pretensions and dissimulations of the existing social order. He was revealing the harsh realities of life in the urban ghetto. He was helping to create a new culture reflecting the everyday experiences of the impoverished Jews of Poland and Russia. The controversy surrounding Asch's drama was a sign of the bitter struggle within East European Jewry between opposing values, loyalties, beliefs, and aspirations. It was part of a conflict between ancestral faith and modernist rebellion that continued until the destruction of the Jewish community during the Second World War.

That the modernists were gradually gaining the upper hand in this conflict seems indisputable. And yet the old order retained considerable strength. It may have had greater support in the smaller towns and villages than in Warsaw, Lodz, Bialystok, or Lvov. But it had its followers in the large cities as well. They could be seen everywhere in interwar Poland, wearing those distinctive black coats and hats, with long beards and earlocks, scrupulously observing the intricate rules and ceremonials of their orthodox faith, studying the sacred writings with tireless zeal, regarding their rabbi with almost the same reverential devotion as God himself, maintaining in public the strict separation of the sexes, and insisting on a purely religious education for their children, an education undefiled by secular knowledge. They lived in a world of their own, determined to defend the one true faith against the assaults of skepticism and godlessness. That resolve gave them the strength to maintain their separate identity in the rapidly changing environment of East European Jewry.

To the anti-Semitic movement throughout the Continent, however, the pious Jews were a visible warning against the danger threatening Christian cultural values. They could be seen peering slyly out of countless racist cartoons and caricatures, dressed in those outlandish costumes, hook-nosed and shifty-eyed, servile but cunning, compliant but untrustworthy. How could anyone believe that people so different in character and temperament would ever become truly assimilated into non-Jewish society. They might assume the outward manner and appearance of their Christian neighbors, but inwardly they would remain eternally alien.

This widespread belief also helped deepen the gulf between the pious and the assimilated Jews of Europe. The latter looked down on the former as ignorant, superstitious, crude, and distasteful in dress and speech. But even worse, the pious made more difficult the task of those who were trying to become indistinguishable from educated, well-to-do gentiles. The Jewish communities of Germany, Austria, and Hungary, whose members had tried so long and so hard to find acceptance as real Germans, Austrians, or Hungarians, were embarrassed by their coreligionists to the east who provided a constant reminder of the insurmountable differences between the genuine and the spurious heirs to the nation's cultural legacy. For that matter, the assimilated Jews of Eastern Europe regarded the orthodox believers with distaste as well. Even those members of the Jewish community in Poland who had become secularized without becoming Polonized viewed the pious traditionalists with condescension as uneducated and unenlightened.

The latter responded in kind. Feeling besieged, surrounded by Jewish as well as non-Jewish opponents, they became increasingly intolerant and fanatical. Their anger was directed against secularized Jews even more than against Christians. The Christians after all did not know any better. They simply believed what they had been taught. But the secularized Jews were traitors, apostates. Though brought up in the true faith of the Torah, they had chosen to desert it. That was inexcusable. The pious regarded the impious with loathing; they shunned, cursed, and anathematized them. And yet this intolerance, this zealotry, also made it possible for them to withstand the reality of declining numbers and diminishing influence. It gave them the strength to face bigotry, oppression, and privation. Later it even helped some of them survive the genocidal fury of National Socialism.

At the opposite end of the ideological spectrum of East European Jewry were the assimilationists. They were proportionately not nearly as numerous as those in Central Europe, but their view of the problem of Jewish identity and destiny was basically the same. They too believed that escape from bigotry and discrimination could be found only in a complete identification with the national society and culture. It was therefore of the utmost importance to demonstrate their indistinguishability in speech, dress, custom, and sometimes religion. They were eager to show that they were as loyal, as patriotic, as their gentile neighbors, perhaps more so. They even displayed at times the same disapproval and condescension toward the various ethnic minorities, including the Jews. Cultural and social acceptance became their overriding concern. To gain that acceptance they were prepared to disavow their own origin, background, and tradition.

Some of them were rewarded for their pursuit of assimilation by achieving considerable prominence. They became participants or even leaders in the cultural life of Poland: Julian Tuwim and Józef Wittlin in literature, Szymon Askenazy and Marceli Handelsman in historiography,

Julian Klaczko in literary criticism, Maurycy Gottlieb in art, and Arnold Szyfman in the theater. Careers such as those seemed to demonstrate that identification with the dominant society was the best way to escape from the cultural ghetto of Jewish life. Only the Second World War proved beyond any doubt how tragically mistaken this view was.

Yet there were even earlier signs that assimilation was not a panacea for anti-Semitic discrimination. Those who tried it seemed, like Tantalus in the underworld, so close to their goal and yet never quite able to reach it. Their professions of loyalty to national aspirations and ideals, however sincere, however fervent, could not silence the mutterings and grumblings about the "Judaization" of Polish culture, or about the excessive Semitic influence in public life, or about the cunning exploitation of Christian naiveté by Jewish guile. To most Polish Jews it became apparent that assimilation was not a solution to the problems confronting them.

They would not have been able to adopt that solution in any case, even if they had wanted to. They generally lacked the cultural and financial resources needed for acceptance into genteel Polish society. How could the impoverished Jewish masses, oppressed, scorned, and alienated, regard assimilation as an attainable goal? Nor did they really want to become indistinguishable from the Poles. They were too attached to their own traditions and values. What they sought was to achieve equality as a separate and distinct ethnic community within the national state. Such ethnic communities, each with its own language, tradition, history, and sometimes religion, were common in Eastern Europe. To seek to add one more to the mosaic of autonomous nationalities and cultures did not seem unrealistic. In fact, that became the objective of a growing number of East European Jews.

What they sought, however, was not simply a recognition of the old religious community as an autonomous ethnic institution. They had become too estranged from the orthodox faith for that. Although many of them still observed, sometimes perfunctorily, the important customs and ceremonials of traditional religion, they had no wish to remain under the spiritual supervision of the rabbi and the synagogue. They were becoming, often without fully realizing it, secularized. The period beginning in the late nineteenth century thus became for Polish Jewry a time of heated discussion and controversy regarding its future, the most exciting period since the establishment of the Jewish community in Poland during the Middle Ages. Out of that impassioned debate emerged a new concept of Jewish collective identity and destiny.

This concept represented a sharp break with the beliefs that had molded the cultural outlook of East European Jewry. It did not rest on religious faith as defined in the Torah and the Talmud. It sought rather a new foundation for the spiritual life of the Jewish community in ethical principles independent of divine sanction. The supporters of this transformation were ideological revolutionaries. They wanted to create for the Jews of Poland and Russia a new secular culture the vehicle of which would be the Yiddish language. They regarded the orthodox teachings of Judaism as incapable of providing a sound basis for a modern, enlightened, progressive Jewish society. Such a society required more than piety. It required a faith independent of supernatural forces or scriptural injunctions. If being English, French, German, or Polish was ceasing to depend on religious belief, why should being Jewish continue to depend on it? If the Christians were increasingly willing to divorce morality from theology, why not the Jews?

The elevation of Yiddish from popular jargon to literary idiom was an essential part of the process of modernization advocated by the secularists. Hitherto it had been the common vehicle of communication at home and in the marketplace, without cultural pretensions or scholarly aspirations. The language of learning had been Hebrew. But to the new movement for Jewish secularization Hebrew appeared too closely associated with religious faith and observance. It was the handmaid of piety and orthodoxy. Yiddish, in contrast, was the speech of the masses, familiar, homey, and free of ties to traditional religion. It seemed the natural cultural vehicle for the modernization of Jewish life. Its transformation into a language of literature and learning became therefore an essential part of the movement to secularize the Jewish community without destroying its Jewishness.

Admittedly, not all Polish Jews favored this form of secularization. The assimilationists saw in it an additional obstacle to the only solution for the problem of anti-Semitism, namely, a complete identification with the dominant society and culture. Hence the secularists, because of their insistence on the essential separateness of Jews from Poles, seemed not much better than the religionists. Both were making the task of acceptance through acculturation more difficult. Still, the assimilationists were only a small, isolated group on the fringes of Polish Jewry, prosperous and successful but with little influence over the Jewish community as a whole. Their views carried even less weight among Jews than among Poles.

The opposition of the orthodox believers was more important. The defenders of traditional religion, still numerous and intransigent, saw little difference between the assimilationists and the secularists. Each was an enemy of Judaism, each was a traitor and apostate, because each rejected the true faith of the Torah. The sacred task of every real Jew was to observe strictly the scriptural commandments as expressions of the divine will. Those who failed to do so were traitors to God, whether they spoke Yiddish or Polish, whether they favored cultural assimilation or ethnic separateness. There could be no compromise with them. The struggle between the religionists and the secularists continued without interruption until the German invasion of Poland in 1939 put an end to it once and for all.

By then, however, it was already clear which side was likely to prevail. Throughout the preceding five or six decades the orthodox community had been steadily losing adherents to the secularist movement. To be sure, the religious traditionalists remained a powerful force in Jewish life. They could still be seen in their distinctive dress and demeanor wherever Polish Jews lived, relatively more numerous in small towns and villages, somewhat less visible in the big cities. But even in the largest urban centers there were sizable orthodox congregations fiercely loyal to the ancestral faith and bitterly opposed to the new currents of modernization and secularization.

They were nevertheless clearly losing strength. More and more Jews, especially of the younger generation, were beginning to move away from traditional religion. This did not mean in most cases a sudden and complete rejection of the teachings of Judaism. Yet the observance of those teachings was becoming more sporadic and perfunctory. A newborn male child might still undergo the *brith*, the ceremony of circumcision; on his thirteenth birthday a boy might still celebrate his *bar mitzvah*, his religious admission to manhood; the death of a parent might still be mourned with a recital of the *kaddish*, the traditional prayer for the dead. But weekly attendance at Sabbath services in the synagogue was becoming less common, and the numerous private prayers required of the orthodox were being said even less frequently. For that matter, those pious rites and ceremonials which continued to be observed increasingly reflected habit and custom rather than any profound religious faith.

The other side of the process of secularization was the emergence among the Jews of Eastern Europe of a new, exciting, worldly culture expressed generally in the Yiddish language. It resembled in many respects the older secular cultures of the Continent, although there were also significant differences derived primarily from the unique

social structure of the Jewish community. The gap between high culture and low culture, between the taste of the patriciate and the taste of
the masses, was much narrower in the life of East European Jewry. That
meant that Yiddish literature, Yiddish learning, the Yiddish theater,
and the Yiddish press were more folksy and homey, more accessible and
popular, than in most Continental cultures. Highbrow drama appeared
side by side with lowbrow comedy; edifying serious novels and sentimental short stories, learned disquisitions and sensational shockers,
serious plays and lurid melodramas, all came pouring out in a great
outburst of creative energy suddenly released within the Jewish community. In the course of two or three generations the cultural life of the
Jews of Eastern Europe became transformed.

That transformation was discernible first of all in the new Jewish
press which emerged in the urban centers of Poland, Russia, and Romania. All the big cities and many of the small ones had their daily Yiddish newspaper, sometimes two or three, each with its distinctive style,
outlook, and ideology. There was also a flourishing periodical literature:
weeklies, monthlies, and quarterlies dealing with local or regional or
national affairs, some promoting an appreciation of belles lettres, others satisfying a popular interest in sensationalism, some devoutly pious
in tone, others defiantly secular, some apolitical, others liberal, socialist, or Zionist in sympathy. They provide a revealing insight into the
entire range of concerns of East European Jewry: local gossip and ethnic destiny, work and recreation, experience and aspiration, hopes and
fears, affections and resentments, likes and dislikes. They constitute the
most valuable single source of information regarding the vanished
world of everyday Jewish life.

Today the fragments of this cultural legacy, the parts that were not
destroyed during the Second World War, lie yellowing and crumbling
in obscure archives, neglected not only by non-Jewish scholars in the
countries where they originated, but often also by Jewish scholars in
Israel and America who prefer to deal with other periods and other
regions in the long, sprawling history of world Jewry. For the Jews of
Eastern Europe the tragedy of the Holocaust has meant not only
destruction but to a large extent oblivion.

Some understanding of who and what they were can still be gained,
however, from another source: the brief flowering of Yiddish literature
during the half century preceding the Second World War. Starting with
Mendele Moykher Sforim in the 1870s and ending with Israel Joshua
Singer in the 1930s, a group of gifted writers left a vivid fictional portrayal

of the life and culture of the Jewish community of Eastern Europe. In fact, a few of them, Isaac Bashevis Singer, for example, continued to depict the ethnic milieu in which they had grown up long after the Second World War. Their works provide a moving literary re-creation of a vanished historical reality. They help keep alive the memory of an ancestral way of life which now seems so strange and distant, but which persisted and flourished until almost the day before yesterday.

Admittedly, not everything those authors wrote was a sober, factual account of the Jewish experience. Some of them, especially in the early years, tended to look back with a gentle nostalgia at the social milieu of the shtetl which they had known in their childhood and which was being increasingly replaced by the bleak realities of big-city life. Sometimes they portrayed a pastoral, idyllic past which had never been as rosy or innocent as they recalled. Yet even at their most arcadian, they never ignored or obscured the hardships endured by the Jews of Eastern Europe, the prejudices, oppressions, discriminations, cruelties, and hatreds. Their realism, moreover, their willingness to portray the everyday experiences of the ghetto in unsparing detail, grew with the passage of time. By the 1920s and 1930s the lapses into nostalgia and sentimentality characteristic of the early years of Yiddish literature had largely given way to an unflinching, critical, and sometimes harsh portrayal of life in the Jewish slums of Eastern Europe. The last nostalgic illusions about existence in the ghettos of Poland and Russia were now vanishing.

The new Yiddish theater reflected the changing outlook of East European Jewry almost as vividly as the new Yiddish literature. Both emerged at roughly the same time, the closing decades of the nineteenth century, and from similar sources in the popular culture. In one case, folk tales in the vernacular handed down from generation to generation provided the basis for a formal structure of literary expression. In the other, itinerant groups of players, storytellers, musicians, and dancers became the forerunners of an organized theater through a process similar to that by which theatrical institutions developed in most European countries. Indeed, in the Jewish communities of Poland such wandering companies of entertainers continued to appear before lower-class audiences until the outbreak of the Second World War. They would present funny sketches, tell off-color jokes, perform vaudeville acts, and do risqué parodies for a public whose daily life rarely provided an opportunity for amusement. Without realizing it, they became pioneers of the Yiddish theater, continuing to the end to provide a sizable part of its standard repertoire.

The entertainment offered by these migrant players would typically include some irreverent scenes poking fun at the pious and respectable. A woman comes to the rabbi to complain that she has been treated by her husband so badly that she has started to waste away. To prove her point, she places his hands around her waist, shocking and embarrassing the devout man of God. The audience roars with laughter. Or a good-looking young man appears on the stage, a naughty gleam in his eye, a suggestive smile on his face, to sing about how nice it would be if his sweetheart would only let him do what he would so much like to do. Everybody knows what he means. The men guffaw loudly; the women giggle and titter in embarrassment. Everybody goes home in good spirits, ready to face the trials and tribulations of tomorrow.

The lowbrow theater of the wandering entertainers, however, was soon overtaken by the highbrow theater of formal dramaturgy. About twenty years after Mendele Moykher Sforim became the founder of serious Yiddish literature, Jacob Gordin helped initiate the writing of serious Yiddish plays. A century later those plays seem rather artificial and melodramatic; they sound like the sentimental soap operas of the age of radio and television. And yet they represent a major step beyond the song and dance tradition, the jokes and pratfalls, of the itinerant vaudeville companies. They seek to portray the changing way of life of East European Jews in a new, more realistic style. *Mirele Efros*, for example, Gordin's most popular play, depicts a widowed businesswoman who decides unwisely to yield control over the family's wealth to her weak, indecisive son and his conniving wife, only to discover, like King Lear, that a thankless child is worse than a serpent's tooth. The point, though well-taken, is trite. Three hundred years earlier Shakespeare had said the same thing more eloquently. Still, the real significance of Gordin's drama lies not in its artistic merit but in its evocation of the social milieu of Jewish merchants, shopowners, brokers, and promoters in czarist Russia.

In any event, within a decade the concept of the Yiddish theater as a vehicle of gentility and uplift was challenged by the appearance of Scholem Asch's *God of Vengeance*. A vast gulf separates the well-bred, respectable Mirele Efros from the guilt-ridden brothel owner Yankel Chapchovich. Defying the Victorian sensibilities which still dominated the European stage, Asch rudely tore away the veil of reticence surrounding the criminal underworld of the Jewish community whose existence had until then not even been acknowledged. The new currents of realism and naturalism transforming European dramaturgy now reached the Yiddish stage as well. Its willingness to declare openly that not all Jews were chaste, pious, and saintly, that there were also thieves and whores and pimps among them, was a measure of the growing self-confidence of the youthful secular culture of East European Jewry.

Not long after the appearance of Asch's scandalizing play, another major contribution to the new Yiddish dramaturgy portrayed an entirely different aspect of Jewish life. Peretz Hirschbein's *Green Fields* is far removed from the harsh existence of the urban slums depicted in the *God of Vengeance*. It resembles rather the nostalgic, sentimental accounts of life in the small towns and villages of Poland and Russia written a generation earlier by the pioneers of Yiddish literature. Hirschbein tells the story of a shy young religious student who is invited to stay with a family of Jewish farmers, simple folk with little education and less refinement, but kind and goodhearted. Little by little he becomes accustomed to their rustic ways, their innocent piety and joy in life, deciding in the end to marry one of the daughters and become part of their community. The play could easily have degenerated into just another sunny, heartwarming depiction of bucolic contentment. But it is written with so much charm, so much genuine warmth and affection, that it is bound to win over the grumpiest, the most dyspeptic of theatergoers. It is something rare in Jewish literature: an endearing pastoral idyll.

The best-known achievement of the Yiddish theater, however, the one which has endured the longest and has gained the greatest acclaim, is *The Dybbuk* by S. Ansky, the pen name of Solomon Zanvel Rappoport. A story of Hasidic mysticism, of broken vows and divine retribution, of wandering spirits and tormented ghosts, of rabbinical spells and religious exorcisms, it has fascinated audiences of Jews and non-Jews alike with its evocation of the exotic world of Jewish orthodoxy. Truth to tell, some of its admirers, especially those who did not know much about the spiritual world of East European Jewry, found the play interesting for the same reason they found Japanese kabuki theater or traditional East Indian choreography interesting. It was so unusual and outlandish, so different from what they were accustomed to seeing on the stage. But to those familiar with the religious beliefs and traditions of Hasidism, Ansky's drama was a brilliant artistic evocation of the orthodox Jewish community whose faith remained undiminished even while its following was slowly shrinking.

An even more important source of information regarding the changing world of the Jews of Eastern Europe is Yiddish scholarship, not as colorful or dramatic as Yiddish literature or Yiddish theater, but more comprehensive and balanced. Beginning in the second half of the nineteenth century, three successive generations of Jewish historians, economists, sociologists, and political scientists undertook a critical examination of the ethnic community of which they were part. Some of them wrote in Russian, Polish, or German, but most used Yiddish for the first time as a language of learning. The best-known of these scholars was Simon Dubnow, who for more than fifty years studied and depicted the historical experience of East European Jewish society, perishing in the end amid the terrible catastrophe which had overtaken that society. For him, as for almost all other members of the new school of Jewish learning, the ultimate goal was the establishment of a secular ethnic community institutionally autonomous and culturally distinct, employing Yiddish as its principal means of expression and communication.

The achievement of that goal became the primary purpose of various learned organizations and societies, most of which emerged during the interwar period. Chief among them was the Jewish Scientific Institute (YIVO) founded in Vilna in 1925 for the purpose of encouraging the study of the culture and history of the Jews, especially in Eastern Europe. It sought to perform for the Yiddish world of learning the organizational and promotional functions that comparable institutions in the leading countries of Europe had been fulfilling for more than a century. But there were also a number of other scholarly foundations, not quite as ambitious or influential as YIVO, but equally devoted to the task of creating a new cultural environment for East European Jewry. They too became part of that brief, brilliant flowering of Jewish artistic and intellectual creativity which was so cruelly destroyed during the Second World War.

All in all, the direction in which the culture of the Jewish community was moving is clear. The process of secularization had by the 1920s become irresistible, although its development did not signify an eventual absorption into non-Jewish society but rather the continued maintenance of ethnic distinctiveness and separateness in a new form. The still unanswered question, however, was, What would become the dominant political outlook of this emerging secularized Jewry? What would be its civic ideals? Where would its ideological sympathies lie?

The answer was far from clear. Jews were torn and divided by opposing views regarding the social foundation and economic structure of the new autonomous community which they hoped to create. Should they retain or reform or abolish the existing class system? Should they preserve or modify or do away with the institution of private property? Should they embrace the principles of liberal parliamentarianism or the teachings of democratic socialism or the doctrines of militant communism? Should they subordinate the interests of the Jewish community to the needs of the nation as a whole or should ethnic issues become the primary concern of their policy? And what about their relationship to non-Jewish political parties? Should they join parliamentary coalitions crossing cultural and linguistic boundaries or should they avoid entangling partisan alliances? Those were the problems being weighed, pondered, and debated by the Jews of Eastern Europe, problems which they never succeeded in resolving.

Important differences, moreover, continued to separate the civic outlook of most members of the Jewish community from that of their non-Jewish neighbors. Jews tended much more to sympathize with the parties and ideologies in the center or on the left of the political spectrum. In other words, they were by and large more liberal or more radical than the population at large. That was true everywhere in Europe, in France and England as much as in Poland and Russia. But it was especially true in Eastern Europe, because a close and direct connection existed between the intensity of anti-Semitic bigotry on one side and the degree of left-wing sympathy on the other. Each fed and reinforced the other.

Still, a few exceptions to this generalization should be acknowledged. Among the assimilationists were some so eager to be accepted as true Poles or Russians that they were willing to embrace all the doctrines of the ultranationalist conservatives, sometimes even including anti-Semitism. They were occasionally rewarded for their conformist zeal with a measure of prominence in the politics of the right, but more often they merely earned the scorn of both the Jews, whose identity they wanted to renounce, and the non-Jews, whose identity they sought to assume. To the former they became traitors, to the latter, toadies. They too were in a sense victims of the ethnic bigotry so deeply rooted in the soil of Eastern Europe.

More important were the members of the orthodox Jewish community, who remained in general indifferent to national politics except as they affected religious interests. Liberalism did not appeal to them any more than other secular theories of government, and as for the various forms of socialism, those were totally unacceptable because of their avowed materialism and godlessness. Devout Jews sought salvation in obedience to the divine will, not in a transformation of the social system. What the civil authorities did was as a rule of little concern to them. Yet they were not entirely uninterested in public affairs. In fact, they carefully studied the policies of those in authority, sometimes even organizing parliamentary parties of their own. But the goal of those parties was narrowly restricted to the defense of the religious autonomy of the Jewish community.

To achieve that goal, the orthodox believers were prepared to cooperate with whatever regime was in power, whether right or left, conservative or liberal, nationalist or progressive. In Poland, for example, they supported the semi-dictatorship of Joseph Pilsudski in return for the government's agreement that attendance at a Jewish confessional school satisfied the general requirement of compulsory elementary education, and a promise that the authorities would not interfere with the dietary laws prescribed by divine commandment, especially ritual slaughter. Otherwise, devout Jews remained largely indifferent to the issues around which national politics revolved. What mattered to them was not material progress in this world but spiritual salvation in the next. Everything else was of secondary importance.

Most Jews in Eastern Europe were more worldly, however. They were increasingly concerned with the problem of how to create a political system in which religious and ethnic differences would cease to be a barrier to social equality. Many of them, like their fellow Jews in Western Europe, became attracted to the egalitarian doctrines of liberalism. That was understandable. How could they resist an ideology which preached that all people, regardless of religion or race, were created equal? How could they remain indifferent to the principle that all people are endowed with inalienable rights which the state has no right to suppress or curtail? How could they dispute the proposition that government should represent the people, all the people, and that it should accordingly be chosen by the people? All they had to do was look at the Jewish community in France or England and compare it with the Jewish community in Poland or Romania to see the fundamental difference between a liberal and a conservative form of authority. What drew East European Jews toward liberalism was not only its abstract principles but the practical implications of those principles for their own position in the social order. In essence, they saw in it the promise of emancipation.

There was still another reason why many secularized Jews, especially those of means and education, embraced liberal ideas. Here was an ideology advocating political equality without preaching economic equality, an ideology seeking fundamental change in the structure of authority without urging fundamental change in the system of ownership. That was important. Jewish merchants, industrialists, bankers, and entrepreneurs could support liberalism without endangering their own financial interests. In a period of growing class consciousness, of intensifying social discontent and conflict, most affluent Jews preferred to maintain a clear separation between religious and material equality, between change in government and change in economy. The spread of radicalism among the urban working classes alarmed the Jewish as well as the non-Jewish bourgeoisie of Eastern Europe. But whereas the latter generally sought security in the maintenance of the existing system of authority, the former hoped to combine the introduction of political parity with the preservation of economic disparity. The answer seemed to be liberalism.

Jews therefore became prominent in the liberal movements of Eastern Europe. A few of them, mostly from the assimilationist fringe, even emerged during the interwar years as leaders in the various national parties advocating the principles of liberalism. But most Jewish liberals remained cultural separatists, expounding their doctrines in Yiddish and directing their appeals primarily toward fellow Jews. They founded several important "folkist" political organizations, the People's Party in Poland, for example, which advocated the establishment of a secular, autonomous, and progressive Jewish community within the framework of an enlightened, tolerant, and democratic non-Jewish state. The victory of liberalism, they argued, would put an end to the religious hostilities and ethnic divisions threatening the collective sense of national unity. It would free Jews and non-Jews alike from the burden of mutually destructive suspicions and resentments. It would lead to the emergence of a new, liberating awareness of common purpose.

The Jewish lower classes, however, especially the urban industrial workers, found the doctrines of socialism much more persuasive. They tended to support organizations like the "Bund" in Poland, the Jewish Workers' Union, which insisted that the problem of reactionary anti-Semitism could not be solved without solving the problem of parasitic capitalism. Hostility toward the Jews, they maintained, was being deliberately kept alive by landowners, industrialists, and financiers, the exploiters of the common people, who used ethnic prejudice to divert the resentment of their victims from an unjust economic system toward an innocent, defenseless minority. Only a new social order based on the collective ownership of the means of production and transportation could end the persecution of Jews by ending the purpose served by that persecution. Ethnic justice, in other words, was inseparable from social justice; the liberation of the Jewish proletariat was unattainable without the liberation of the non-Jewish proletariat. The conclusion seemed clear: "Workers of the world, unite!"

To Jews in the big-city slums, and even to many members of the Jewish intelligentsia, this line of reasoning made eminent sense. They were too weak to change the established system by themselves, yet the established system showed no sign of a willingness to change on its own. That left only the use of force as an instrument of reform. Accordingly, around the turn of the century Jewish socialist parties were founded throughout Eastern Europe. Though maintaining close ties to the non-Jewish socialist parties, they sought to preserve their separate linguistic and cultural identity. Their goal was autonomy, not assimilation, autonomy to be achieved through a transformation of the existing social system. They were willing to use parliamentary means to achieve their goal, where that was possible. But they never rejected revolution as the ultimate weapon in the class struggle. They were thus more militant than the socialists of Western Europe. There were very few Fabians among them. Their weakness tended to make them intransigent, their isolation helped to make them uncompromising. Theirs was the socialism of desperation.

Yet to many Jewish workers they seemed to offer hope for the future. In place of the messianic vision of a better life in the hereafter, which inspired the orthodox believers, the socialists presented the revolutionary vision of a better life in the here and now. Once the established system of authority had been overthrown, all peoples and nationalities would live in peace. There would be no more wars, oppressions, persecutions, or pogroms. Socialism would realize at last Isaiah's prophecy in the Old Testament; the wolf would dwell with the lamb and the leopard lie down with the kid. It all seemed so promising, so exciting. In order to achieve the emancipation of the exploited masses, Jewish socialists were prepared to adopt revolutionary methods, to organize demonstrations, to take up arms, to build barricades, to fight and die. They were willing to pay any price, make any sacrifice, to overthrow a system of authority based on bigotry and oppression.

Still, the spread of revolutionary ideas among the Jewry of Eastern Europe also had the effect of intensifying the anti-Semitic prejudices of the non-Jewish population. The Jews were increasingly perceived, often with encouragement from the authorities, as not only alien and rapacious but destructive and subversive. The secularization of their community led logically to the secularization of the hostility directed against that community. They were now seen less as infidels refusing to acknowledge the true faith, and more as conspirators seeking to undermine the foundations of national loyalty. But the Jewish socialists refused to be intimidated. They continued to preach, agitate, denounce, demonstrate, and organize. They remained convinced that the enmity of the defenders of the established order was a price worth paying for the achievement of social justice. The growing political support they found in the urban ghettos was evidence of the influence which their doctrines were gaining among the secularized Jewish proletariat.

The outbreak of the Russian Revolution, however, led to a division of the socialist movements in Poland, Romania, and the Baltic States which was as bitter as in France, England, and the Low Countries. Yet in the East the underlying reasons for the split were less ideological and more strategic. Left-wing parties in the countries bordering the Soviet Union, including the Jewish left-wing parties, were generally willing to approve the methods adopted by the Bolsheviks in the struggle against czarism. They agreed that the overthrow of the old order by violent means had been justifiable. They maintained that the establishment of a dictatorship of the proletariat was unavoidable, at least as long as the new regime in Russia remained engaged in a struggle for survival. They even conceded that harsh repressive measures against the antirevolutionary forces of the aristocracy and the bourgeoisie were necessary. How else was the Bolshevik government to defend itself against the attacks of domestic and foreign reactionaries?

The break between the socialists and the communists came rather over the right of sympathizers with the Russian Revolution to express open criticism of its leadership. Should lifelong left-wingers, men and women who had fought and suffered in defense of the Marxian ideals, be free to voice disagreement with the policies of Lenin and later Stalin? Or should any opposition to the official line of the Kremlin, however loyal to radical doctrines, however committed to the interests of the proletariat, be regarded as a threat to the unity of the revolutionary movement? Such was the main issue leading to the break between socialism and communism, a break almost as sharp as that which separated each from the old prerevolutionary order.

The Jewish socialists of Eastern Europe, like socialists everywhere, were deeply affected by this dispute. Most of them turned against the

Bolshevik regime because of its intolerance of dissent even by those who sympathized with its underlying principles and ultimate goals. But a minority composed of the most radical and uncompromising supporters of the socialist movement seceded to join various national communist parties whose loyalty to the Soviet Union was unquestioning. Those parties welcomed members from all ethnic, religious, and cultural backgrounds, as long as they were willing to accept without reservation the ideology and leadership of the Kremlin. This new variety of intransigent radicalism was especially attractive to those secularized Jews of the younger generation who had begun to despair of ever achieving social justice under the existing system of authority. Many of them came to believe that only the violent overthrow of the old order and the establishment of a communist dictatorship could lead to the emancipation of the oppressed and exploited masses. This belief inspired the political activities of radicals like Leon Trotsky in Russia, Henryk Henrykowski in Poland, Ana Pauker in Romania, Bela Kun in Hungary, and Eugen Leviné in Bavaria.

For the conservatives of Eastern Europe this prominence of Jews in the various communist parties provided additional evidence of the destructive influence of Jewry in Christian society. There was thus a clear reciprocal interaction between right-wing anti-Semitism and Jewish radicalism. Bigotry, hostility, and discrimination on one side fed resentment, defiance, and rebelliousness on the other. Nationalists and traditionalists ceased to view the Jew as typically a grubby moneylender interested only in profit, a comical figure wearing an outlandish costume, cringing and obsequious, afraid of his own shadow. Now he was seen more and more as a sinister conspirator encouraging subversion and fomenting rebellion in order to gain dominance over good-natured, unsuspecting Christians. The contention that "where there's a Jew there's a communist, and where there's a communist there's a Jew" became a commonplace in the political rhetoric of conservative circles in interwar Poland. And similar views could be heard elsewhere in Europe, and not only in the East.

It did no good to point out that while communism had broader appeal among Jews than non-Jews, the great bulk of the Jewish community remained noncommunist or anticommunist. The Communist Party of Poland, for example, never had a membership of more than 20,000—by the middle 1930s the figure had dropped to about 10,000—although the Jewish population of the country was close to 3,000,000. In the Polish parliamentary elections of November 1922 the communists and their front organizations received only 1.4 percent of the vote. In the elections of March 1928 their percentage did rise to 6.7, but in the following elections of November 1930 it fell again to 2.5. And this in a nation where Jews constituted more than 10 percent of all inhabitants, and where at least some non-Jews joined or voted for the Communist Party as well. Statistical data from other countries in Eastern Europe point to the same conclusion. Jews were proportionately more favorable to communism than non-Jews, but most of them remained anticommunist.

Statistics, however, meant little to inveterate anti-Semites. Their hatred of Jewry had become a psychological necessity whose grip could not be broken by mere facts. It helped them find a simple explanation for all the bewildering problems facing their country. The bitter political disputes of the interwar years, the economic hardships caused by war and depression, the growing social unrest of the lower classes, even the rebellion of the younger generation against time-honored conventions and traditions, all of that could be ascribed to the corrupting influence of Jewry. The portrait of the Jew haunting the anti-Semitic imagination combined disparate elements, some of them even inconsistent or incompatible, but all mutually reinforcing. The Jew was at one and the same time clannish and fawning, greedy and ostentatious, superstitious and materialistic, clever and insensitive, liberal and selfish, nouveau riche and communist. However illogical, this juxtaposition pointed to a satisfying preordained conclusion. The Jewish and the non-Jewish character were so fundamentally different that they could not be reconciled. Hence there had to be some form of exclusion or expulsion of the Jews from Christian society. The separation should be accomplished by consent, if possible, or by force, if necessary. But there had to be a separation.

The various political organizations of the secularized Jewry of Eastern Europe, with one exception, rejected this view categorically. They insisted that Jews had as much right as non-Jews, based on history, law, and tradition, to remain in the country of their birth. Their ancestors had also lived there for centuries, they too had contributed to its growth, been part of its culture, and shaped its thought and character. By what authority then could anyone tell them that they were aliens who must be segregated or expelled? They did seek cultural and administrative autonomy for their community, but only as a free and equal constituent part of the national state. They would settle for nothing less.

Even religious Jews shared this view. They may have been less interested than the secularists in the right to take part in political life. But they also believed that the land where they lived had become theirs, though by the will of God rather than through a historical process, and that they should therefore remain there until the Messiah came to lead them to the promised land. Unlike the secular Jews, they were willing to accept something less than full civic equality. Participation in public affairs did not mean very much to them. Yet they were all the more determined to maintain a communal autonomy reflecting their distinctive religion, tradition, and culture. Accordingly, they too insisted on their right to live in the country of their birth. They too argued that their nonconformity in faith and custom was not incompatible with the maintenance of national unity. And they too rejected the contention that Christians and Jews were so unlike that only complete segregation, whether achieved by agreement or force, could protect the former against the latter.

Yet there was one political movement among the Jews of Eastern Europe which agreed with the far right that the differences separating Jews from non-Jews were too profound to be overcome by greater tolerance or deeper understanding. Zionism emerged around the turn of the century as a significant part of the process of secularization transforming the Jewish community. It reflected the ideas of modern nationalism, which were steadily increasing their influence throughout the Continent, though in a form expressing the unique experience of European Jewry. Its basic argument was that oppression of the Jews would never end as long as they remained a minority in the countries in which they lived. Neither liberalism nor socialism, neither segregation nor assimilation, could alter their position as scorned and resented outsiders. Their only escape from discrimination lay in the establishment of an independent state in which Jews would form the bulk of the population. Such a state should obviously be located in Palestine, the ancestral home from which they had been driven out almost two thousand years before. Its ideological foundation, however, should be secular rather than religious, and its cultural outlook modern rather than traditional.

Still, what the Zionists wanted to establish was more than a new Jewish state. They wanted to create a new Jewish character, a new Jewish mentality, a new Jewish spirit. They felt that the experience of the Diaspora had destroyed the heroic qualities of biblical Jewry. The Jews had become timid, submissive, and cringing. That would have to change. The emphasis of Zionism on the need to transform the essential nature of the Jewish community accounts for its lack of sympathy for cultural expressions of the traditional way of life of East European

Jewry. It displayed little interest in the new Yiddish literature or dramaturgy or scholarship. Critics of the Zionist movement even charged that the choice of Hebrew, which had not been spoken since biblical times, as the language of the future Jewish state rather than the vernacular Yiddish reflected a tacit resolve to purge the new national culture of all reminders of the long, bitter experience of exile.

Before long, however, serious internal disputes began to divide the Zionists of Eastern Europe into sects and factions: moderates against militants, liberals against socialists, and secularists against religionists. Some maintained that a Jewish state could be created only through cautious diplomacy, by following a tortuous course between the conflicting policies of the Turks, the Arabs, and the British. Others insisted that only the creation of a strong quasi-military force could defend Jewish interests not only in the Middle East but in Eastern Europe as well. Some argued that the system of government to be established in Palestine should be democratic and the system of property capitalistic, while others favored the public ownership of the means of production and transportation. Some believed in a separation of politics and religion; others found it inconceivable that a Jewish state should be indifferent to the Jewish faith. Zionism became torn by the same sharp differences of opinion dividing the various other political manifestations of Jewish secularization.

Yet in spite of that, it managed to gain considerable popular support among the Jews of Eastern Europe, though for reasons which were often more emotional than rational. The vision of an independent Jewish state to be established in their ancestral homeland seemed to most of them noble but impractical. How could the concept be translated into reality? Would not the present inhabitants of Palestine resist with force their displacement by the former inhabitants? And even if that obstacle could be overcome, was it realistic to believe that the millions of European Jews would leave their homes, belongings, and occupations in order to settle in a strange and inhospitable land? Sober reason insisted that the Zionist goal was simply unattainable. Still, the sight of young Jewish men and women abandoning the life of exile in order to pioneer in building a better existence in the country of their ancestors was inspiring. That was why many of those who remained skeptical about the feasibility of a Jewish state in Palestine would occasionally drop a coin or two into the tin collection boxes being rattled by Zionist sympathizers at street corners and tenement gates in the ghettos of Eastern Europe.

There was yet another reason why Zionism appealed even to those Jews who had serious doubts about its ideology or its strategy. To those who had been treated by hostile neighbors with contempt, who had been scorned as submissive and cowardly, there was something stirring, something heartwarming, in the sight of young Jews marching in uniform, with military precision, all in step, heads high, shoulders back, carrying white and blue banners with the Star of David, proud and defiant. They looked almost as fearless, almost as invincible, as similar marching formations of nationalistic young Poles or Romanians or Lithuanians. Even pious Jews, those who believed that they would be led to the promised land not by Theodor Herzl or Chaim Weizmann but by the Messiah, were often deeply moved. Zionism had become for them, as for so many other Jews, a form of emotional or psychological liberation. Their response to it reflected the long, bitter experience of ethnic oppression and humiliation.

And so the Jewry of Eastern Europe went on and on, in a state of mounting excitement, arguing, preaching, agitating, appealing, and agonizing over the future of its community, over its destiny. What should be the nature of Jewish culture, of Jewish character, of Jewish life? Should it reflect the values of ancestral faith or the challenges of modernist rebellion? Should the Jews seek liberation in their devotion to God, or in a reform of the non-Jewish society which had treated them with such hostility, or in the establishment of a Jewish state in the Middle East? The great debate raged on, growing ever louder, fiercer, and more passionate. And in the meantime, amid the unending arguments and debates, an unspeakable horror was beginning to assume shape over the horizon, a horror which would soon overtake and overwhelm and finally destroy the East European Jewish community. But the members of that community did not know what awaited them. They continued to discuss, hope, and dream, still convinced that they could sometime, somehow, create a better future not only for themselves but for all of society.

That was the vanished Jewish world into which I was born on August 24, 1920, in Warsaw.

Chapter 1

The Patrimony of a Lithuanian Ghetto

Both of my parents were participants in that youthful rebellion around the turn of the century against the traditional beliefs and pieties of East European Jewry. They both embraced the ideal of a secular Jewish community; they both shared the vision of a new Yiddish culture. More than that, they both decided at an early age to devote their lives to the attainment of that ideal, to the realization of that vision. Yet they were not rigid or dogmatic in their views. They were prepared to tolerate the religious convictions and social values of the older generation. After all, they told themselves, that generation could not be expected to reject the faith in which it had been brought up. But young people like my parents felt themselves more enlightened, more modern, more progressive than their elders. Before them rose the exciting challenge of creating a new, a better society, on a firmer ethical and cultural foundation, tolerant, liberal, and just, fundamentally different from the old, drab world of Jewish orthodoxy. For them, as for Wordsworth a hundred years earlier, it was bliss to be alive in that dawn.

Although my father and mother shared this bliss, they arrived at it by different paths. My father's was the more familiar one. He was born in a small town called Kovnata in the Lithuanian region of the Russian Empire. It seems to have been very much like hundreds of other towns and villages with a sizable Jewish population scattered throughout Eastern Europe. He thus grew up in the environment of a typical shtetl of czarist times. As for my paternal grandfather, he died shortly before I was born. In fact, I am named after him. He was apparently quite poor, although I never learned what his occupation had been or how he had earned his livelihood. I do know that he was a widower when he married my grandmother, and that he had children by his first wife who were as old as or even older than his second wife. Those children eventually emigrated to Denmark, where, to the best of my knowledge, their descendants still live. I actually met one of them once, while he was visiting the United States not long after the Second World War.

I know, moreover, what my grandfather looked like from an old photograph in the possession of one of the members of the family. It shows an elderly man with a grayish beard, wearing the familiar black cap and long coat of a pious Jew, seated in an easy chair, while a portly, middle-aged woman, my grandmother, stands beside him, her hand resting lightly on his shoulder, in a pose favored by photographers of family portraits a hundred years ago. It is hard to tell from their stiff bearing and impassive expression how they felt about each other. Nor do I remember hearing much from my grandmother about her marriage, whether her relationship with her husband had been harmonious or strained, whether he had treated her with kindness or harshness, whether he had been affectionate or indifferent, and whether she had been contented or dissatisfied. Questions of that sort were not generally discussed in the orthodox Jewish community. Matrimony was viewed as providentially ordained, like social position or economic status. It was something to be accepted, not analyzed or questioned or debated.

This view was also reflected in the common practice of arranging a marriage through negotiations between the parents of the prospective bride and groom, often with the help of a professional broker. The two young people whose union was being contemplated would see each other only infrequently prior to their wedding, and never alone. There would be time enough for them to get to know one another afterward. Still, the fact that romantic love was not regarded as a requirement for marriage may actually have helped make such unions more stable, more enduring. There were fewer expectations and illusions, and therefore fewer disappointments and dissatisfactions. Marital discord may have been common, but divorce or abandonment was quite rare.

In the case of my grandparents the pattern was somewhat different. He was a middle-aged widower who, in the opinion of the community, needed a wife to give him support, comfort, and protection against sinful temptation. But since he was not wealthy, he would have to settle for a bride who could offer him little besides herself. My grandmother's prospects were equally bleak. A young woman who had been left an orphan, she was expected to marry as soon as possible in order to escape loneliness, subservience, or even worse. Yet because she could bring no dowry, her expectations had to be modest, restricted to someone who was in all likelihood poor, much older, and previously married, in short, someone like my grandfather. And so the community elders arranged for their marriage in accordance with the established practice in cases of this sort.

Seven children were born of that marriage. This was about an average number in Jewish families in Eastern Europe during the nineteenth century. Quite often there were many more. The pattern was the same in the Christian community, especially among the lower classes. Pious Jews as well as pious Christians regarded procreation as a gift from above bestowed on man and woman by divine providence. To interfere with it in any way, to restrict it because of insufficient financial resources, or to treat it as simply a means of amorous gratification would be worse than immoral. It would be sinful. Consequently, families were large as a rule, even more so among the poor than among the well-to-do, although the high rate of infant mortality served to some extent to limit the growth of the population. By the turn of the century the sharp differences between the older generation of orthodox believers and the younger generation of secular modernizers could also be seen in their opposing views of sex and procreation.

Those differences were apparent on a small scale in my father's own family. My grandparents had seven children, but these in turn, though each of them married, had a combined total of only eleven children, not even enough to maintain a balance between births and deaths. Five of the seven had only one child apiece, another had two, and another four. This striking disparity in the family size of two succeeding generations reflected in part a basic change in attitude toward procreation. But there were other factors as well. The younger people were willing to limit the number of their children in order to provide a brighter future for them, a better education, a richer opportunity, and a higher standard of living. The declining birth rate thus indicated a rising level of expectations. And finally, the sharp reduction in the number of children resulted in part from the changing position of women in the social and economic order. My grandmother spent most of her life performing household duties, fulfilling the needs of a large and growing family. Of her seven daughters and daughters-in-law, on the other hand, six found employment outside the home, primarily because of financial need, but partly also because of a new quest for independence and

equality. Here too was one of the major generational differences transforming the way of life of the East European Jewish community.

There were others. I remember as a child hearing from my grandmother how my uncle Max, the only one of my father's siblings whom I
never met, returned to the parental home for a visit shortly after starting
out on his own. To display his new freedom, and perhaps also to show
his defiance of paternal authority, he casually took out a cigarette, lit it
slowly and deliberately, and proceeded to smoke. And this on the Sabbath, of all days. Others in the room froze in apprehension, dreading a
terrible scene between the devout father and his blatantly irreligious son.
But nothing happened. The old man, after a long silence during which
he tried very hard to control himself, returned to whatever he was doing,
pretending not to notice the shocking display of filial disobedience. As
for the son, he kept on smoking nonchalantly, relishing the victory he
had just won in his struggle for independence. It was a scene which must
have been repeated in various forms in countless Jewish homes.

A decade later that same Max provided an even more shocking display of indifference to the orthodox pieties. He was the only member
of the family to remain in Eastern Europe during the interwar period.
In fact, he left Lithuania shortly after the Russian Revolution and settled in the Soviet Union, whether out of ideological conviction or for
economic reasons. From there he continued to write to his mother,
sometimes displaying a touching concern for her well-being by enclos-
ing a few rubles, although she was by then living much better than he,
thanks to my father's financial support.

In one of his letters he attached a photograph of himself, his wife,
whom the family had never met, and their child. I remember my
youngest aunt Rivke or Irene, who lived with us, whispering agitatedly
to friends and relatives that Max must have married a gentile. And
indeed, the woman in the picture had blue eyes, blond hair, and unmis-
takably Slavic features. Could my grandmother have failed to recognize
that her new daughter-in-law was a shikse? Whether she did or did not,
she said very little, behaving as if nothing untoward had happened.
Probably, like my grandfather confronted with his son's defiant cigarette smoking on the Sabbath, she preferred to look the other way. As
for Max himself, he was killed in the late 1930s in one of Stalin's murderous purges. The reason was never revealed to the members of his
family. Perhaps there was no reason.

Max was not the only member of the family to reject the precepts of
the ancestral faith. His sister Mushel, whose name was later Americanized

to Martha, defied them as well, though in a less blatant form. When I first got to know her, she was almost middle-aged, but even then it was apparent that as a young girl she must have been very attractive. She still had a mischievous, flirtatious look with twinkling, smiling eyes, an invitingly plump figure, and a bold but engaging and amusing way of speaking. She looked like a woman who would enjoy good food and drink, a good joke, especially if slightly off-color, a good laugh, and good male company. Men must have found her irresistible.

The evidence supporting this surmise is convincing. Mushel was married three times. I never met her first husband, because their marriage lasted only a few years, but he was apparently something unusual in the East European Jewish community. He was an alcoholic. Pious Jews did not regard the habitual consumption of hard liquor as a convenient means of forgetting troubles or overcoming inhibitions or displaying manliness. They saw in it rather a sinful indulgence. Drunkenness among them was therefore very rare. Even among secularized Jews alcoholism was and still is much less common than in most other ethnic groups or national cultures. But Mushel's husband was an exception. His addiction to drink proved in fact so powerful and uncontrollable that before long she was forced to get a divorce under circumstances about which I have little concrete information.

I know more about her second marriage. Since it lasted much longer than the first, I had ample opportunity not only to meet Mushel's next husband but to see and talk with him quite frequently. The two had met during the First World War, after the Germans occupied Lithuania. He was a soldier in the imperial army, a tall, blond, blue-eyed specimen of Aryan manhood, but without the aloofness or stiffness which is often ascribed to this type, not always fairly. Robert Fernholz was in fact gentle, pleasant, fun-loving, and likable, a man who enjoyed having a good time and who could not always resist temptation, whether amorous or financial. Shortly after their first meeting, he and Mushel formed a close partnership, partly commercial, partly romantic. They began to dabble in the black market, illegally selling foodstuffs which were in short supply on the civilian market but which members of the occupying German forces could obtain more easily. This association, formed initially for the purpose of material gain, turned little by little into a passionate love affair.

Robert, however, was not content with secret trysts and hurried embraces. He wanted to do the honorable thing, he wanted to get married. While Mushel did not require much persuading, there was one

serious obstacle: her father's religious scruples. The old man was prepared, though without much enthusiasm, to accept a non-Jewish son-
in-law, but only on the condition that he convert to Judaism. To Robert
that seemed to be no problem. His confessional loyalties were lukewarm
at best, so that he was willing to promise to obey the teachings of the
Jewish faith with the same lack of conviction with which he had previously promised to obey those of the Christian faith. But becoming a Jew
was not that simple. It also required the rite of circumcision, and for a
grown man this could prove not only awkward but quite painful. Still,
Robert was prepared to submit to a distasteful alien ritual for the sake
of his beloved, and shortly after his ordeal he and Mushel were married.

It would be nice to report that they lived happily ever after, but life
is not like the movies. The marriage soon began to unravel under the
pressures of adversity and disappointment. After the war the newlyweds
settled down briefly in Robert's hometown in Westphalia, but then
during the 1920s they emigrated to the United States with the help of
my father. Yet once again, life in the New World did not prove as easy
as they had hoped. Robert, still affable and charming, also turned out
to be feckless and ineffectual. He simply could not hold on to a job for
any length of time, so that during the depression the burden of supporting the family, which now included two young daughters, fell
almost entirely on his wife.

Facing mounting financial and marital problems, Mushel displayed
remarkable and unexpected strength. She found employment in the
garment district, almost single-handedly providing the household with
a modest but adequate income. After work she would rush home, cook
dinner, do the dishes, dust the furniture, shop for food, and perform
the countless other time-consuming chores needed to maintain the
appearance of petit-bourgeois respectability. It was an impressive feat,
but it took its toll on the marriage. Robert and Mushel eventually
divorced, he moving away from the Jewish neighborhood in Brooklyn
to the Yorkville section of Manhattan, the favorite gathering place of
German immigrants. As for her, she did not remain single very long.
Soon a third husband came along, an American Jew considerably
younger than she, with whom she then continued to live in seeming
harmony and contentment for the rest of her life.

Mushel's experiences were not rare among the hundreds of thou-
sands of Jewish families that embarked on that arduous geographic
and cultural odyssey from the shtetls of Eastern Europe to the Brook-
lyns and Bronxes of the New World. Nor were they very different

from those of her three younger sisters, Esther, Hanke or Anna, and Rivke, who had left Lithuania soon after her, but for a different destination, France and Poland rather than America. I never got to know Esther or Hanke very well, but I gather that they settled down in Paris with the help of friends or distant relatives who had emigrated from Eastern Europe a few years earlier. They became part of that far-flung Jewish diaspora of the twentieth century which scattered various members of my father's family to Denmark, Russia, France, and the United States, thereby saving most of them from the deadly fury of National Socialism.

Of those three aunts, the one I know least about is Esther. I met her briefly, for only a few days, in the course of my journey in 1930 from Poland to America. But on the basis of occasional bits of information provided by various relatives, I learned that, either shortly before or shortly after settling in Paris, she married another immigrant from Eastern Europe, and that they had a son, their only child. I also gathered that this son became an ardent leftist while still a teen-ager, and that his parents sympathized to some extent with his radical political views. During the German occupation of France in the Second World War, all three were arrested as Jewish aliens and deported to the eastern killing fields. They never returned. The story of their migration in search of freedom and opportunity, their rejection of traditional religious piety, their adherence to a new secular faith, and their ultimate death at the hands of murderous anti-Semites is a familiar one in the experience of modern European Jewry.

My aunt Hanke, whom I came to know a little better, was more fortunate. She too defied the commandments of orthodox Judaism, but not by embracing socialism or communism. Rather, shortly before the Second World War she married a Frenchman, and that proved to be her salvation, at least her secular salvation. Her identification papers now showed that she was a French citizen, not an alien. More important, they made no mention of the fact that she had been born in Lithuania or that she was Jewish. That enabled her later not only to lead a fairly normal life while her husband was a prisoner of war in Germany, but also to assist the more vulnerable members of the family. She took in the young son of her sister Rivke, who had been sent to a concentration camp with her husband, saying that he was actually her own child. Even more remarkable, she was able to protect her mother by placing her in an old people's home run by a Catholic religious order. Since my grandmother could not speak French, Hanke told the head nun that she was Russian. Whether the latter really believed this story seems doubtful; she must have guessed the truth. But she pretended to believe it, and so the uncomprehending, bewildered old woman spent the war years in relative comfort and safety. No one said anything; no one betrayed her. When I saw her while on a few days' leave from the army shortly after the war, she told me that she had rather enjoyed her stay in the home. Amid so many accounts of tragedy and horror during the preceding six years, her story is heartening.

As for Rivke, the youngest of my father's siblings, she had to endure much greater hardship. Only about ten years older than I, she had lived in Poland with my grandmother and me through most of the 1920s, supported by the generous remittances which my parents sent every month from across the Atlantic. But when in 1930 they could finally take me with them to live in the United States, Rivke was forced to make an important change in her life. She decided to emigrate to France along with her mother and the young man to whom she was engaged, joining her two older sisters in Paris. She married her fiancé soon after arriving there, and the two of them had a son, again an only child. But then the Second World War disrupted her new life, just as my departure for America a decade earlier had disrupted her old life. Her little boy remained safely in Paris under Hanke's protection, but Rivke and her husband were deported to the death camps in Eastern Europe. He perished there, but she somehow survived a long stay in Auschwitz, returning to France in 1945 with a tattooed prisoner's number on her arm and terrible stories of cruelty and suffering, stories which she would often recount in a surprisingly offhand, almost matter-of-fact tone.

Compared to these experiences, Rivke's life after the war was anticlimactic. She soon found new employment in Paris as a teacher in a trade school, and at about the same time she found a new husband as well, another concentration camp survivor. She became, moreover, a dedicated communist, whether as a result of her wartime experiences or of her prewar political leanings. Perhaps a little of each. What is clear is that she eventually had to pay a price for her embrace of radicalism. When Hanke decided to emigrate to the United States after her husband's death in a motorcycle accident, Rivke tried to follow. After all, most members of her family were by then living on the other side of the ocean. But she discovered that while she was free to visit them as often as she liked or could afford to, she was prohibited from becoming a permanent resident. The American laws excluding communists were quite explicit. Rivke managed to overcome her disappointment, however, continuing to lead a modest but comfortable existence in France, and railing even more loudly than before against the injustices of capitalism, especially in the United States.

Almost all of my father's siblings thus expressed their rejection of the ancestral faith by either marrying a gentile or adopting a radical political ideology. But one of them, his youngest brother David, did so in a way which was more common among the younger generation of East European Jews. He did not openly defy or disavow the teachings of his religion. He simply ignored them. His indifference to orthodox Judaism could even be detected in the photograph that I once saw of him as a young man, in his late teens or early twenties. No traditional black hat and long coat for him. There he stood in a relaxed, nonchalant pose, leaning indolently against a horse-drawn wagon, a sporty cap at a rakish angle on his head, wearing a short natty jacket and polished black boots, with a roguish grin on his face. The young girls of Kovnata must have found him irresistible.

Indeed, there is incontrovertible evidence that at least one of them could not resist him. Many years later my mother told me in a half-whisper, with a knowing look and faintly mischievous smile, that Uncle David and Aunt Havel had gotten married because they had to. That came as something of a revelation to me, since awkward occurrences of that sort had never been mentioned in the many stories I had heard about life in the old country. The accepted view in the Jewish community of Eastern Europe was that extramarital intimacies were something in which drunken farmhands and shameless barmaids engaged. Jews, including young Jews, were too busy pondering the mystery of salvation and reflecting on the meaning of the Torah to yield to temptations of the flesh. But that was another of those convenient fictions with which the pious establishment sought to disguise the unedifying realities of life in the shtetl. Behind the facade of otherworldliness, East European Jewry harbored thoughts, feelings, and instincts which were worldly and human, sometimes all too human.

In the case of my uncle David, his beloved's father seemed to know exactly what to do. Apparently hers was not the only incident of youthful indiscretion which had ever occurred in their town. He went directly to my grandfather, told him what had happened, and the two promptly agreed that the errant couple must marry as soon as possible. The prospective bride and groom offered no objections. They may in fact have been quite pleased, although their feelings would in any case have had to yield to religious and social convention. The wedding took place almost at once, and a few months later their first child was born safely within the bounds of respectable matrimony.

Establishing a family, however, proved easier than supporting one. After struggling in vain to make a go of it in Lithuania, David emigrated to the United States with the help of some of his wife's relatives, and after becoming an American citizen he also brought her and his son over. But life in the New World presented problems and difficulties as well. He tried his hand at various occupations: clerk in a grocery store, superintendent in an apartment building, and finally driver of a delivery truck. This last job proved the most enduring and rewarding. It provided his family, which by now included four children, with a measure of security, inspiring in David a profound admiration for Jimmy Hoffa, the militant leader of the teamsters' union, who had won important gains for his members by means which were not universally regarded as irreproachable.

By now David had become quite Americanized. Like so many immigrants from Eastern Europe, he settled down in a Jewish neighborhood in Brooklyn, spoke in fluent Yiddish to his wife and in shaky, labored English to his children, continued to enjoy traditional dishes like gefilte fish and cheese blintzes with sour cream while also learning to like strange, exotic beverages like Dr. Brown's Cream Soda, and he soon became completely addicted to pinochle. For him as for most of the others, Jewishness had gradually become transformed from a profound commitment to religious faith into a cozy, homey ethnic loyalty.

But not for my father Chaim Shneyer, the oldest of my grandparents' children, whom relatives and friends always called by his middle name. Paradoxically, he was the one who rejected the ancestral religion most demonstratively, yet sought to preserve the ancestral culture most persistently through secularization. A taciturn man, aloof and withdrawn, he avoided all displays of emotion, preferring to keep his feelings hidden behind a facade of silence or even gruffness. I once heard my grandmother tell that whenever Shneyer as a young man would come to visit her, he always brought some small gift, whereas Max usually came empty-handed. Yet she preferred Max's company, because he was jovial and lively, full of jokes and entertaining stories. Shneyer, on the other hand, would sit quietly, looking a little glum or preoccupied, speaking only when spoken to. I think I know what she meant.

To account for my father's stubborn, distrustful reserve is more difficult. Could it have been a result of the poverty in which he had grown up? Did that teach him to endure in silence any resentments or disappointments he might have felt? The family lived in a state of permanent privation, forced to endure not only the lack of amenities and conveniences but at times even the pangs of hunger. That must have left its mark. Perhaps more important, the young boy could not have found much parental affection or emotional support while growing up. Long afterward my mother told me that in a rare display of personal feeling he had described to her how, whenever he would return home for a visit while still a teen-ager forced to live on his own, his parents seemed to have less and less time for him. There was always a new child in the family, a new brother or sister to nurture, a new mouth to feed, a new cry for attention, a new demand for affection. To the youngster who had looked forward so eagerly to a reunion with his father and mother, their habitual inattentiveness must have come as a bitter disappointment. That sense of disappointment helped shape the character of the brooding, introverted man I came to know many years later.

As for my father's formal education, it was not only brief but narrowly limited. Like all boys of his cultural and social background, he went for a few years to a heder, a religious school whose curriculum consisted of a little Hebrew and the rote memorization of the numerous prayers which pious Jews are required to recite. Worldly subjects like literature, history, and geography were excluded as mere distractions from the true purpose of learning, namely, salvation. Then, at the age of thirteen he was apprenticed, as was common in poor families, to a tailor in Vilna. From that time on he was on his own. He would visit his parents only two or three times a year, during the major religious holidays. The master craftsman whose apprentice he had become was supposed to provide the young boy, barely an adolescent, with guidance and supervision. He was supposed to treat him as a member of his own household. But in fact all he was interested in was squeezing as much work out of his youthful helper as he could. What the youngster did in his meager spare time was not the master's concern. My father grew into manhood lonely, ignored, and neglected.

Toward the end of his life he told my mother, in another of his infrequent confessions of private emotion, that it was a wonder he did not turn into a petty criminal during those early years in Vilna. Many other young men in his situation drifted into the sizable urban underworld of amateur pickpockets, shoplifters, burglars, thieves, pimps, and extortionists. They would spend their off-hours and their meager earnings in back alleys, seeking the pleasures and amusements offered by sordid establishments eager to exploit their loneliness. But my father was not one of them. Driven by some inexplicable inner hunger for learning, without outside guidance or encouragement, he resolved to acquire an education on his own. He became something quite rare: a true autodidact. He learned to read Russian, thereby opening the door to a world of ideas, beliefs, hopes, and aspirations closed to him in the narrow cultural environment of the small town in which he had been born. Those lonely years of apprenticeship in Vilna became the years of his intellectual awakening.

To be sure, he did not do it all on his own. Various political and social organizations dedicated to improving the living conditions of the Jewish workingman, organizations like the socialist "Bund," for example, offered evening courses designed to raise the level of culture in the ghetto. My father became one of their most devoted pupils. With the help of the classroom instruction he received and especially of his own studiousness, he managed to acquire a remarkably broad education. He was most familiar with literature, not only Russian literature, not only Tolstoy and Gogol, but German, French, and English literature as well: Hauptmann and Sudermann, Hugo and Zola, Dickens and Shaw. His knowledge of dramaturgy in particular was both detailed and cosmopolitan. I remember how toward the end of his life, hearing me once complain about some plan of mine that had miscarried, he casually quoted a line from one of Molière's lesser plays of which I had never even heard: "You've asked for it, Georges Dandin, you've asked for it." I was impressed.

He would also surprise me occasionally with his familiarity with history, American as well as European, while his knowledge of world geography was not only broad but almost always accurate. His education in the natural sciences was inevitably more limited. There were no laboratories in the evening classes he had attended, no telescopes or microscopes, not even test tubes. Still, he managed to acquire through extensive reading a clear understanding of the contributions of Copernicus and Galileo to astronomy, Newton and Einstein to physics, Darwin to biology, and Freud to psychology and psychiatry. Only in mathematics did his knowledge remain pretty much confined to elementary arithmetic. Otherwise, the scope of his learning equaled or exceeded what most American college degrees represent.

During those years in Vilna, moreover, my father acquired a political education, becoming a convert to socialism, though only a lukewarm convert. Like many of the young men and women in that great migration at the turn of the century from towns and villages to the big cities, he came to believe that salvation for the poor and oppressed was to be found not in the Old Testament but in the *Communist Manifesto*. His experience as a tailor's apprentice helped persuade him that the system of private property should ideally be replaced by a collective ownership of the means of production. Yet he was no rigid doctrinaire in his view of economics or politics. By the time he came to the United States, his devotion to socialism, never very ardent, had become vague and tepid. During the 1930s he, like most Jewish immigrants, including those who had formerly been quite militant in their ideological convictions, supported the New Deal and voted religiously for Roosevelt every four years. Nevertheless, his loyalty to the Democratic Party in America was not much stronger than his loyalty to the Socialist Party in Lithuania had been. He always remained skeptical and suspicious of abstract social theories, willing only to concede that a compassionate but judicious reformism was on the whole preferable to a rapacious rugged individualism.

My father found something else in Vilna which attracted him far more than politics, something to which he became passionately devoted, something which changed his life. Those same political and social organizations which sought to raise the level of education in the Jewish community through evening classes also hoped to stimulate its interest in culture by establishing societies or clubs in which men and women from the working class could discuss literature, study art, learn to appreciate music, and perform in amateur theatricals. My father joined one of the dramatic clubs, thereby finding at last an outlet for thoughts and emotions he had found it impossible to express in daily life. Like many people drawn to acting, he discovered that he could say and do things on the stage which he could never bring himself to say or do in his everyday existence. And that discovery became a source of liberation for him.

Outwardly he remained unchanged, the same taciturn, gloomy young man, unwilling or unable to reveal his inner feelings, hiding his loneliness behind a show of gruffness. But once the curtain rose, he became transformed. The parts which he liked to play, in which he displayed the greatest talent, were not those of the dashing adventurer or romantic lover. He was essentially a character actor, preferring to portray clumsy, slow-witted country bumpkins or portly middle-aged householders or, best of all, gray-bearded sages and patriarchs. His choice of roles revealed something of his own personality and character.

My father's talent for the stage brought him into contact with other young men and women in Vilna who shared his interest in the theater and his commitment to a new form of Jewish dramaturgy. They were a remarkable group, bright, gifted, idealistic, and full of youthful enthusiasm. Almost all of them came from middle-class families; almost all had received at least some formal education. My father was something of an oddity among them: a man of working-class background, poor, self-educated, without social polish or family connections. And yet they accepted him as an equal, while he in turn came to feel at ease in their company, probably for the first time in his life. Their shared devotion to an inspiring cultural ideal made them equals. They began to perform together on the stage, first as amateurs and then as a professional theatrical ensemble, the best-known theatrical ensemble in the history of the Yiddish theater: the Vilna Company.

Faithful to their artistic vision, they organized their group on principles different from those of most stage companies. There were to be no stars and no bit players, no leading parts, no supporting roles. The names of the actors were to appear on programs and posters in strictly alphabetical order and in letters of equal size. As for salaries, all members of the ensemble were to be paid the same, the profits being divided among them evenly. The Vilna Company would have no room for professional jealousies or artistic rivalries, for oversensitive egos or temperamental personalities. Private feelings would have to be subordinated to the great cause of Yiddish culture.

I met some of the members in the 1930s and 1940s, long after the company had ceased to exist. Among those I remember best was David Herman, its artistic director, a tall man, stoutish and dignified, graying at the temples, nothing very dramatic or theatrical about him, looking rather like a prosperous businessman or a successful stockbroker. Noah Nakhbush, a gifted character actor, was quite different. A lively little man with an infectious sense of humor, full of amusing stories and mischievous jokes, he delighted in recalling funny little incidents from the good old days, when they were all so much younger and better-looking and so full of hope. Sholem Tanin, handsome, distinguished, and slightly aloof, was born to play a star-crossed lover or some refined patrician intellectual in a Chekhov play. When I got to know him, he still had the bearing of a proud Russian aristocrat from the last twilight years of czarism. What impressed me most about Leib Kadison at our first meeting during my early adolescence was the sharp glance, the furrowed brow, the bushy eyebrows, and that huge head of frizzly gray hair. But all of them without exception seemed to me so interesting and colorful, so polished and sophisticated, so completely out of the ordinary.

Yet the two members of the Vilna Company I wanted to meet most were actually the ones I met last. I had often heard my parents speak of Alexander Azro and Sonia Alomis, the "beautiful" Alomis, as she was frequently described by those who had known her. When as a young man I was finally introduced to them, she was already well into middle age. But even then it was apparent that in her younger days she must indeed have been a beauty. She and her husband had had some falling-out with my father and mother. What the reason was remains unclear to me; my parents were reluctant to talk about it. But professional rivalries and jealousies had no doubt been the root cause of the quarrel. Both Azro and my father were leading members of the company, both were talented character actors, both were ambitious, both were headstrong. Alomis and my mother were competitors as well, attractive young women appearing on the stage in similar roles, eager for the limelight, hungry for recognition, each jealous of the success achieved by the other. The result was an estrangement which lasted for some twenty years. Only around the time of the Second World War did the former rivals become reconciled, witnesses now to the destruction of the Jewish community in which they had grown up, mourning amid the ruins of their youthful hopes and aspirations.

The repertoire of the Vilna Company reflected its vision of what the new Yiddish theater should be. Its members looked down on the popular lowbrow tradition, on the song and dance numbers, the vaudeville sketches and burlesque parodies, and especially the coarse jokes and risqué stories. They found all that demeaning. They were more tolerant, but not much more, of the genteel Victorian melodramas and tearjerkers which had become popular in the last decades of the nineteenth century. Those seemed to them maudlin and artificial. What they wanted was a radically different form of Jewish dramaturgy, a form which would respond to the new currents of realism, expressionism, and symbolism transforming European culture. They found what they were looking for in the plays of Peretz, Asch, Hirschbein, and Leon Kobrin, later in Ansky, and sometimes in the Yiddish translations of Schnitzler, Sudermann, and Artsybashev. Armed with a new cultural ideology, a new acting technique, and a new dramatic repertoire, they set out to conquer and reshape the Jewish theater.

In 1917 the Vilna Company came to Warsaw. By then its reputation had spread throughout the Jewish community of Eastern Europe. It had

for some time been receiving urgent invitations from various cities in
the czarist empire to display on the local stage the exciting achievements
of the new Yiddish dramaturgy. But travel was difficult for an ensemble
of Jewish actors. The authorities were indifferent and sometimes suspicious of efforts to promote secular culture among the uneducated
masses of Russian Jewry. They felt that there was something vaguely
subversive about an attempt to popularize a modern form of dramatic
art in the ghetto. A rejection of established values in literature and
drama, they feared, might encourage a rejection of established values in
society and politics. And they were of course right. The implications of
secularized Yiddish dramaturgy were in fact revolutionary, and not only
in the arts and letters. The reluctance of Russian bureaucrats to allow
the company to perform outside Vilna was quite understandable.

That changed, however, when the German army occupied Poland
and Lithuania during the First World War. For one thing, the new mas-
ters of Eastern Europe had a greater respect for artistic achievement
than the old ones. They believed that the spread of education and culture among the lower classes should be encouraged, not only in their
own fatherland but in other countries as well. The Vilna Company
found support, moreover, among Jewish officers in the occupying forces,
most of them reservists called to active duty when the war broke out,
who were interested in the artistic aspirations of their eastern coreligionists. Even some of the non-Jewish members of the German military administration proved sympathetic to a movement seeking to raise
the cultural level of East European Jewry. The Vilna Company could
finally undertake regular tours to other cities in its artistic crusade to
bring the new Yiddish drama to the masses.

That was what enabled it to accept an invitation in 1917 to make a
guest appearance in Warsaw, the city with the largest Jewish population
in Europe. For most of its members this trip to the Polish capital was
memorable because it represented a recognition at last of the cultural
importance which their ensemble had achieved. But for my father it
meant even more than that. For him it became a turning point in his
life as crucial as the one a dozen years earlier when he had left Kovnata
for Vilna. For during that visit to Warsaw he met my mother.

Chapter 2

Those Patrician Rubinlichts of Gesia Street

Bella Rubinlicht came from a family which at first glance seemed to resemble that of Chaim Shneyer Hamerow. Her father, like his, was a pious Jew with the usual long, gray beard, wearing the familiar black hat and long coat, and reciting every morning, afternoon, and evening those endless prayers and blessings required of the devout. Her mother, like his, was pious as well, modest and respectable in appearance, maintaining order in the household, blessing the candles on Friday night, dutifully sitting in the women's gallery of the synagogue on the Sabbath, and faithfully repeating the prescribed religious supplications which, though not as numerous as those expected of her husband, were numerous enough. The two families resembled each other, moreover, in their large size. My paternal grandparents had seven children, while my maternal grandparents had sixteen, twelve of whom reached adulthood. That was an impressive number, even by the prolific standards of the orthodox Jewish community.

But there the resemblance ended. For while my father's family lived in poverty and hunger, my mother's was well-to-do, even affluent. Her father had been a real-estate broker, shrewd, energetic, and successful. My paternal grandmother, who for some reason was not very fond of her Warsaw in-laws, would grumble occasionally that he was a little devious and untrustworthy. What is undeniable is that he acted with determination and vigor in defense of his business interests. Speaking fluent Polish, he would often appear in court in person in order to plead his case in the many financial litigations in which he was involved. That must have been an interesting sight: a Jew dressed in the traditional costume of religious orthodoxy, but proud and dignified, standing before a panel of stern, aristocratic Polish judges, expounding some abstruse point of the law. Whether he ever equivocated or dissembled may perhaps be open to question, but there can be no doubt about his boldness.

His mother, my great-grandmother, came from a prosperous family as well: the Vinavers. I am not sure how they made their money, but they had apparently been successful in business for several generations. My mother even used to tell me that one of our ancestors had been the proprietress of an inn in Praga, the eastern suburb of Warsaw, and that in 1812, during his retreat from Russia, Napoleon had stopped at that inn and had actually played a game of chess with her, hoping no doubt to take his mind off his troubles. I always found that story fascinating. To think that a forebear of mine had actually met and talked to the great French emperor, the conqueror of Europe. The mind boggled. I suppose that later I could have checked on the accuracy of this account. There are after all detailed descriptions of Napoleon's flight from Moscow. But I could never bring myself to do it. Why spoil a good story?

By the time I got to know my maternal grandparents, their wealth had largely disappeared. They had invested heavily in czarist government bonds, which became worthless after the Bolshevik revolution. But even in the 1920s there were signs of their former affluence. They still lived in a spacious apartment at 29 Gesia Street in the heart of the Jewish quarter of Warsaw. The parquet floors continued to gleam brightly in a rich brown hue, some of the furniture still looked elegant and expensive, and the huge grand piano in the living room was as resplendent as ever, although I cannot remember hearing anyone play it. More impressive to me as a child was the flushing toilet, situated not on the landing, where it would have had to be shared with other tenants in the building, but inside the apartment itself for the exclusive use of its residents. That was a rare luxury. The most persuasive evidence that the family had once been affluent, however, was the secular education which each of the twelve children received, usually at a *gimnazjum*, one of the exclusive secondary schools in which not only the curriculum but also the tuition was exacting. To pay for such an education must have taken a lot of money.

That my grandfather was willing to pay it reflected his determination to open to his children social advantages and professional opportunities which had been inaccessible to him. But how could he, the shrewd, experienced businessman, not have foreseen that the secular education he was providing for them would inevitably lead to a secular outlook? Perhaps he hoped to preserve their loyalty to the orthodox faith through habit, example, and exhortation. But he had miscalculated. The younger generation of Rubinlichts became alienated from the religious tradition in which it had grown up. On Jewish holidays and festivals my aunts and uncles would still visit the home of their parents, taking part in the various ritual celebrations, but only as an expression of filial duty. Otherwise, they never went to the synagogue, they ignored the orthodox dietary laws, and they spoke only Polish among themselves. If my father's siblings, who had received a strictly religious education, became nonbelievers almost as soon as they left the parental household, how could my mother's siblings, who had attended secular schools, be expected to go on believing in the Torah?

The process of secularization, moreover, had the same effect on the family size of the younger Rubinlichts as on that of the younger Hamerows. My parental grandparents had seven children, who in turn had a combined total of eleven children. My maternal grandparents, on the other hand, who had sixteen children, twelve of whom reached maturity, had only six grandchildren. The sharp difference in the reproductive rate of the two generations was the result of a sharp difference in their attitudes, feelings, and beliefs. The young people no longer regarded procreation as a religious obligation but rather as a rational, calculated decision. They hoped, moreover, that by restricting the number of their children they could provide them with a higher standard of living and a greater chance of success. Above all, their view of the role of women in the social order was changing from that of mothers and homemakers to that of independent, self-supporting breadwinners. This was one of the most significant aspects of the great transformation which the East European Jewish community was beginning to experience around the turn of the century.

Important differences remained, however, in the way the two families responded to the new forces of secularization and modernization. The Hamerows, though rejecting the religious faith of their ancestors, remained closely attached to their Jewishness, not as a matter of principle or conviction but out of habit. They continued to speak Yiddish, at least among themselves, they liked to recall incidents and tell stories about life in the Old World shtetl, they continued to enjoy traditional Jewish cooking, and occasionally they would even go to a Yiddish theater to hear the "mother tongue" spoken on the stage. The Rubinlichts, on the other hand, became Polonized. They spoke in Polish not only to one another but even to their parents. They became devout admirers of Polish literature, poetry, drama, music, and art. And they no longer remembered, or at least they pretended not to remember, the Yiddish they had heard at home as children. To be sure, Polish society would not let them forget that they were still Jews. But their hope was that someday they and others like them would be accepted as full and equal members of the national community without regard for origin, religion, or ethnic background. Only the tragic experience of the Holocaust taught them how futile that hope had been.

The differences in the educational and cultural environment of the Hamerows and the Rubinlichts account largely for the differences in their social and economic position. My father's siblings were employed mostly in manual occupations, the women in the garment industry as a rule, the men in factory production, maintenance work, or delivery service. Only my father succeeded in gaining admittance to one of the professions. In contrast, my mother's siblings were almost all in occupations requiring at least some higher education or technical training. Of her four brothers, one was a chemist, another a sculptor, a third a businessman, and the fourth a bank accountant. The sisters were generally employed in cultural or artistic occupations: publishing, stage design, dress styling, and children's theater. Only one worked in a more down-to-earth but equally skilled profession: medical testing. All of them were proud of their accomplishments, perhaps too proud. They tended to look down on those who had less education or less sophistication or less refinement. Behind my father's back they would sometimes refer to him, half humorously, half condescendingly, as the "little ruffian." Although he soon found out what they were saying, and I can guess who told him, he always described the Rubinlichts as a "highly talented family." His resentment of their assumed superiority did not blind him to their merits and accomplishments.

The most important difference between the two families, however, the most profound, the most tragic, derived from their differing experiences during the Second World War. Since by then three of my paternal grandmother's six living children resided in the United States, they were safe from the fury of National Socialist anti-Semitism. Even of the other three, the ones who lived in France, only one perished in a German death camp. Counting all members of the extended family who were living in Europe at the outbreak of hostilities—my grandmother, her daughters in Paris, their husbands, Max's widow in Russia, and the three grandchildren—seven out of eleven survived. In my mother's family the ratio of survivors to victims was the reverse. Of the eighteen Rubinlichts who lived in Poland in 1939—my recently widowed grandfather, nine of his children, their five spouses, and his three grandchildren—only three were still alive in 1945. Those proportions were not unusual in the Jewish community of Eastern Europe. The implacable resolve of the Third Reich to achieve a "final solution" to the "Jewish question," and the willingness of a large part of the non-Jewish population to contribute to its success, resulted in the extermination of between 80 and 90 percent of the Jews living in the region.

The members of the Rubinlicht family whom I remember best are those who either escaped or survived the Holocaust, since they were the ones with whom I could meet and converse after the war. My mother's older sister Cesia had received the same secular education as her siblings, and had like them become assimilated and Polonized. But around 1920 she married a young man who was an ardent Zionist, and shortly thereafter the two of them emigrated to Palestine. That changed her life completely. Her husband died unexpectedly in the 1930s, leaving her alone to raise two small children, earn enough money to support her family, and adjust to a new and strange way of life. Yet adversity brought out hidden qualities in the young woman, revealing not only considerable courage but considerable resourcefulness as well. She gradually shed the elegant manner and clever banter of polite Polish society, she soon found steady employment, some of it rather menial, she managed to earn a modest livelihood, and she succeeded in providing her sons with a warm, loving environment. She never complained, never regretted, never reproached. When I got to know her, she was in her sixties, but still cheerful and pleasant, still full of good spirits, still determined to enjoy to the full whatever was left of her life.

Her younger sister Felice or Felka was both more and less fortunate. Tense, nervous, discontented, and resentful, she suffered from a perpetual sense of alienation. That was no doubt a result of the fact that as a young girl she had been chosen by her parents to go and live in Ozorkov with an aunt whose maternal instincts had remained unfulfilled. The experience must have been devastating for Felka. The feeling that she had been rejected, that while her brothers and sisters were playing, joking, laughing, and having fun in Warsaw, she had been condemned to live alone, away from her family, that feeling embittered her life permanently.

During those lonely years in Ozorkov she met a young man who became attracted to her, and the two soon fell in love, swearing eternal devotion to one another. They proved more faithful to their vows than is usually the case. Even after he emigrated to America, even while he was working as a printer by day and studying for a college degree at night, they continued to exchange assurances of undying affection. After graduating cum laude, he went to France to enroll in the school of medicine at the University of Nancy. Felka, who had in the meantime been training to become a dress designer, joined him and they were married. Shortly before the outbreak of the Second World War they returned to the United States, just in the nick of time. Their love, however, though tested by a long separation and considerable hardship, was not enough to ensure a happy marriage. Felka became increasingly moody, restless, resentful, and bitter, while her husband grew little by little disenchanted and withdrawn. Eventually they divorced. She spent her last years in loneliness, childless and friendless, alienated from her surviving brothers and sisters, still brooding over the cruel rejection she had suffered long ago, during her solitary, unhappy childhood in Ozorkov.

Of the Rubinlichts who remained in Warsaw, the ones I remember best are the two survivors, Henryk or Heniek and Leon. Although Heniek became estranged from his sister Felka late in life, they actually resembled each other in many respects. He too was tense, unstable, insecure, and often resentful. He devoted his restless energy to being or rather attempting to be a shrewd businessman. All his life he pursued success relentlessly, trying his hand at venture after venture, now one dubious investment, then another, first this project, then that, then a third, each invariably turning out badly. Yet he refused to become discouraged. The next time would be different; he would soon become wealthy, respected, admired, and envied. He went on to the end desperately chasing the will-o'-the-wisp of fortune.

When the Wehrmacht occupied Poland in 1939, Heniek was forced to work for starvation wages in a factory manufacturing military supplies which the German authorities had established. But he soon recognized that the ultimate purpose of the conquerors was not oppression or exploitation but extermination. Indeed, his wife and daughter were eventually deported to a death camp from which they never returned. He decided therefore to leave the ghetto illegally and cross over to the "Aryan" side with the help of forged identity papers. Still, life there proved dangerous as well. Constantly threatened with betrayal by implacable bigots and rapacious extortionists preying on the victims of Nazi racism, he finally found refuge with a Polish woman who became successively his protector, his beloved, and finally his wife. Amid the cruelties and horrors of genocide, she and others like her, men and women who risked their lives to help save fellow human beings, who defied not only German commands but Polish prejudices, attest that even the most ruthless tyranny cannot completely silence the voice of conscience. They belong to that small company of the righteous who will someday sit at God's right hand. Indeed, by now most of them do.

After the war Heniek, his new wife, and their infant daughter emigrated to Canada. But the end of the dangers they had faced for so long also led to the reemergence of their less heroic qualities. Both he and she were too insecure, nervous, obsessed, and driven to adjust to the humdrum existence of peacetime. There were arguments and quarrels, reproaches and accusations, then a separation, and finally a divorce. Heniek lived to a ripe old age, still pursuing his dream of a successful business career, full of projects, plans, designs, and schemes for getting rich, refusing to be discouraged by their invariable failure. But he also continued to be haunted by terrible memories of the destruction forty years before of the world of his youth, traumatized to his dying day by the horror of the Holocaust.

Leon, only a year or two younger than Heniek, was different. I still remember him as a young man, elegant, well-bred, blond, blue-eyed, and rather haughty, looking "good," as assimilated Jews used to say, that is, not looking Jewish. He was then a devoted admirer of Polish culture, speaking, writing, and thinking in Polish. He even composed poetry in Polish. His service in Pilsudski's army during the war with Russia in 1920 helped him obtain a position as accountant in a government bank, a rare distinction for someone with his name and background. He married a young woman very much like him, the daughter of a well-to-do Jewish family, also assimilated and Polonized. Both regarded themselves as examples of how high Jews could rise in Polish society, provided they looked, talked, believed, and thought like Poles.

The war changed Leon's outlook. He escaped the Holocaust by illegally crossing from the German to the Russian zone of occupation shortly after the Polish defeat. The Russians, however, regarded refugees from Hitler's oppression, whether Jews or Poles, as hostile aliens. Leon was sent to a remote settlement in Siberia along with other Polish fugitives, where for almost two years he was employed at hard manual labor. There he began to see the cruel realities which he had preferred to overlook in the days before the war. Many of the Polish refugees, though forced to endure the same hardships and injustices, still regarded him as an outsider, as an interloper who could never really become one of them, sometimes even as a Judas responsible for the defeat of their country. Leon gradually came to feel that his earlier views regarding assimilation were not only wrong but demeaning.

His situation improved with the outbreak of hostilities between the Third Reich and the Soviet Union in the summer of 1941. The Russians suddenly started viewing the refugees from Poland not as dangerous aliens but as potential allies. They even formed a Polish army under the command of the Soviet general staff to participate in the struggle against what had now become the common enemy. Leon, who had been a reservist in the armed forces of prewar Poland, became a member of this new Polish army. He returned to Poland in 1944 with the advancing Soviet troops to find that all the members of the Rubinlicht family whom he had left behind in Warsaw four years earlier were now dead except Heniek. Leon's wife had also managed to survive, thanks to the bravery of a Polish woman who risked her own life to save one of those despised Jews. She too belongs to that small, select company of the righteous. But to Leon the heroism of the few was outweighed by the complicity of the many. Not only had there been widespread collaboration by Poles in the Nazi campaign of extermination against the Jews, but even after the defeat of Germany anti-Semitic attitudes and activities persisted in Poland. Leon and his wife decided to emigrate.

They went to Israel, where her brother had settled shortly after the war. Yet although Leon could finally resume a more or less stable existence, the elegant young assimilationist so proud of his Polishness was now completely changed. He suddenly began to remember the Yiddish he had heard as a child in his father's house, the Yiddish he had tried so hard to forget. In conversing with his surviving siblings, he would still occasionally lapse into Polish, yet he preferred as a matter of principle to speak and write in Yiddish. He even resumed composing poetry, though only in the language of his parents and grandparents. He found a secure but modest livelihood working as an accountant or bookkeeper for a large baking company. His major occupation, however, one which interested him far more than calculating expenditures or estimating profits, was recalling the world of his youth. Like Heniek, he spent the remaining forty years of life mourning the tragic fate of the family and the community into which he had been born.

Of those Rubinlichts whom I never saw again after leaving Poland, the ones who stand out most clearly in my mind are two of my aunts: Judith or Jadzia and Halina or Hala. Jadzia, the eldest of my mother's sisters, was a little like Leon: reserved, stern, dignified, and proud. Like Leon, moreover, she had become completely Polonized and had even worked for a time as editor for a Polish newspaper. I remember overhearing my aunt Rivke, my father's youngest sister, who liked to gossip, especially about my mother's family, confide to an acquaintance that Jadzia had once fallen in love with a young man, a Pole who worked for the same publishing house, but nothing had come of their romance. The parents on both sides objected to their marriage, not only for religious reasons but because the young lovers came from "two different worlds." I cannot vouch for the accuracy of that story. But I do recall that by the time I got to know Jadzia, she was facing an even greater misfortune than the unhappy end of a love affair. She had developed a progressive arthritic degeneration which gradually deprived her of the use of her hands. Since she could no longer work, she was forced to live with her parents, dependent on the generosity of the family, lonely, despondent, frightened, and resentful.

When I left Poland, she gave me as a farewell present a book she had once edited, all about the heroic struggle of the Poles in the nineteenth century against the tyranny of those awful Russians. It was the only thing left that she could still give me, she remarked with some bitterness. But even worse things were in store for her. After the Germans occupied Poland, her relatives decided, according to Heniek's account years later, that the best thing would be to put her to death quickly by poison, presumably without her knowledge. Could he have been fantasizing? Perhaps, although euthanasia of the sick and crippled was not uncommon in the ghettos of Eastern Europe under the genocidal rule of the Third Reich. In view of what happened to the other Rubinlichts, it would have been an act of kindness.

My favorite among the aunts and uncles in Warsaw was Hala, only three or four years younger than Jadzia, but altogether different in character and temperament. She had little of her sister's elegant reserve; she was more natural and spontaneous, more approachable, more down-to-earth. Even her appearance was simple and unpretentious. Someone who had known the family before the war remembered afterward that Hala was "the plain-looking one" among all those attractive Rubinlicht girls. But what she lacked in prettiness she more than made up in kindness and cheerfulness. Whenever I visited my grandfather's home in Warsaw, she was the one who would display the greatest interest in how I was and what I was doing. She would show me the sights of the big city, take me to the movies, cook some favorite dish of mine, offer me chocolate goodies, and best of all, she would let me explore her mysterious, fascinating laboratory.

Hala was a medical assistant, trained to examine and evaluate biological specimens obtained by physicians from their patients. She had established a small laboratory in one of the rooms of my grandfather's apartment, and here she would show me how the microscope worked, let me whirl the centrifuge, teach me how to light the Bunsen burner, and point out the strange, wondrous bottles, tubes, beakers, and dishes lining the walls. I found all that entrancing. Before I left Poland, Hala even typed up at my request a solemn vow by which I and one of her male friends swore to continue to correspond for the rest of our lives. She then used her lancet to draw a drop of blood from each of us which was smeared next to our signatures as a token that we really meant it. I am sorry to have to report, however, that this oath was broken very soon after my departure.

Hala's subsequent life followed the familiar tragic pattern. During the 1930s she married a doctor whom she had come to know in the course of her professional career. Just prior to the war they had a child, a son whom I never had a chance to meet. Then the German occupation of Poland put an end to all their hopes and expectations. According to Heniek, whose memory was not always reliable but who lived in Warsaw during that time, Hala could not endure the horror of what was happening. She suffered a nervous or mental breakdown, and was deported to a death camp early in the Nazi campaign of extermination. Her husband and child held out a little longer, but eventually hunger and privation drove them from their hiding place outside the ghetto. They were promptly arrested by the Polish police, handed over to the Germans, and sent to perish in Treblinka. Details about the time, place, and circumstances of Hala's death, as of almost all victims of the Holocaust, remain unknown. But I will always remember her kind generosity, her good nature, and that marvelous, exciting laboratory of hers which a long time ago filled a little boy with such wonderment.

My recollections of the other Rubinlichts are rather vague. On rare occasions, usually at a family gathering in the home of my grandparents to celebrate some religious holiday, I would see my uncle Moritz, the oldest of my mother's many siblings. Shy, timid, and withdrawn, something of a mama's boy all his life, he was easy to overlook. Indeed, he seemed almost to ask to be overlooked. A chemist by profession, he had married a woman very much like him, just as shy, timid, and withdrawn. Predictably, they had no children, and just as predictably, he became the first member of his family to perish in the Holocaust. Perhaps he had been destined from birth to end up a victim. He died as he had lived, quietly, unobtrusively, unprotestingly. No one knows how, when, or where. Many years later Leon dedicated one of his poems of lamentation to his brother Moritz: "It must have been hard for you to die without us, /But it is harder still for me to live without you."

My recollections of my uncle Felix or Felek are equally hazy. He was a few years younger than Moritz, whom he resembled in some ways. But Felek was otherworldly rather than shy, impractical rather than timid. He was a sculptor, neither highly successful nor entirely unsuccessful, managing to earn a modest livelihood by his art. I remember visiting his studio once and being impressed by the various plaster heads and torsos scattered at random around the room. More lasting reminders were the casts he had made of the fifteenth-century wood carvings by the German sculptor Veit Stoss which adorn the high altar of the Church of the Virgin Mary in Cracow. Felek gave some of those casts to my mother, who displayed them proudly on the walls of our living room. He never married, determined apparently to devote himself solely to his art. When the war broke out, he became the first of the Rubinlichts to die, even before the Germans conquered Poland. During the siege of Warsaw in September 1939, Felek was mortally wounded by a bomb fragment. At least he did not have to witness the horrors of the next few years, horrors which would have broken his kind, gentle spirit.

My aunt Ruth was a little younger than Felek, closer in age to my mother. The two sisters were in fact both friends and rivals, the prettiest of the Rubinlicht girls, constantly praised, flattered, admired, and courted. But Ruth was different from Bella, in appearance as well as temperament. She was a pale, cool, blue-eyed beauty with a faint Gioconda smile, whose serenity and remoteness only seemed to enhance her attractiveness. Of her many suitors, the one she consented to marry was Boaz Karlinski, a journalist for the *Moment*, the leading Yiddish newspaper in Warsaw. I remember during my teens seeing a photograph of the two of them, his head resting gently on her bosom, her arms encircling his neck and shoulders. To my adolescent sensibilities there was something very intimate, almost suggestive, about that picture of marital bliss.

Still, the bliss did not last very long. Boaz died of leukemia shortly before the war, while still middle-aged, thus being spared the anguish of witnessing what was about to happen. When the Germans came, Ruth and her son managed to survive for a while, largely because he was serving as a member of the Jewish police force which the Nazi occupation established in the ghetto to enforce its will. But when the Third Reich's official policy of segregation and exploitation turned into outright genocide, they too became its victims.

Francisca or Franka, next to the youngest of my mother's sisters, resembled Ruth in appearance more than in character or temperament. She too was pale, serene, elegant, and a little aloof, though not quite as coolly attractive. She had a natural talent for art, especially painting, which helped her find employment as a stage designer in a Polish theater. She never married, but I remember overhearing gossip that she had had several suitors, Poles as well as Jews, and that she had even lived with one of them in an extramarital relationship. That would not have been surprising, since she was a committed leftist, a communist or at least a communist sympathizer, and she moved in circles in which unconventional unions were by no means uncommon.

That probably saved or rather prolonged her life. When the Germans occupied Warsaw, she found refuge on the "Aryan" side with the help of Polish friends. Here she lived for a time with her brother Heniek, who had also managed to escape from the ghetto. But the constant gnawing fear of being discovered or betrayed or blackmailed or abused, not to mention the knowledge of what was happening to her family on the other side of the wall, undermined Franka's health. She died quite suddenly of some unexplained seizure or stroke. Her death can be described as natural only if terror, brutality, oppression, and anguish can be described as natural.

The youngest of my mother's siblings was Natalie or Nacia, whom I remember as a shy young girl, pretty, with sparkling dark eyes and long brown hair, speaking only Polish, like all the Rubinlichts, and hungrily reading Polish novels, short stories, poems, plays, histories, biographies, and autobiographies. While I was still in Poland, she became engaged to a young man who came from a well-to-do business family. What I remember about him best is that despite his eyeglasses, which gave him a studious, almost rabbinical look, he was reputed to be an expert horseman. That impressed me, even though I never actually saw him in the saddle. Still, I could never quite overcome a certain sense of incongruity between his wearing of spectacles and the idea of his galloping through woods and fields on a wild, fiery steed.

Shortly after I left for America, Nacia and her fiancé were married. They apparently lived harmoniously and comfortably until the war, but they had no children. In spite of that, or perhaps because of it, she devoted herself to running a children's theater intended to serve the cultural needs of the youngest members of the Jewish community. But their quiet, contented existence came to an end with the outbreak of hostilities in 1939. I have little information about what happened to them afterward. Nacia apparently continued for a while her efforts to provide theatrical entertainment for the most vulnerable, most pitiable inhabitants of the ghetto, who were now even hungrier for diversion than before. But then the final destruction of the Jewish community put an end not only to her work but to her life. She too became one of the six million.

Of all the Rubinlichts, the one I knew best, the one I remember most clearly, and the one who influenced me most profoundly was of course my mother. She and Ruth were in the middle age range of my grandparents' eight daughters, younger than Jadzia, Cesia, and Hala, but older than Felka, Franka, and Nacia. Although they were by general agreement the two most attractive ones, there were significant differences between them, in personality even more than appearance. One was aloof, the other outgoing; one was serious, the other playful and mischievous; one was cool and reserved, the other warm and ingratiating. Bella exuded, not unawares, a charming spontaneity. There is a photograph taken during her late twenties or early thirties in which she poses as an endearing little girl, wearing a short dress, long hair flowing down her back, holding a ball in one hand and a toy in the other, looking into the camera with a roguish smile. Those who knew her, women as well as men, found her enchanting. Long afterward they would describe her as "lovable," "sunny," "lively," and "captivating." She had discovered early in life the precious secret of popularity.

Her appeal was not entirely artless, however. She knew quite well what made her so attractive; she knew what was required to make people smile, to gain their favor and admiration. That does not mean that her gaiety was artificial. She genuinely liked to be with others, she liked to amuse and entertain. She had a sharp sense of humor, a knack for storytelling, an eye for the incongruous and picturesque, a talent for imitation and caricature. But she needed an audience, she needed to be surrounded by companions, listeners, devotees, and admirers. Alone, she would often lapse into brooding, sometimes even bitterness. That kind of personality is common among people who are drawn to show business.

The education my mother received was similar to that of the other members of her family: comprehensive, highly demanding, and purely secular. She attended one of those exclusive secondary schools for girls to which well-to-do Jewish parents in Poland were by the turn of the century beginning to send their daughters. Here she acquired her flaw-less command of Polish, the language in which she felt most comfort-able throughout her life, even after she had become an actress on the Yiddish stage. It was the language into which she would frequently lapse when conversing with her surviving siblings after the war. In writ-ing Yiddish, moreover, she always used the Latin rather than the Hebrew alphabet, another legacy of those early years in a Warsaw *gimnazjum*. She also acquired a good command of foreign languages, not only Russian, which was a requirement in the curriculum of the sec-ondary schools of Poland under czarist rule, but French and German as well, even a smattering of English.

Her favorite subject, however, was literature, especially European drama, from Shakespeare to Chekhov, from Molière to Ibsen. She was almost equally fond of history, especially the tragic romances of roy-alty: Henry VIII and Anne Boleyn, Napoleon and Maria Walewska, and Archduke Rudolf of Austria and the beautiful Countess Vetsera. Yet she also knew quite a lot about the major developments in the warfare, diplomacy, and politics of Europe. Her education extended in fact beyond a sound knowledge of world geography to a good grasp of intermediate algebra and even a broad understanding of the major discoveries and theories of modern science. The *gimnazjum* she attended was clearly more than a finishing school.

But what was to be the purpose of her education? Her parents assumed that she would sooner or later marry and have a family of her own. Yet they also wanted all their children, daughters as well as sons, to be prepared to pursue some practical career. Therefore, after com-pleting her secondary schooling, Bella decided to study to become a teacher. There is an old photograph taken during the First World War, after the Germans had occupied Warsaw, showing her class in the school of education which she was attending to earn her teaching cer-tificate. Seated in the middle is a stiff, erect, stern man in uniform, looking directly into the camera, with a neatly trimmed mustache and close-cropped hair, a picture of the haughty Prussian army officer. Actually, he was the German instructor appointed by the occupation authorities to teach education courses. Grouped around him in various graceful poses are about fifteen or twenty young women, most of them seemingly Jewish, trying to look both serious and attractive in their commitment to pedagogy. And there among them is my mother, as serious as and even more attractive than any of the others.

Yet she must have realized quite early that the prim, strait-laced life of a schoolteacher was not for her. She needed something more exciting, something unusual, unconventional, and unpredictable, something defiantly bold. And so, at the same time that she was attending classes in pedagogy and child psychology, she also joined an amateur theatrical group in Warsaw, the "Artistic Corner," which had been formed to promote the ideas and ideals of the new Yiddish drama. It was at this time that she adopted the stage name Bella Bellarina. She did so, she explained later, in order to keep secret from her parents her resolve to devote herself to the theater. Especially her pious, respectable father would have been scandalized to learn that his daughter was risking her reputation by displaying herself publicly on the wicked, immoral stage. There may have been more to it than that, however. Perhaps she also found the sound of Bella Bellarina more euphonious than Bella Rubinlicht. In any event, whatever ideas she might have entertained at one time of becoming a teacher were soon discarded. She was now unalterably determined to become an actress, regardless of what it might cost. And that was when she met my father.

In 1917 the Vilna Company came to Warsaw for a guest appearance. For the members of the cultural elite of the Jewish community this was a festive occasion. The foremost dramatic group in the new secular Yiddish theater had arrived to display its repertoire on their city's stage. There were speeches, celebrations, dinners, and banquets. I still have in my possession a memento of those exciting days which I inherited from my father: a silver ornament for a fob chain inscribed to "Ch. Shneyer" with "thanks and remembrance" from the "Society of Jewish Writers and Journalists" in Warsaw. It was at this time also that the pretty young would-be actress Bella Bellarina first met one of the stars of the Vilna Company, a man now appearing on the stage as Chaim Shneyer, without the family name Hamerow. And before long—I cannot be sure exactly when or how—a passionate love affair began.

That love affair, however, was not only passionate; it was also stormy. My mother apparently had several other suitors. There was one in particular, a well-to-do professional or businessman with a serious interest in Yiddish culture, who could offer her position, comfort, and security. She and my father had a serious quarrel—I always thought it best not to ask why—and when the Vilna Company left Warsaw for an engagement in Lodz, she did not come to the railroad station to see him off. The romance was seemingly over.

But not really. Now that my father was gone, my mother had to face an agonizing choice. On one side stood stability and respectability with perhaps a touch of stodginess. On the other was excitement, challenge, adventure, and defiance of convention. Did she love my father or did she really love what he represented: commitment to art, life on the stage, limelight, applause, admiration, popularity, and fame? Probably both. In her mind they must have seemed inseparable. In any event, the young woman of twenty-one did something extraordinary, given the environment in which she had grown up, something requiring remarkable courage and determination. She ran away from home. She packed a small valise, left a note for her parents explaining what she was doing, and took the next train to Lodz. There she found out where my father was staying, went there, and offered to share his life on the basis of "free love," without the restricting bonds of formal marriage.

My father was taken aback. Not that unconventional unions of that sort were unusual in the world of the Yiddish theater. Far from it. In later years I would often hear from my parents how so-and-so in the Vilna Company had left his wife for someone else, someone who had in turn left her husband. Subsequently the two might become reconciled with their legal spouses or they might find new love partners or they might simply continue to live with the old ones. Show business, whether Jewish or non-Jewish, was never too punctilious about romantic attachments. Yet my father, despite his many years on the stage, always displayed a certain bourgeois propriety, almost a primness, in his personal relationships. What attracted him to the theater was the actor's art rather than the actor's life. He therefore proposed to my mother that they be married by a rabbi, not because either of them had serious religious scruples, but because that would make a reconciliation with his new in-laws easier. Since their marriage was never recorded with the civil authorities, it had no legal validity. But for my pious grandparents, a rabbinical blessing was enough. The newlyweds were now able to return to Warsaw, where the Rubinlichts could finally see and inspect the most recent addition to their family.

That initial meeting was not without strain or tension. My grandfather found it hard to accept that his daughter had run off to get married without his approval or even his knowledge, and to a "Litvak" at that. My mother's siblings, moreover, discovering that their new brother-in-law was an autodidact, without formal education or social polish, made little effort to disguise their sense of superiority. They would whisper and titter loudly about the "little ruffian" whom Bella had married, loudly enough for the "little ruffian" to overhear. He in turn resented their superciliousness and condescension. The mutual disapproval which became apparent at that first meeting remained a permanent feature of the relationship between my father and the Rubinlichts.

Still, the first few years of the marriage lived up more or less to my mother's expectations. She now became a member of the Vilna Company, though not without opposition. Some of the others regarded her as an outsider, an interloper. There were grumbles and complaints, rivalries and quarrels. The hard feelings between my father and mother on one side and Alexander Azro and Sonia Alomis on the other, feelings which persisted for more than two decades, were largely a result of those early tensions. But there were also gratifying experiences. My mother was now a professional actress, traveling all over Eastern Europe, appearing on the stage, earning applause, winning admiration, exciting envy, hobnobbing with actors, artists, writers, and intellectuals, leading the carefree life of Bohemia. It was all so exhilarating, so exciting.

There was one subject, however, on which my parents disagreed almost from the outset. My father wanted children; my mother remained reluctant. Their differences were understandable. Having a family would not interfere with his career, but it would clearly impede and restrict hers. She would have to bear the chief burden of parenthood. And so this became the source of frequent disputes between them. Long afterward my mother confessed to her daughter-in-law that during the early years of her marriage she had undergone several abortions. But finally in 1920, after becoming pregnant once again, she somehow reconciled herself to motherhood. I will never know exactly how or why I escaped the fate of my unknown, unborn brothers and sisters. What is clear, however, is that late in August, barely a week after the "miracle on the Vistula" in which Pilsudski's Polish troops defeated the Red Army, a second miracle occurred on the Vistula, historically not as important as the first, but a miracle nevertheless. For that was when I saw the light of day for the first time.

Chapter 3

Migrations, Metamorphoses, Memories

Being good parents is much more difficult for people who are in show business than for those who are not. While there are undoubtedly many exceptions to this generalization, both experience and logic support its overall validity. The actor's way of life is so different from that of other occupations and pursuits that it makes the successful rearing of children very hard. Those who choose it must get ready to go to work when everybody else is coming back from work. They climb into bed when everybody else is climbing out of bed. When their child returns from school, they are busy preparing for that evening's performance, and when their child starts out for school, they are still asleep after the previous evening's performance. The ordinary responsibilities of parenthood are thus almost impossible to reconcile with the daily demands and requirements of the stage. Parents and children tend to become more distant from one another, more detached, perhaps even more estranged than in most families.

What makes a normal parental relationship still more difficult is the character or personality or psychology of many of the people who are attracted to show business. They generally find it harder than others to subordinate their own needs and wishes to those of their children. They are frequently too hungry for the limelight, too eager for attention and applause, to perform uncomplainingly the many ordinary, unglamorous tasks required for the proper care of the young. They tire more quickly of feeding the baby, soothing its pain, drying its tears, changing its diapers, and providing it with a general sense of security. Nor do they always have the patience to supervise the growing child, to offer guidance and instruction, wait at the school door, visit the zoo, arrange the music lesson, or prepare for the birthday party. The knowledge that not far away, behind the footlights or in a nearby café, colleagues and rivals, as witty, charming, clever, and sophisticated as ever, are being admired and applauded, that knowledge makes successful parenthood still harder for actors. Their affection for their children may be as great as that of other parents, but their way of life renders it difficult for them to become closely involved in their children's upbringing.

My own parents are a good example. They were both happy to have a child; they both loved their newborn baby. Yet for them too parenthood presented serious problems. Who would take care of their son? Who would provide for his needs? Who would assume responsibility for his health and well-being? Those questions were especially troubling for my mother. She was the one who was expected, tacitly but universally, to assume the primary duty of nurturing and rearing the newborn infant. But what would that do to her career as an actress? What would it mean for her own ambitions and aspirations? For my father the situation was less difficult. He was free to pursue his profession without violating the implicit obligations of parenthood. Usually taciturn and introverted, always reserved, he displayed as much affection toward his son as he was capable of displaying. He would from time to time hold the baby, bounce it, coo at it, and make halfhearted, soothing noises. That was about as much as was expected of him. The duties facing my mother were more demanding. To perform them she would have to abandon, at least for the time being, the career on which she had just embarked, the career which had provided her with a new feeling of excitement and fulfillment. In its place she would have to accept the common, tedious routine of motherhood. The prospect was dismaying.

She tried to pretend to others that being a mother was a deeply satisfying experience, that it gave her a sense of accomplishment she had never experienced before. Perhaps she even half believed what she was saying. She certainly did not lose her sense of humor. She reported to friends, for example, that while she was walking with a distinguished elderly playwright through the streets of Warsaw during the latter stages of her pregnancy, a truckload of Polish soldiers heading for the front to battle the Russians made loud, coarse comments about her condition, congratulating her sexagenarian companion on his remarkable manly prowess. Even at this juncture in her life she remained outwardly as charming, amusing, playful, and mischievous as ever.

Yet those were actually very difficult days for my mother. The prospect of exchanging the glamor of the stage for the tedious obligations of parenthood troubled her far more than she was willing to admit. She could see all her achievements of recent years, all that glitter and excitement and applause, slipping away. Nor were her friends and relatives very helpful. She always remembered how shortly after I was born Ruth, her sibling rival, would remark, casually or teasingly or perhaps with a touch of spite, that it was a pity she had been unable to attend so-and-so's party or such and such a banquet. It had been so much fun; they had all wondered why she did not come. My mother would respond with some dismissive quip or a pious observation about the joys of motherhood. But inwardly she must have been profoundly perturbed by those reports of what she was missing.

She did not have to miss it for very long, however. In the struggle between maternal instincts and artistic aspirations, there could be little doubt which would ultimately prevail. As soon as feasible, perhaps even sooner, she returned to the life of the theater to which she had by now become completely addicted. And yet a feeling that she had somehow shirked her parental responsibilities for the sake of her professional ambitions continued to trouble her for the rest of her life. Years later she would often tell me the story of how she had been unable to breastfeed me when I was born because of some vague, unspecified, temporary ailment or incapacity. I therefore had to be entrusted to a wet nurse, a Polish woman who understandably chose to feed her own baby before feeding me. As a result I was perpetually hungry and frequently in tears. It almost broke my mother's heart, she insisted, to see her child in such a sad, unhappy state.

At first I used to wonder why she kept telling me this story over and over again. After all, I had no recollection of my infancy, and the inadequate care I may have received at that time had no lasting adverse effect on my health. Why then did she keep coming back to those painful early experiences of her motherhood? Why did she continue to dwell on the neglect with which the Polish wet nurse had treated me? Why did she go on describing the sorrow she had felt at seeing her baby forlorn and in tears? In retrospect, I suspect that she may have been trying indirectly, maybe subconsciously, to excuse her inability to subordinate her artistic aspirations to the obligations of parenthood. Perhaps that mysterious illness which made her incapable of breast-feeding was really a metaphor for her reluctance to jeopardize her career for the sake of her maternal duties. Perhaps she was in a roundabout way apologizing to me. Who knows?

In any event, the conflict between theatrical ambitions and maternal obligations was soon resolved, at least practically, if not emotionally or psychologically. I was not left to the care of unconcerned wet nurses or indifferent nannies for very long. A much more satisfactory arrangement was found. Shortly before my birth my paternal grandfather had died. That left his widow penniless. To make matters worse, although most of her children were by then on their own, the youngest one, my aunt Rivke, was only ten or eleven years old, incapable of supporting herself. Hence my father, the oldest son and most affluent member of the family, had begun to provide his mother and sister with financial assistance. Now the birth of his son offered an obvious answer both to his parental obligations and to their economic needs. Why not invite his mother and sister to come and live with us? While my parents were traveling all over Europe with the Vilna Company, my grandmother could stay home and look after me. They would no longer have to worry about nannies and nursemaids, and she would no longer have to worry about where the next meal or the next rent payment would come from. It seemed an ideal arrangement. And so at the end of 1920 or beginning of 1921 my grandmother left Kovnata for Warsaw, thereby becoming the most important person of my childhood.

She was by then in her fifties. Her life had been hard, spent in an unending struggle to raise seven children, supply them with food and clothing, provide them with shelter and a rudimentary education, and prepare them to earn their own livelihood. She had received little support from her elderly husband, who always remained remote and standoffish. The family lived in permanent poverty. One of my aunts remembered how one day, while the children sat at the table hungrily waiting for their meager dinner, their mother was as usual spreading the butter on their slices of bread thinner and thinner, trying to save as much as possible for the next meal. Finally the father, unable to contain himself any longer, burst out in a loud voice that she was to stop at once this scraping and scrimping and start feeding the family. She complied, silently but resentfully. She too loved the children, she too was hurt by the privation they had to endure. But what could she do? Bitter experience had taught her that being half hungry was better than facing outright starvation. The harsh circumstances of her existence had forced her to suppress her maternal feelings, to be stern and severe with those most dependent on her affection.

But that changed when she was invited by my parents to come and look after me. Now at last, well into middle age, she could express those

My father and my grandfather in Vilna in 1906.

Photograph of my father's family, taken around 1914, with my grandfather and grandmother in the center and, standing right to left, my father Chaim Shneyer, David, Mushel, and Max, and, left to right in front, Esther, Hanke, and Rivke.

Photograph of my father taken in Warsaw around 1917.

Photograph of my mother taken in Warsaw around 1918.

A photograph of the Vilna Company around 1918–19; sitting at right my father
Chaim Shneyer, sitting at left Boaz Karlinski, a journalist who married my aunt Ruth;
standing at far right is David Herman, third from right is Sonia Alomis,
fourth from right is the well-known Yiddish writer Jacob Dineson,
and at far left is Noah Nakhbush.

My father in the 1920s in the role of the saintly rabbi in S. Ansky's *The Dybbuk*.

natural emotions of motherhood against which she had fought so hard as a young woman. There was no longer any need to worry about food or shelter, clothing or education. She was able for the first time to lavish on her grandchild the care and affection which she had been forced to deny to her own children. Not that she suddenly began to coo or croon or speak in baby talk. She always remained a little strict, a little stern. She never hesitated to reprimand me for not finishing my soup or for dawdling over the chicken. Occasionally she would even tap me lightly on the backside for being more naughty than usual. And yet I always felt that she loved me. She would cook huge meals, perhaps to make up for the meager diet she had provided for her own family years before, meals which I was expected to finish to the last bite. In summer she would push the swing on which I sat, silently pleased with the appreciation I demonstrated by squeals of delight. In winter she would pull through the snow-covered streets a small sled with me on top, an elderly woman, grave and portly, providing fun for a little boy who rewarded her with loud shouts of merriment. Even now it seems rather touching.

My aunt Rivke, however, found it very irritating. She was not quite a teen-ager when she came to live with us, but she already had vivid and unpleasant memories of life in the parental home. She still remembered the poverty which she and her brothers and sisters had to endure. Even more bitter was the persistent feeling of rejection by her parents, who had been so busy trying to make ends meet that they had little time to show affection for their children. Her years of privation had finally come to an end, but Rivke felt that the maternal love which had been denied to her was now being lavished on her little nephew. He was the one who was getting all the attention, who was being comforted and soothed and praised and loved. Was that fair? She harbored an understandable resentment which I sensed even then. Though never actually mean, she remained as a rule cool and distant, often dissatisfied, and sometimes morose. The sense that she had been illtreated by fate remained with her for the rest of her life. Those who came to know her later would generally ascribe her gloomy disposition to her experiences during the Holocaust. But the actual source of her perpetual disgruntlement was in all probability the rejection she had encountered much earlier, during those impoverished, loveless years of her childhood.

While I was growing up in this strange *ménage à trois*, my parents were reaching the high point of their careers as actors on the Yiddish stage. The years immediately following the First World War were the most exciting period in the brief, brilliant flowering of secular culture in the Jewish community of Eastern Europe. The undisguised hostility toward Jews displayed by the czarist authorities was replaced by the outwardly more conciliatory attitude of the succession states of the Russian Empire. The constitutions of Poland, Lithuania, and Latvia as well as new liberal laws in the enlarged Romanian kingdom proclaimed that all citizens, regardless of religion or ethnic origin, were to enjoy equal protection under the law. To be sure, those avowals of tolerance toward the various minorities in the region represented a change in official policy rather than in popular attitude. They were part of a political strategy designed to gain the support of the democratic victors in the recent war. Beneath the surface of progressive legislation, anti-Semitic prejudices remained deep-seated not only among the masses but also in the government and the bureaucracy. Yet at least Jewish theatrical ensembles like the Vilna Company were now free to travel from city to city, from province to province, even from country to country within Eastern Europe. That was significant progress.

Still greater opportunities for the Yiddish theater were opening up farther west. The newly established democratic regimes in Central Europe, especially in Germany and Austria, relaxed many of the earlier restrictions against immigration from the east. At the same time the chaotic political and economic conditions resulting from the Russian Revolution, aggravated by military conflicts between the Bolshevik regime and the succession states, generated a large-scale westward migration of East European Jews, not only to cities like Berlin and Vienna, but beyond that to Paris, Brussels, Amsterdam, and London. The extent of this migration was greatly exaggerated by ultranationalistic parties and anti-Semitic organizations, which never tired of issuing dire warnings against the imminent Judaization of the national culture. But the postwar Jewish diaspora was in fact large enough to provide significant new support for Yiddish art and Yiddish culture.

Many of the migrants, isolated and lonely in their new, unfamiliar environment, hungered for the sound of the language which had been spoken at home. They wanted to see on the stage scenes of life in the shtetls of Poland and Lithuania to which they now looked back with a feeling of nostalgia. Their hope was that by going to a Yiddish theater they would recapture the feel, the flavor, the bittersweet experience of their youth. Many of them thus became ardent supporters of the new secular Jewish drama. What had started out forty or fifty years earlier as a primitive form of popular entertainment for the masses of East

European Jewry was now maturing into a serious expression of dramatic art capable of contributing to the culture of Europe as a whole.

My parents witnessed firsthand this exciting artistic and geographic expansion of the Yiddish theater. They traveled with the Vilna Company all over the Continent, first to Germany and then farther and farther west to France, Belgium, Holland, and finally Great Britain. Wherever they went, they found a warm, welcoming reception among expatriates from Eastern Europe hungry for a glimpse of the life they had known in the old country. And whenever they returned from one of those triumphal tours, they would bring back with them souvenirs and stories of the wondrous distant regions they had visited in the service of their art.

Hanging for years from the ceiling of our living room was one of those dark-green glass globes encased in a protective layer of cordage which Dutch fishermen used to float on the North Sea to mark the location of their nets. As a boy I often contemplated that mysterious globe, wondering what it would be like to be on a fishing boat in the ocean, defying the wind and the rain, ignoring storms and blizzards, hauling in enormous catches of sardines, herring, and salmon. Even more interesting was an illustrated guide to the works of art in the famous Rijksmuseum in Amsterdam, which my parents had acquired during one of their tours. In my teens I would sometimes leaf through its pages, studying the black-and-white reproductions of the paintings of Rembrandt and Hals, Vermeer and Ruisdael, fascinated by their evocation of Dutch life three hundred years before. At those times I wished my parents had taken me with them on those exciting trips of theirs.

They would often return from a tour, moreover, with interesting observations and stories. My mother in particular would years later still tell anecdotes about her travels, anecdotes which were amusing, charming, slightly embellished, and sometimes mischievous or even unkind. She liked to make fun, for example, of the way East European Jewish immigrants in Paris mispronounced and mangled the elegant French language. They transformed *joujou*, for instance, the word for a toy, into *tchutche*, while the fashionable rue de Rivoli became "Rivele gass" in their homely Yiddish.

My father, on the other hand, rarely told stories about his travels, and he never joked about the plebeian tastes and manners of Jewish emigrants from Eastern Europe. That was partly, but only partly, a reflection of his habitual reticence, his characteristic introversion. More important, while my mother was expressing, probably without realizing it, the sense of superiority, the condescension, with which many members of her family regarded their poor and uneducated fellow Jews, my father was more understanding, more sympathetic. He had after all grown up among them, he had been one of them, indeed, he still identified with them to a considerable extent. And besides, he too had occasionally been the butt of Rubinlicht superciliousness. Here then was another of those issues on which my father and mother so often disagreed.

They were in general agreement, however, regarding the country which was the most interesting, the most congenial, of all those they had visited during their professional tours. It was Germany. That may seem surprising in view of what was to happen only about a decade later. But the early years of the Weimar Republic were a period of exciting change and experimentation, culturally and artistically as well as politically. There were brave hopes that out of the military defeat of the old order, out of humiliation, privation, bitterness, and upheaval, would emerge a new social order based on liberty and justice. The national culture would be transformed as well, becoming less rigid and conventional, becoming more venturesome, imaginative, and daring. For a few exhilarating years the new democratic Germany, especially Berlin, provided a home for the youthful, defiant avant-garde of European arts and letters. All expressions, all forms of artistic insubordination, of cultural innovation and rebelliousness, were welcome. There was even room for a theatrical ensemble of young, self-taught actors from the backwaters of Eastern Europe who wanted to display before a cosmopolitan audience the proud achievements of the new Yiddish dramaturgy.

What my parents found especially impressive about Germany was the respect with which most people, even members of the working class, regarded cultural pursuits and accomplishments. In Poland, Lithuania, or Romania Jewish actors, like Jews in general, were usually treated with sullen indifference and sometimes with undisguised hostility. But in the Weimar Republic the prevailing attitude was quite different. One of the few stories about his travels which my father liked to tell dealt with a train ride which was taking the Vilna Company to Berlin. The conductor, noticing that a group of foreigners was occupying one of the coaches, inquired politely who they were and what they were doing in Germany. Having learned what their occupation was, he whispered solemnly to another railroad official that those passengers sitting back there in the rear compartment were "performers on the stage," indeed, they were "artists." He seemed genuinely impressed, and so was my father. Nothing that flattering had ever been said about him by a conductor on any of his many train rides to Vilna or Warsaw or Bucharest.

Even more gratifying was the warm, friendly reception which my parents found among German actors. In Eastern Europe there was a sharp division between the Jewish and the non-Jewish theater. The two carefully avoided any contact. One looked down on the other with scorn and condescension; the other regarded the first with resentment and bitterness. They were entirely separate worlds, mutually suspicious and hostile. In Germany the situation was different. There the members of the Vilna Company were greeted warmly as colleagues, as comrades, and as partners in a great and noble artistic enterprise.

The Jewish actors on the German stage were especially cordial. My parents would later recall meeting Alexander Granach and Fritz Kortner, two highly popular young performers in the Berlin theater. But there were also introductions to prominent non-Jewish actors, among them the famous Käthe Dorsch, one of the brightest stars of the theatrical world during the 1920s. The theater critics, moreover, the commentators, reviewers, journalists, and columnists, were in general very favorably impressed by the ensemble of young Jewish actors from distant Lithuania who had come to Germany to portray the strange, exotic world of East European Jewry. Toward the end of the decade the well-known writer Arnold Zweig devoted a chapter of his book on Jews in the German theater to the Vilna Company, mentioning among others a character actor whose name he spelled or rather misspelled as "Schnëur." For my parents that brief period immediately following the First World War was the most gratifying of their theatrical career.

Some thirty years later I saw Fritz Kortner, now close to sixty, perform in Munich in Friedrich Hebbel's *Herodes und Mariamne*. As I watched the demented Biblical king declaiming his dramatic lines on the stage, I wondered whether he ever thought about that earlier postwar period, so much more exciting, so much more challenging and promising, than the present one. And then I wondered whether he still remembered that small band of players from far-off, provincial Vilna who had come to Berlin to show the world that Yiddish dramaturgy could enlarge and enrich European culture as a whole. I would have liked to meet him so that I could ask.

But I felt no need to ask him about the audiences which had come to see the Vilna Company perform. The recollections of my parents had been informative enough. Those who flocked to the Yiddish theater in Germany were largely though not entirely emigrants from the ghettos of Eastern Europe. They had sought to escape the postwar chaos in what had once been the Russian Empire by moving westward. Now they hoped to recapture the flavor of the life they had left behind, the feel of the old country, the old community, the old faith. Still, they were not the only ones sitting in the theater. Many Germans, non-Jews as well as Jews, attended the performances of the Vilna Company. The two languages, Yiddish and German, are similar enough so that some-one familiar with one can follow without much difficulty what is being said in the other. To the German Jews this was an opportunity to learn more about their coreligionists from the east, whom they regarded as a rule with curiosity, sympathy, superiority, and a vague uneasiness. To the non-Jews, on the other hand, the repertoire of the Yiddish stage offered an insight into the mysterious, exotic world of traditional orthodox Judaism. Here then was one of those rare occasions when the German passion for cultural achievement and the Jewish obsession with the Diaspora experience met and interacted, enlightening one community, gratifying the other.

The actors of the Vilna Company also had frequent opportunities to meet German Jews socially, through contacts outside the theater. Those were interesting encounters. Members of the Jewish community of Central Europe generally viewed their coreligionists to the east with mixed feelings: inquisitiveness and superciliousness, friendliness and embarrassment, compassion and aversion. Having tried so long and so hard to win acceptance as real Germans, they felt vaguely uncomfort-able in the presence of their country cousins, their poor relations from the backwaters of the former Russian Empire. In the faces of the hum-ble expatriates they could see their own ancestors, many of whom had migrated to Germany only two or three generations before, sometimes more recently. Occasionally they would even catch a sudden glimpse of themselves as they had once been or as perhaps they still were, stripped of the airs, pretensions, and protective affectations of cultural assimila-tion. It was a rather disturbing experience for them.

Worse still, the presence of Jewish immigrants from Eastern Europe seemed to intensify the dangers by which the Jews of Central Europe felt themselves surrounded. Anti-Semitism in Germany, though not as deep-rooted as in Russia or Poland, was a significant social force fed constantly by the bitter experiences of defeat, revolution, humiliation, and economic chaos. The efforts of the Weimar Republic to remove the remaining legal as well as extralegal restrictions on the Jewish community encouraged the view among many conservatives that while the Germans were suffering under the rule of the new democratic order, the Jews were prospering and rejoicing. Indeed, they were gaining a decisive influence in politics, economics, and culture. And yet they remained an alien force in national life, fundamentally and unalterably different from the Germans. Anyone who doubted that only had to look at that flood of Jewish immigrants from the east, growing, multiplying, overrunning the country, coarse, ignorant, greedy, and cunning. To a bewildered and embittered people, this view did not seem altogether farfetched. The German Jews thus tended to regard East European Jews not only with patronizing condescension but with embarrassment, uneasiness, and concern.

The East European Jews in turn were no blind admirers of their German coreligionists. They often resented the tone of condescension adopted by them, their air of social and cultural superiority. Behind their backs they would make fun of their pomposity and self-importance. Those same proper, respectable forms of behavior which the Central European Jews cultivated to make themselves acceptable to their non-Jewish neighbors made them seem affected, pretentious, or even faintly ridiculous to the East European Jews. The latter would frequently tell jokes, some of them quite caustic, about the eagerness of the former to conform, adapt, submit, and acquiesce. The two Jewish communities remained deeply divided by their differing experiences and aspirations in the Diaspora.

Even those East European Jews who had themselves become secularized, who had abandoned the beards and earlocks, the somber coats and black hats, often found the German Jews alien and not always likable. By the time the Vilna Company came to Germany, for example, my father had long since become indistinguishable in appearance from the members of the Jewish community of Central Europe. He too wore a suit and tie. He too was fluent in a major European language, Russian, not to mention his passable knowledge of German and Polish. He could certainly cite Shakespeare, Molière, Goethe, and Tolstoy with the best of them. And yet he too found the German Jews strange and even a little ludicrous. He was amused rather than irritated by their formality and ceremoniousness. And the devout attachment to the ancestral religion which many of them retained seemed to him odd, almost incomprehensible. He had of course known many pious Jews in his life, but those had been entirely different in speech, education, dress, and manner. To see Jews, however, who were so very modern and secular in appearance still repeating traditional prayers and observing orthodox rites, that he found quite surprising.

There was a story my father used to tell about how he and some of the other actors in the Vilna Company had been invited for an informal visit to the office of a prosperous Jewish businessman in Berlin. After carefully closing the door to make sure that the clerks and secretaries could not see what he was doing, the host opened a drawer in his desk, took out a yarmulke, put it on his head, and began reverentially to invoke the blessing of "our fathers Abraham, Isaac, and Jacob, from whom all of us here are descended." His guests were taken aback, but being experienced actors, they did what was expected of them. They assumed a pious, otherworldly expression of religious devotion. Yet inwardly they thought it grotesque. Here they were, a group of young rebels, freethinkers and nonconformists, many of whom had left the parental home precisely because of their rejection of orthodox beliefs and customs, listening in respectful silence to a devout sermon about the Biblical patriarchs of Israel. And that from a man who shaved every morning, who always wore an elegant business suit, and who did not even know a single word of Yiddish. It seemed almost funny.

Still, my parents found postwar Germany more congenial than postwar Poland, more tolerant and more democratic, not as authoritarian or nationalistic. Therefore, when I was about a year old, they decided to move their domicile—"headquarters" might be a more accurate term—westward to Berlin. To be sure, the progressive outlook of the early Weimar Republic was not their only inducement. The Vilna Company was by then making regular tours of Western Europe, and travel to France, Britain, or the Low Countries would be easier from Germany than from Poland. That was another reason for moving from Warsaw.

And then there was the problem of my grandmother. Recently widowed, separated from all her children except Rivke, she found life in Poland lonely and depressing. Her relationship with her Rubinlicht in-laws was strained almost from the beginning, and for the same reason as my father's: on one side a feeling of superiority, on the other a feeling of resentment. Not knowing a word of Polish intensified her isolation. Even the Jews in Poland seemed different from those in Lithuania. Their Yiddish was not quite the same, they were more voluble, more excitable, more importunate; they did not seem as reliable and trustworthy as the Jews back home. In Germany, on the other hand, she would be close to her oldest daughter Mushel, who was then living in Westphalia in the hometown of the husband she had married during the war. There would be an exchange of visits, short excursions, longer vacations, perhaps even occasional trips to see the relatives in Paris. A move to Central Europe seemed advantageous from every point of view.

And so in 1921 our family left Poland for Germany, where we were to remain for the next three years. That was the country in which I grew from infancy into childhood. That was the period of my life about which I have my earliest memories. And the language which I learned to speak there became the first of my three successive mother tongues. After we returned to Poland in 1924, I seemed to forget almost everything that had happened during those years in Germany. And yet they kept coming back to me in sudden spurts, in little bits and pieces, at the most unexpected times throughout the rest of my life.

For the first year or so after our departure from Poland we lived in Berlin. I have only the haziest recollection of our stay there. I learned from my mother afterward that we lived in the fashionable Charlottenburg district of the city. I have some vague memories, moreover, of being in a tall apartment building and looking down from a window to the pavement three or four floors below. What does stand out vividly in my mind is the sight of a fascinating sweeping machine coming down the street, a huge truck with a long horizontal broom attached to its front bumper, gathering and removing the litter which had accumulated in the course of the previous day or two. Not that there was much to remove. The reputation of the Germans for meticulous, passionate cleanliness is not undeserved. Compared to the streets of Warsaw or even Paris, those in Berlin sparkled. And the unremitting effort to keep them that way, to remove every last cigarette butt, apple peel, peanut shell, charred matchstick, broken twig, and fallen leaf, was a source of delight to a lonely little boy glued to the window of an apartment in the big, bustling city.

Still, we did not stay in Berlin very long. Sometime in 1922 my family moved again, this time to a small community in Westphalia called Kückelheim where my aunt Mushel was living. The chief reason was once again my grandmother. The poor woman found Berlin even less to her liking than Warsaw. At least in Warsaw there were Jews, even if they did speak a funny Yiddish and you had to watch your purse when dealing with them. At least in Poland there were in-laws, even if they were uppity and stuck-up. But in Berlin there was no one, no relatives, no in-laws, no friends. Even the Jews were indistinguishable from the goyim. My grandmother felt that she was wasting away, that she had to get out.

There was also another reason why we moved. My father, like many East Europeans, believed that it was unhealthy for small children to grow up in a big city. Big cities were insalubrious, full of refuse and fumes and odors. There was no opportunity for youngsters to play among the trees, to run in the grass, to breathe fresh air, find wholesome amusement, and draw close to nature. As they grew older, moreover, they might be exposed to harmful moral and psychological influences. They might come in contact with undesirable social elements, with hustlers, gamblers, swindlers, racketeers, panders, and seducers. There was no telling where they might end up. The countryside, by contrast, was the home of simple virtue and unblemished character. It bred honesty, simplicity, trustworthiness, and responsibility. Could there be any question which would be better for a young boy entering his formative years? Hence at the age of two I was moved again, this time from wicked and corruptive Berlin to rustic, virtuous Westphalia.

My recollections of Kückelheim are more distinct than those of Berlin. It was a small, sleepy community, not much more than a village, far removed from the hustle and bustle of the big city. The railroad did not even stop there, so that those who wanted to catch a train had to go to Plettenberg, a nearby larger town. We lived on the second floor of a two-story house belonging to a well-to-do farmer. I still remember vaguely Herr Zobel, a sturdy, stoutish, middle-aged rustic whose one overriding passion was hunting and fishing. I can recall more clearly his two daughters, Erna and Klara, sedate young women in their late teens or early twenties, wearing long black skirts and high-necked white blouses, their hair brushed upward and back to form a modest, virtuous bun. But the member of the Zobel family I can see most distinctly in my mind is the son, whose name unfortunately continues to elude me. That is a pity, because he was the one who was nicest, kindest, and most affectionate. He would carry me on his shoulders, run with me, play with me, and tell me amusing stories. All of the Zobels seemed in fact to be genuinely fond of their youthful tenant, calling me by the pet name "*Bubi*" or "laddie," a name which my parents soon adopted and which they continued to use throughout their lives, sometimes to my embarrassment.

Many of the other residents of Kückelheim, mostly farmers and laborers, also discovered that there was an unusual visitor among them, a young boy from a foreign country, cute and endearing, who had learned to speak German and had even acquired some of the local mannerisms, customs, and idioms. To them I became "the little Pole." That was of course a euphemism, and both the members of my family and the Kückelheimers knew it. But I suppose that it sounded better than

"the little Jew." In any case, I was delighted to receive so much attention and affection from the Westphalian rustics among whom I was living. I had gotten little of that from my absentee parents or my severe,
reserved grandmother or my surly aunt.

And so I enjoyed mingling with the locals as they sat in the beer garden with their steins and sausages. I liked talking to them, joking and
laughing with them, and singing with their encouragement some children's ditty they had taught me. I remember, for example:

Hans, my son, what are you doing there?
I am flirting with my grandmama.
No, my son, you are not allowed to do that;
Your grandpapa does not permit it.

It sounds better or at least cuter in German than in English. I can also
recall singing before an appreciative audience a popular folk tune which
first asks rhetorically why it is so nice to be on the Rhine, and then
answers that the girls are so merry and the lads are so thirsty, that is
why. The Kückelheim farmers, their enjoyment enhanced no doubt by
a few glasses of beer, would applaud loudly, while the diminutive artist
reveled in their approbation. They became part of some of the pleasan-
test memories of my peripatetic, solitary childhood.

We remained in Germany for a relatively short period of time, only
about three years. Soon after we left, I seemed to forget almost
entirely the landscape, the language, and even the people of that
country. And yet they kept coming back to me again and again at various junctures in my life, sometimes without my fully recognizing
their nature or source. Some two decades later, for example, while
serving in the American army during the Second World War, I was
admitted to a program which provided instruction in four of the
major European languages: French, Spanish, German, and Russian.
The ostensible purpose was to create a reservoir of manpower trained
for intelligence work or the administration of occupied enemy terri-
tory. The real reason, I suspect, was to help the colleges, which had
lost most of their student body to military service, survive the crisis in
higher education. They could now make ends meet by providing
instruction to members of the armed forces. I was assigned to the
German curriculum for beginners, since I had never studied the language and had long since forgotten what little I had learned as a child.
For the next eight months I devoted myself to mastering the intrica-
cies of German, until preparations for the invasion of Normandy

unfortunately required the redeployment of the soldier students to more strenuous and hazardous duties.

During that brief period of linguistic study I displayed a remarkable aptitude for German. Indeed, I became the best pupil in the class, praised by my instructors and secretly envied or resented by some of my fellow students. On two or three occasions I was even chosen by the faculty to address in German a group of exiles from the Third Reich in order to demonstrate how effective the program was in transforming raw beginners into fluent speakers. The approbation I received was so generous in fact that I myself began to believe that I had some remarkable talent for foreign languages. And yet, while basking in those words of praise, I had the uneasy feeling that my mastery of German was not simply a result of natural brilliance. I suspected vaguely even then, and I am convinced of it now, that the true source of my fluency in German lay in those long-ago days when the farmers of Kückelheim were being amused and entertained by "the little Pole" who had briefly lived among them.

There is still another influence which my childhood stay in Germany has had on my life, an influence whose extent and depth I cannot describe with precision, but whose existence seems to me undeniable. Unlike many Jews, I have never held the Germans collectively responsible for the atrocities committed by National Socialism. Nor do I believe that they have historically been more authoritarian or more nationalistic or more anti-Semitic than most of the other peoples of Europe. I like to think that I base these views on my study of the history of Germany and on my extended visits to that country after the Second World War. Yet occasionally another idea pops into my head. Could it be that behind that image of the brutal storm troopers and murderous SS men I can still see the farmers of Kückelheim laughing and singing, friendly and kindhearted? Could it be that some of those nice farmers later became ruthless Nazis or even that some of those ruthless Nazis later became nice farmers? Could it be that good and evil, virtue and corruption, righteousness and wickedness do not exist at opposite poles but rather side by side, one turning into the other and then back again, parallel, complementary, and almost interchangeable? And could it be that this parallelism, this interchangeability, characterizes not only some but most of us, perhaps all of us? And in contemplating the Germans, should we not then conclude, like Pogo in Walt Kelly's cartoon, that "we have met the enemy and he is us"? I have often wondered about that.

But enough philosophizing; back to the hard, palpable facts. Sometime in 1924 our family moved once again, this time from Germany back to Poland. There were several reasons. My aunt Mushel and her husband Robert were about to emigrate to the United States or they may already have departed. And that left my grandmother even more isolated, lonely, and dispirited than in Berlin. She must have complained constantly to my father, who felt that he could not simply ignore her endless pleas and lamentations. Not that he needed much persuading. After all, both he and my mother had dedicated themselves to the cause of Yiddish culture. They naturally wanted their child to grow up sharing their ideas and ideals. But the Westphalian countryside was far removed from the Jewish community of Eastern Europe. Staying in Germany meant that I would be more likely to learn songs about little Hans flirting with his grandmama or about the merry girls who help make life on the Rhine so pleasant than to study the writings of Sholem Aleichem or the plays of Peretz Hirschbein. Only a return to Poland could save me from the danger of becoming completely and irreversibly Germanized.

There was also something else. My parents had concluded that the financial future of the Weimar Republic was grim. They had lost some of their savings during the catastrophic inflation there of the early postwar years, and that helped persuade them that even the wobbly economy of the Polish Republic was not as risky as that of unstable, unpredictable Germany. Clearly, their talent as dramatic actors exceeded their shrewdness as economic prognosticators. Just as the republican regime in Berlin was beginning to achieve financial stability, just as it was about to enter a period of booming prosperity, my father and mother decided that their prospects would be brighter farther east. They packed up their paintings and sculptures, their books, albums, and photographs, and their few random pieces of household furniture, and returned to Poland. The German chapter in their life as well as mine was over.

There may have been still another reason for their decision. By now the Vilna Company had begun to disintegrate. It was falling victim to its own success. The youthful idealism of its members during the early days of the ensemble had gradually become eroded by jealousies and rivalries, quarrels and intrigues. Why should the stars, who attracted the large audiences crowding into the theater, be paid no more or little more than the bit players? Why should the names of the leading actors appear on the posters no larger than the names of those performing minor roles or even of mere walk-ons? Was that fair? The company became increasingly torn by disputes, cabals, secessions, and schisms. My parents were among those who left the group sometime during this period. That meant that they would now have to plan their own engagements, organize their own tours, negotiate their own contracts. And since they had become self-employed, it was important for them to be close to the center of the Yiddish theater, to live in Poland rather than in distant, alien Germany. That consideration helped persuade them in 1924 to return to Warsaw.

My adjustment to this new situation took close to a year. But in the end I became as completely Polonized as I had previously been completely Germanized. Indeed, I was to remain Polonized until the age of ten, when I slowly began to become Americanized, though never quite to the same extent as in my two previous cultural incarnations. In any event, during the first few months following our return to Poland I continued to speak only German. My mother later told me a little story about my reunion with my grandfather shortly after we arrived in Warsaw, a story which was amusing and charming but with a faint touch of malice, like many of her stories. The old man, it seems, putting on his prayer shawl, asked me to kiss it in keeping with religious custom, as a sign of reverence for our ancestral faith. But I protested vehemently. The cloth was old and worn, stained with years of perspiration, and to be quite frank, it was faintly malodorous. An orthodox Jew never washed his prayer shawl, since its soiled condition attested to his piety and devotion. That line of reasoning failed to impress me, however. "But mommy," I whispered loudly to my mother in German, "that thing is so smelly." My grandfather must have heard what I said, and he knew enough German to understand it. I cannot be sure what his reaction was, although I strongly suspect that he was shocked by his grandson's precocious religious skepticism.

Some of the details of this story may have been embellished for comic effect. My mother often did that with stories she liked to tell. Yet I also remember clearly another incident which confirms my continued use of German well after our return to Poland. One day my parents were visited by a friend, an elderly, portly, dignified gentleman who carried a handsome walking stick. Since I was in bed with a cold or some minor childhood ailment, our guest was brought to the bedroom which I shared with my grandmother. We were introduced, and after a brief, desultory conversation, I asked whether I might examine his cane. When he agreed, I put it to my shoulder, pointed it at him, and shouted in peremptory German: "You are a Frenchman. I am going to shoot you." That sudden outburst of martial ferocity was inspired no doubt by the war stories I had heard the Westphalian veterans tell during their frequent visits to the beer garden. It too is part of the Kückelheim legacy which transformed "the little Pole" into an ardent German patriot. A considerable period of time was to elapse, almost a year, before I became retransformed into an equally ardent Polish nationalist.

While I was going through this difficult cultural adjustment, my father was trying once again to ensure that I would grow up in a healthy, wholesome, clean, and secure environment. The same concerns which had persuaded him two years earlier that I should not remain in Berlin convinced him now that I must not stay in Warsaw. The Polish capital was no better than the German one. Both harbored harmful moral influences and undesirable social tendencies to which a young boy should not be exposed. He was probably thinking of his own youth in the slums of Vilna, determined to protect me against experiences of that sort. But this time, instead of sending me to a remote and alien Westphalian backwater, he arranged for me to live in Otwock, a small town some fifteen miles southwest of Warsaw with a population of about thirteen thousand inhabitants, most of them Jewish. There I was to spend the next six years, until my departure for the New World in 1930 put an end to my strange childhood in Poland.

Otwock had all the bucolic virtues which my father considered essential for the proper upbringing of his son. There were pine woods, green grass, and clean, white sand. The air was fresh, the sun bright, the sky blue, and many of the streets were not even paved. Here was an unspoiled, rustic environment ideally suited to nurturing a Jewish Tom Sawyer or Huckleberry Finn. But the town's proximity to Warsaw also attracted big-city influence and big-city money. It had become a favorite vacation spot for many of the capital's residents, mostly Jews, nothing fancy like Zakopane or Zoppot, but homey, pleasant, and comfortable.

A rickety train ran between Warsaw and Otwock, a kind of Toonerville Trolley, making five or six stops along the way and taking almost an hour to cover the few short miles. Still, the head of a middle-class family in the capital could send his wife and children to the unpretentious nearby country resort for a few weeks or months during the summer, joining them on weekends. Or he might decide to stay with them in Otwock and commute daily to Warsaw. For that matter, even some workers were able to afford modest vacation accommodations in the town, bare and admittedly a little drab, but still a welcome change from the crowded streets of the big city. At the other end of the social scale, Otwock had a few hotels with pretensions to elegance: bright, sparkling dining rooms, orchestras of four or five pieces, and even dancing in the evening. What it did not have was much ethnic diversity, for the prevalence of Jews ensured a paucity of Poles.

My father decided for a variety of reasons—moral, cultural, geographical, and financial—that Otwock would be an ideal place to raise his child. Soon after our return from Germany, he bought a house there situated on a sizable plot of two or three acres. Actually, there were two houses which, though adjoining, had separate entrances, separate designs, and separate purposes. Facing the street from a distance of roughly two hundred feet stood a wooden building, with five spacious rooms and a veranda in front, which served as the family home. Behind it was a three-story structure containing several smaller rooms, each with a separate door to the hallway, which were rented out to vacation guests of rather modest means. And still farther to the rear, at some distance from the two main buildings, was a small hut which served as the home of the caretaker, a Polish peasant. The most attractive feature of the property was the land on which these buildings stood, with a grove of tall pine trees, a large green meadow, and patches of white sand here and there in which a growing child could play to his heart's content. Our new residence in Otwock seemed to fulfill exactly my father's quest for a healthy, wholesome rural environment for his son.

His resources were too limited, however, to enable him to finance the purchase on his own. He was therefore forced to enter into a partnership with a certain Mr. Gelbfisz, whom I do not remember ever meeting, but whose name I heard quite frequently, accompanied as a rule by condemnations and imprecations. Apparently the two co-owners had a falling-out almost as soon as they became partners. I am not sure what the cause of their dispute was, but I suspect that it had something to do with their differing objectives and expectations. For my father the purchase had been intended primarily to provide a secure and comfortable home for his family. Mr. Gelbfisz, on the other hand, was interested above all in making a profit on his investment. This divergence in the goals of the two proprietors led to mounting differences, complaints, quarrels, and threats.

The dispute culminated eventually in bitter litigation. After my father left for America, my grandfather, who was something of an expert on conducting cases before a Polish court, took charge of the legal campaign. But that did not lead to any prompt settlement. Far from it. The controversy dragged on and on, through the 1920s and almost to the end of the 1930s. Then the coming of the Second World War resolved the issue once and for all. I never found out what happened to Mr. Gelbfisz, although I think I can make a pretty good guess. As for my father, not long after the war, following the decision of the new communist government of Poland to seek normal diplomatic relations with the United States, he received a check for two thousand dollars as compensation for his expropriated property. His unfortunate venture into landownership thus outlasted by a few years his ill-fated career on the Yiddish stage.

For me those early years in Otwock were a very pleasant experience, as pleasant as my previous stay in Kückelheim. I enjoyed walking among the tall pine trees, playing in the grass, and digging tunnels in the sparkling sand. I also liked to sit on the veranda, listening to the conversation of relatives and family friends from Warsaw, occasionally asking questions or expressing opinions, feeling quite comfortable in the company of my elders. I do not recall wanting to be with other children, wanting to play games, or wanting to shout, laugh, run, and roughhouse. Perhaps because I had previously had very little contact with other youngsters, perhaps because I had been almost exclusively in the company of adults, I felt quite at ease in the presence of grown-ups. They did not inhibit or intimidate or bore me. In fact, I found their conversation with each other rather interesting. Sometimes I would even add my own observations. Not only was I never shushed, but my views were often solicited, seriously and without condescension. In short, I did not feel lonely growing up in what I can now see as an unusual environment for a young child.

The only source of dissatisfaction I can remember, vague at first but then increasingly persistent and troubling, was the frequent absence of my parents, especially my mother. My grandmother was a kind, well-intentioned woman who loved me in her own stern way. I never felt abandoned or neglected. For that matter, my aunt Rivke, though often disgruntled and aggrieved, was rarely mean, though she must have regarded me with at least some resentment as a successful competitor for her mother's affection. In fact, she would occasionally play or chat with me, take me for a walk, or even help me wash and dress. And yet I became increasingly aware that my parents were away a great deal of the time.

Worse still, I began to have the uneasy feeling that perhaps they preferred to be away, perhaps they found me a burden or a nuisance.

When they were at home, my father was almost as reserved and taciturn with me as with most other people, whereas my mother displayed an overflowing, almost ostentatious affection, hugging, kissing, coddling, and caressing me. And yet even while being kissed and hugged, I could not overcome a sense that both of them had other interests, other concerns, more important to them than spending time with me. Perhaps that was mostly an expression of childish possessiveness, but could there have been more to it than that? I suspect so.

There is one incident which still sticks in my mind, reflecting this growing feeling of abandonment by my parents. It must have been shortly after we moved to Otwock. We were all sitting in the kitchen one evening, while I was preparing to go to bed. I wanted my mother to stay with me until I fell asleep, to tell me a fairy tale or sing some soothing lullaby. She tried to comply, but I could feel that she was growing impatient, that she was anxious to get away. Indeed, she was already late for a social engagement or cultural event she very much wanted to attend. It became clear that we were facing an imminent crisis. If she did not leave soon, she would miss the train to Warsaw. But if she did leave, I would make a terrible scene. What to do?

After a hurried, whispered conference between my mother, grandmother, and aunt, they decided to distract me. Rivke urged me in a tone of feigned excitement to go quickly into the adjoining living room, where I would find something quite unusual, even extraordinary. I hesitated for a moment, troubled by a faint suspicion that maybe they were playing a trick on me, maybe they were simply trying to get me out of the way. But suppressing my doubts, I ran into the other room wondering what I might find: a highwayman perhaps or a pirate or a hussar or an uhlan. At that moment of eager anticipation, anything seemed possible.

But when I rushed in to behold this hidden marvel, all I could see was the familiar table and chairs, the pictures and decorations, and the tall, white, tiled oven. I stood still for a moment, disappointed and bewildered, and then it suddenly hit me. They had tricked me, they had lied to me. There was no highwayman or pirate, no hussar or uhlan. They had simply wanted to get rid of me. I ran back into the kitchen just in time to catch a glimpse of my mother leaving by the back door to escape the scene which she knew I was about to make. She was so right. I let out a piercing howl of rage, pain, bitterness, and frustration. I cried for half an hour or more, while my grandmother and aunt tried to console me. This incident is the only one I can recall which expresses directly the growing feeling on my part of parental alienation or deprivation. But without quite realizing it, I must have gradually become aware that the circumstances of my upbringing were different and unusual.

I could not have known, however, that the intermittent absences of my parents for weeks or months were about to culminate in a separation which would last for five years. The postwar diaspora of East European Jewry had led not only to the expansion of the Yiddish theater into Western Europe, but also to a growing cultural exchange between the Jewish theater in the Old World and the New. The currents of theatrical influence were alternate and reciprocal, now flowing in one direction, now in the other. The more than two million Jewish emigrants from Eastern Europe who came to the United States in the three decades preceding the First World War comprised not only workers, artisans, tradesmen, and shopkeepers. They also included people in show business—playwrights, actors, directors, and impresarios—who promptly established in their new environment the familiar, popular variety theater they had known in the old country. Here the recent arrivals could enjoy the same forms of entertainment as back home in Poland or Lithuania, the Ukraine or Bessarabia. They could see the same song-and-dance numbers, laugh at the same risqué stories and jokes, and watch the same pranks and pratfalls. They could satisfy for an hour or two their feeling of nostalgia for what had once been.

But then, toward the end of the nineteenth century, the Yiddish stage in America began to develop a new melodramatic genre which soon found widespread interest and support in Eastern Europe. Most of the playwrights and actors who popularized this theatrical repertoire were actually born in the old country, but their talents matured and flowered in the new. What they presented on the stage seems today theatrical, oversentimental, almost mawkish. The kindhearted mother or unselfish father betrayed by a thankless child, the good brother deceived by the bad one, the innocent sister cheated by the wicked one, and worst of all, the honorable husband or wife deserted by a faithless spouse, all that seems in retrospect artificial and unconvincing. And yet in its own day it represented a major step beyond the vaudeville singers and dancers, the buffoons and clowns, and the jesters and jokesters who had previously dominated the stage.

After the opening of the twentieth century, still another theatrical genre began to emerge on the Yiddish stage, starting in Eastern Europe but soon winning an appreciative audience in America as well. It arose in response to the growing demand for a different form of Jewish drama which would respond to the new currents of realism and symbolism reshaping the culture of the Continent. Its models were not Victorian melodramas like *East Lynne* or *The Second Mrs. Tanqueray*, and certainly not the waggishness, naughtiness, and clownishness of the popular music hall. It found inspiration rather in the naturalistic dramas of Chekhov and Hauptmann, Ibsen and Strindberg, and sometimes in the expressionist plays of Maeterlinck, Andreyev, and Pirandello. The ultimate goal of this new school of Jewish drama, was to integrate the Yiddish theater into the broad sweep of European cultural development, portraying the specific collective experience of East European Jewry in a way which would transcend the boundaries of religion or ethnicity.

Although the center of this movement to modernize the Yiddish theater remained in the Old World, it also attracted considerable support in the United States. The most devoted or at least the most consistent and successful of its American champions was Maurice Schwartz. No sensitive aesthete or refined intellectual, he was a man driven by a curious combination of diverse and sometimes incompatible impulses and purposes. He was at one and the same time an actor and an entrepreneur, a director and a bookkeeper, an impresario and a salesman. Add to that an inflated ego and an imperious personality, a constant need to be the center of attention, a deep-seated suspicion of potential rivals or dissenters, and a dismissive intolerance for any disagreement, however slight, however well-intentioned, and you have Maurice Schwartz. Yet throughout the interwar years he also remained resolutely committed to the new Jewish drama, not overly subtle or perceptive in his view of the artistic function of the theater, but convinced that the Yiddish stage must become open to the new forces of reformism and modernization. With all his faults, he made a major contribution to the cultural life of immigrant Jewry in America.

In 1924 Schwartz invited my parents to join his Yiddish Art Theater in New York for a season, appearing in David Pinski's *King David and His Wives*. It was an invitation they could not afford to turn down. They were no longer part of the Vilna Company, which had by then lost many of its founding members. Although various splinter groups still continued to perform under the name of the original ensemble, their composition, direction, and dramatic inspiration were not the same. As for my parents, they were now on their own. Thus the opportunity to appear before new audiences on the other side of the ocean seemed irresistible. To be sure, they would have to leave me behind, but it would be for only eight or nine months, not much longer than their previous tours of England, France, or the Low Countries. In any case, the American immigration laws, which permitted the temporary entry of artists and performers from abroad, did not allow them to take dependents with them. Even if an exception could be made, who would look after me? It seemed best to leave me in Otwock, where I would be safe, sheltered, comfortable, and reasonably content.

And so, only a few months after leaving Germany, my parents left again, this time for the United States. I have no recollection of their departure. A deliberate effort had been made not to arouse uneasiness or apprehension on my part at the prospect of a new separation. This trip, I was assured, would be just like the many previous ones, to Warsaw or Lodz, Bucharest or Berlin, London or Paris. In fact, although none of us knew it at the time, my parents were to remain away for five years. Their departure late in 1924 thus marked, as it turned out, the real beginning of my unusual childhood in interwar Poland, comfortable yet isolated, secure yet deprived, and, despite everything, interesting, stimulating, enlightening, and in a strange way satisfying.

Chapter 4

Living the High Life of Otwock

The 1920s were a golden decade for the Yiddish theater in America. The restrictions on immigration were still too recent and the pressures to assimilate were as yet too weak to reduce significantly the number of Jewish expatriates from Eastern Europe eager to hear the mother tongue spoken on the stage. The economic prosperity of those years, moreover, made it possible for even the humblest of the newcomers to afford a seat at a performance of a Yiddish theatrical company, if not in the front row of the orchestra, then at least somewhere in the second balcony. Many of the large cities in the United States and Canada, cities like Chicago and Detroit, for example, Philadelphia and Boston, or Montreal and Toronto, had each its own ensemble of Jewish actors, many of them professionals, but some semiprofessionals and quite a few dedicated amateurs. The Yiddish stage thrived and flourished.

The center of Jewish dramaturgy in the New World was New York or rather Manhattan. Some of the outlying boroughs of the city had Yiddish theaters as well; there were two in Brooklyn and one or two in the Bronx. But the largest number by far was in Manhattan, concentrated along the Yiddish Broadway, the stretch of Second Avenue from Fourteenth Street to Houston Street, a distance of barely a mile. Even in 1930 when I came to the United States, after the start of the Great Depression, five Yiddish theaters were crowded into this small area, standing almost side by side, some offering serious drama, others specializing in sentimental tearjerkers, and still others presenting old-fashioned vaudeville shows. Squeezed in among them, competing for the attention and the pocketbook of the theatergoing crowd, were Jewish restaurants, Jewish delicatessens, Jewish grocery stores, and Jewish bakeries and pastry shops.

In the midst of this ethnic hubbub, at the corner of Twelfth Street, stood the favorite gathering place of the Yiddish intelligentsia, the Café Royal. Here Jewish actors, playwrights, directors, producers, authors, poets, journalists, bohemians, literati, and cognoscenti would meet in the evening to drink tea, eat apple strudel, and talk, talk, talk. There was even a room in the back, its door discreetly covered with a curtain, where patrons of more plebeian taste could sit and play pinochle for modest stakes. But for all of them, for those with cultural or artistic aspirations as well as those without, the Café Royal was the favorite rendezvous.

Even the newsstands along Second Avenue reflected the kaleidoscopic ethnicity of the immigrant milieu. Almost all of them displayed prominently the leading Yiddish dailies: the socialist *Forverts*, the liberal *Tog*, the communist *Freiheit*, and the apolitical, moderately orthodox *Morgen zhurnal*. Then came the newspapers of various non-Jewish minorities living in New York, newspapers like the *Novoye russkoye slovo*, the *Progresso italo americano*, and the oldest and most venerable of them, the *New-Yorker Staats-Zeitung*. Peeking out timidly from beneath this babel of foreign tongues and cultures could sometimes be seen a few newspapers in English, the *Daily News*, for instance, the *New York Times*, and the *Herald Tribune*. On Second Avenue even the most recent immigrant from Eastern Europe could feel equal to any native-born, purebred, 100 percent American.

My parents, arriving in New York in the fall of 1924, must have found the city a pleasant surprise. They had come expecting a strange, alien metropolis, as foreign in spirit and culture as Berlin, Paris, or London. Instead, they discovered that they had never really left Warsaw. The New World seemed almost indistinguishable from the Old. The Jewish theater district, where they soon found a furnished apartment, resembled the East European neighborhoods in which they had previously lived. The food they ate in the local restaurants was the same. The newspapers they read presented the same news in the same way from the same point of view. The friends and acquaintances with whom they mingled were largely the same, most of them having also arrived recently from Eastern Europe. The atmosphere, clientele, and conversation in the cafés they frequented were the same as well. Even the language was the same. My parents found that you did not have to know a word of English to make yourself understood in New York, at least not on Second Avenue. Almost everyone spoke some Yiddish, even those who at first pretended to be completely Americanized.

But the familiar atmosphere of the city was not the only thing which appealed to my parents. There were also professional and financial attractions. They had come to America for an engagement which was to last no more than a season. That engagement proved highly successful, however, too successful to end as originally planned. The verdict of both critics and audiences had been quite favorable, and offers to remain for another season, some of them very generous, began coming in. My parents could not resist them. They agreed to prolong their stay, first by a year, then by another year, and then by still another year. At some point, moreover, they learned that it would not be very difficult to change their legal status from that of temporary visitors to resident aliens. And that in turn meant that five years after their arrival in the United States they could become eligible for American citizenship. But there was a catch. During those five years they must not leave the country, not even for a few weeks. The period of residence had to be uninterrupted. Nor could they bring over any dependent until they had been declared citizens. In short, the price of naturalization would be a separation from their son for five years. What to do? After some difficult, perhaps agonizing deliberation, they decided to stay in the United States.

This decision did not entail any material hardship for me. My parents were able to provide a very comfortable life for their family in Otwock. Still, they did not resign themselves to waiting patiently until they had acquired American citizenship. Some fifty years later an acquaintance of mine, a historian studying the migration of East European Jews to the United States, sent me a copy of a letter he had found in the records of the Immigration and Naturalization Service. It had been submitted by a lawyer whose clientele consisted largely of expatriates from Russia, Poland, and Romania. He was appealing in behalf of my parents for special permission to admit their son to America, piteously describing the emotional pain of parenthood without a child and childhood without a parent. The authorities remained adamant, however. I never saw the reply my parents received, but their appeal must have been rejected, since we were not actually reunited until 1929.

Our separation was no doubt more difficult for them than for me. Although I gradually became aware that their absence this time was much longer than any in the past, I was never told exactly how long it was likely to last. And so, little by little, I forgot what they looked like, what they sounded like, how they had behaved toward me, and how I had felt toward them. They became faint, shadowy figures in a distant memory. That was partly the result of a deliberate policy adopted by my grandmother. She feared that it might be harmful for me to think too much about my absent parents. It might make me lonely or melancholy or dissatisfied or resentful. Maybe she was also trying, without quite realizing it, to play the role of a surrogate mother without competition from the actual mother. The Rubinlichts, to be sure, did their best to counter this strategy, sensing perhaps what its underlying motive was. Whenever I visited them in Warsaw or they visited me in Otwock, they would make it a point to talk to me about my father and mother, especially my mother, much to my grandmother's disapproval. Yet their efforts proved in the long run futile. With the passage of time my recollections of my parents became fainter and fainter, until they almost disappeared.

But not quite. As I grew older, I became increasingly aware that my home environment was different from that of other children. While they often talked about their fathers and mothers or their brothers and sisters, all I could boast of was an elderly grandmother and a sour aunt. That bred in me a vague sense of deprivation and dissatisfaction, perhaps even resentment. I remember that after I started school at the age of five or six, I liked to shock my classmates by telling them that my parents were somewhere far away, that I was not sure what they looked like, that I did not even know when I would see them again, and that I did not really care whether I did or not. Consciously, I was simply trying to surprise the other children, gain their attention, strut and posture, show off. But could there have been more to it than that? Could I have also been expressing a subconscious hostility toward my parents for having left me, for depriving me of the kind of upbringing other children received and enjoyed? Possibly.

At least I did not have to worry about financial security. My parents saw to that. Every month they would send my grandmother the sum of a hundred dollars for the support of our household. Today that may seem paltry, but during the 1920s it was a respectable allowance even in the United States, and in Poland it was a small fortune. It enabled us to gain admission to the Otwock patriciate, to join the small elite whose members could afford live-in maids, private tutors, music lessons, taxi rides, and tea dances. We were among the few, the happy few, of our community. Never before or after did my grandmother or my aunt achieve the same relative level of affluence and distinction. As for me, although in later years I had access to many more conveniences and comforts, I never enjoyed the same lofty social position as in my childhood. During that brief period of my life I was Little Lord Fauntleroy.

Others were not as fortunate. Society in Otwock was divided by sharp differences based on origin, class, and education. The most obvious one separated Jews from non-Jews. At the bottom of the social scale were the impoverished, unskilled, uneducated, and barely literate Polish peasants who eked out a meager livelihood as janitors, porters, draymen, servants, and day laborers, hungry and oppressed, brutalized and brutal. Affluent, educated Poles generally avoided Otwock. It had too many Jews. The only ones I ever remember seeing or hearing about were a few physicians and pharmacists, an occasional lawyer or notary, the priests of the local Catholic Church, the officials of the municipal government, and the numerous policemen charged with enforcing law and order. But these were not the friendly neighborhood cops portrayed in Hollywood movies. Proud, arrogant, and surly, dressed in dark-blue uniforms and high, shiny boots, armed with pistols and sabers, they resembled rather the popular image of haughty, imperious Prussian officers. They were feared and disliked by lower-class Poles and even more by Jews of all classes.

Social divisions in Otwock, however, were not based solely on ethnicity or religion. Within the Jewish community itself sharp distinctions existed. On one side of the railroad tracks lived the poor Jews, popularly called the "bazaar" Jews because of the weekly market held there in the central square where grocers, butchers, fishmongers, bakers, tailors, and shoemakers hawked their wares, hustled, haggled, bargained, and dickered. Some of them were orthodox, dressed in the somber costume of traditional piety. But most were clean-shaven and in modern dress, speaking not only Yiddish but Polish, in some cases fluent, educated Polish. What distinguished them from the Jewish elite was not religious observance or even formal schooling but economic status. They may have been better-off than the impoverished peasants, but not by much.

The patricians of Otwock lived in another part of town, separated physically from their plebeian fellow Jews by the railroad tracks, but socially and economically by their relative affluence. They included first of all the owners and managers of the fashionable hotels, restaurants, cafés, and bars which formed the mainstay of the town's economy. Then came the small-town financiers, mostly local bankers, brokers, agents, investors, and speculators. They in turn were followed by the commercial elite, by wholesalers, distributors, merchants, shopowners, and salesmen. And finally, there was a sizable group of

professionals: physicians, dentists, lawyers, accountants, teachers, journalists, and writers. Our household did not belong to any of these cat-
egories, but we gained admission to the *haut monde* partly because my
father was a houseowner and landlord, even though his property was
encumbered with a sizable mortgage and he had to share his ownership
with an uncongenial partner. But even more important, I suspect, were
those remittances which kept coming month after month from the
other side of the Atlantic. They must have made a deep impression on
Otwock's patriciate.

The new social eminence of our household affected its members in
distinctly different ways. The one who remained almost unchanged was
my grandmother. She continued to be what she had always been: a simple, pious, hard-working woman from a small, impoverished town in
Lithuania. Although we now had a maid, she continued to perform
many of the chores for which she had been responsible throughout her
life. She would supervise and sometimes participate in the daily task of
housecleaning. She would do most of the shopping, visiting every week
the Jewish marketplace on the other side of town and returning home
loaded down with bags and bundles of groceries. Above all, she would
assume sole responsibility for cooking our meals, since the Polish maid
could not be trusted to observe all the strict requirements of a kosher
cuisine. This obligation was far too important to be left to anyone else.

My grandmother's commitment to the Jewish faith remained in fact
the guiding spiritual principle of her life, regardless of changing external
circumstances. Every Friday night she would scrupulously observe the
ceremony of blessing the candles. I remember sitting at the table, wide-
eyed and open-mouthed, while the grave, elderly woman, her face
buried in her hands, the faint candlelight distorting her features, whispered pleas and supplications in a strange tongue. What was she saying?
Whom was she imploring? I wondered whether she was communing
with some angel or divine spirit, with fate or destiny, perhaps even with
God himself. Those were wondrous occasions, so different, so unusual,
disquieting and yet fascinating and strangely inspiring.

Saturdays were another story. They were not nearly as interesting.
While my grandmother would of course always go to the synagogue,
she would usually leave me at home. But the few occasions when she
took me with her were almost invariably a disappointment. I would sit
with her in the women's gallery, while down below the men wrapped
in their prayer shawls went on and on with their chants and supplications in some strange language, going through various rituals which I

did not understand or even want to understand. To me it was all just one long bore.

The holidays which we celebrated at home were not as dull, mostly because of the presence of unusual guests. Since some of those solemn occasions required prayers only a man was permitted to recite, and since I was still too young to assume that responsibility, my grandmother, as was customary, would invite one of the religious students from a nearby yeshiva for the observance and the accompanying meal. That was what made those occasions so interesting. The young would-be theologians were invariably thin, pale, and voraciously hungry. They lived largely on the charitable contributions of pious Jews, contributions much too meager to enable them to concentrate exclusively on spiritual matters. Even the saintliest among them were bound to succumb from time to time to mundane needs and appetites.

I remember one occasion, I think it was during Passover, when a rabbinical aspirant, even thinner and paler than usual, was invited to the house for prayer and dinner. My grandmother, after placing on the table a dish of unpretentious hors d'oeuvres consisting of four hard-boiled eggs, one for each of us, returned to the kitchen to finish preparing the main course. I was to remain with our guest and entertain him with lively conversation. But he was not interested in talking. He immediately seized one of the eggs, cracked it open, and gulped it down, then a second, then a third, and finally the fourth, while I watched in awed astonishment. I had never seen anyone that hungry before. When my grandmother returned, she immediately noticed the disappearance of the appetizers, but she said nothing. She watched in silent disapproval while our guest, after rushing through the requisite prayers, stuffed himself with the main course and then the side dishes and then the compote and finally the pastry. Only after he left did I hear her comment to my aunt that it was a pity that the future rabbi seemed more eager to fill his stomach than uplift his soul.

My grandmother's religious devotion was not confined to her own spiritual well-being. She also wanted to encourage in her grandson a sense of loyalty to our ancestral faith. She therefore hired a tutor to come to the house each week to instruct me in the prayers, rites, and rituals of Judaism. But she was enough of a realist to recognize that it would never do to choose an orthodox teacher complete with caftan, beard, and earlocks. There would be loud complaints from Warsaw and even louder ones from New York. She therefore hit on a happy compromise between the secularism of my parents and her own traditional piety. She selected an instructor who wore a suit and tie, who shaved every day, and whose hair was neatly trimmed, but whose head was always covered with a fedora when outdoors and with an unobtrusive yarmulke when indoors. He seemed the perfect choice to initiate me into the mysteries of the Jewish religion.

At the outset all seemed to go well. During the first lesson, while my new teacher was trying to familiarize me with the Hebrew alphabet, explaining what each letter was called, how it was formed, and how it was pronounced, a sudden shower of chocolates wrapped in silver foil fell on the table at which we were sitting. Startled, I turned around to see my grandmother and my aunt standing behind me, all smiles, displaying an uncharacteristic cheerfulness. They explained that whenever a Jewish child began to learn his prayers, an angel came down from heaven to help celebrate the occasion with a gift of sweets. I had just missed seeing him. Though inclined to believe them, I remained troubled by a vague suspicion that perhaps there was a more mundane explanation for the goodies I had so unexpectedly received.

Unfortunately, after that first lesson it was all downhill. My religious instruction consisted almost entirely of repeating and memorizing the innumerable prayers which pious Jews are required to recite at every turn and on every occasion. There are prayers to be said when getting out of bed and prayers when getting into bed, prayers in the morning, prayers in the afternoon, and prayers in the evening, prayers before, during, and after meals, prayers for every daily occurrence, good or bad, prayers for washing and grooming, even prayers for some of the bodily functions. And all this in a language which remained unintelligible to me, since the instruction I received did not include learning Hebrew. Remembering the beginning of each of those prayers was not so bad. All of them started out in the same way: "Praised are you, Lord and God, King of the universe." But after that each went in a different direction, complicated, arcane, and incomprehensible. To a little boy of seven or eight it was simply too much.

The uneven struggle between me and the sacred rites of Judaism continued for about two years, becoming increasingly one-sided, increasingly hopeless. What saved me from total disaster was the return of my parents from the United States. As soon as they saw what the situation was, they put an end to my religious instruction, partly because of my obvious lack of interest in orthodox Jewish beliefs and traditions, but mostly because of their own skepticism regarding organized religion. I felt enormously relieved, and ever since I have remained essentially a secularist in my view of the world.

To my grandmother, however, my abandonment of the faith of our ancestors came as a bitter disappointment, especially since she was experiencing an even more bitter disappointment in her own daughter. The sudden rise in our social and economic status, which had left her basically unchanged, completely transformed Rivke's outlook on life. The latter's early years had been hard, spent in bitter poverty, in hunger and neglect. There had been constant worries about food, clothing, health, and shelter. The sad memory of childhood privation never actually left her. But in Otwock everything seemed to change, at least outwardly. The family suddenly acquired money, status, prestige, and respect, all the things which had seemed beyond reach in the poverty-stricken household in Lithuania.

For Rivke it was intoxicating. Raised largely on bread, potatoes, and watery soup, she could now have as much to eat as she wanted, even exotic delicacies like smoked sprats and salmon, or éclairs and tortes, even oranges and bananas. She no longer had to wear hand-me-down dresses or down-at-the-heel shoes. She could afford fashionable gowns and elegant slippers. She had become Cinderella, the scullion turned into the belle of the ball. The change would have been enough to turn anyone's head. Rivke became increasingly dubious regarding the simple, strict, unbending faith in which she had been brought up. She began to question, dispute, challenge, and finally reject the parental pieties. Like her older brothers and sisters, she became a religious skeptic.

Nor was she content with the purely material advantages of her new social distinction. She also sought to attain the cultural polish appropriate to her station, the cleverness, knowledge, wit, and sophistication expected of someone with affluence and prestige. But that presented a problem. She could not attend some fashionable secondary school for young women, because she had never managed to complete her elementary education. Her parents had been too poor. She would thus have felt out of place among the daughters of other well-to-do families. The only solution was to provide her with private tutors. Those were mostly young men who had been at a university for at least a few semesters, but who could not earn a livelihood in their chosen profession. I remember seeing some of them at our house, elegant in appearance, refined in manner, slightly aloof, somewhat supercilious, and always with an air of intellectual superiority. I was never allowed in the room during the tutoring sessions; the presence of a little boy might have detracted from the solemnity of the occasion. But soon I too recognized that Rivke, though never a brilliant student, was beginning to hold her own with the other young members of the Otwock patriciate.

She proved even more successful at playing the fashionable sportswoman. She owed that to me, though only by accident. My grandmother had decided that I was spending too much time in the hammock reading books. It would be good for me to be more athletic, to spend more time outdoors. She therefore bought a bicycle for me, hoping that it would help cure me of my sedentary habits. A bicycle was very expensive, almost a luxury, in interwar Poland. Still, she felt that the beneficial effects of exercise in the fresh air were well worth the cost. Unfortunately, she had overestimated my talent for the great outdoors. I was too insecure, too timid, to feel comfortable on a bicycle. Athleticism was never my strong point. My strong point was lying in the hammock reading books. My aunt was therefore assigned the thankless task of teaching me to enjoy the unwelcome gift which my grandmother had forced on me.

But that did not help much either. As long as she trotted behind me holding on to the seat of the bicycle, I managed well enough. I was even able to retain my balance, as she would later reveal, after she had withdrawn her support without telling me. The crucial factor was the feeling on my part that someone was there to catch me if I should fall. Once I sensed, rightly or wrongly, that I was on my own, that there was no one to help keep me on a straight course, the bicycle would start to weave, wobble, and spin, finally crashing to the ground with a loud bang. It soon became apparent that despite Rivke's best efforts, I was not likely to become a skilled bicyclist.

For her, however, my failure turned out to be a blessing, at least for a while. She now became the sole proprietor of the bicycle. Free of the fears and inhibitions from which I suffered, she soon revealed an unexpected athletic ability. She would maneuver deftly through the streets of Otwock, partly to display her skill, partly to flaunt her affluence. The poor little girl from Kovnata finally had something to show off. But as the Bible warns, "pride goeth before destruction." One day, tired of parading her good fortune in the well-to-do sections of town, she ventured beyond the railroad tracks to the "bazaar" district. That was a big mistake. To make matters worse, she was wearing shorts, modest shorts, to be sure, drab in color and discreet in cut, reaching down almost to the knees, but shorts nevertheless. And on top of everything else, it was Saturday. What Rivke was doing was an invitation to disaster.

That disaster was not long in coming. Two days later a delegation of pious Jews called on my grandmother. Its members, solemn, stern, and righteous, wearing the distinctive long coats and black hats of orthodox believers, reported what had happened, expressing their profound disapproval. Was it not disgraceful that a young woman of the Jewish faith should violate the Sabbath by riding a bicycle in immodest dress? That sort of behavior might be expected of shameless shikses. But the daughter of a respectable Jewish family? My grandmother was urged in the strongest terms to make sure that no repetition of this inexcusable behavior ever occurred. And having unburdened themselves of their outrage, the members of the delegation left, still grim, still indignant.

Their visit was followed by a long private meeting between my grandmother and my aunt. I can only guess what was said, but I soon noticed a significant change in Rivke's interests and hobbies. She did not stop bicycling altogether, but she exercised far greater discretion. Her excursions became less frequent, and they were now confined to the more affluent and worldly sections of Otwock. Although she still wore shorts occasionally, she became much more careful about when and where she displayed them. And she never again went riding on a Saturday. Outwardly she seemed to conform to the injunctions of her mother's faith, but that memorable bicycle incident reinforced her growing inner rejection of the traditional pieties of Judaism.

It also had another important effect. Rivke's attention now began to shift from athletic to aesthetic accomplishments. Encouraged by the example of her oldest brother, she organized a small group of young men and women interested in the achievements of the new secular Yiddish culture, especially Yiddish drama. Once a week its members would meet in our house to read, discuss, analyze, and rehearse some important play, Asch's *God of Vengeance*, for example, or Hirschbein's *Green Fields* or Ansky's *Dybbuk*. Occasionally they would also stage one of those plays before an audience of local theatergoers who shared their tastes and aspirations. I was never allowed to attend any of their performances; I was considered too young to appreciate serious drama. But I used to see them often as they gathered in our living room, earnest, dedicated young people, mostly of modest background, sons and daughters of shopkeepers, tradesmen, salesmen, or even workers, inspired by a vision of the Jewish society of the future, more cultured, educated, and idealistic than the present one. Their manners were not always polished, their clothes not always elegant. They seemed at times awkward and ill at ease, a little clumsy, a little insecure. But there was something charming and touching, even poignant, about their resolve to transform the Jewish community, to make it better and kinder and nobler.

Rivke, however, did not devote herself exclusively to the cause of Yiddish culture. She also became involved in the social life of the *haut monde* of Otwock. She started to attend dinner parties, dances, and balls. Indeed, mingling with the town's patriciate began to seem to her more interesting, more exciting, than her weekly meetings with the somewhat plebeian members of the amateur theatrical group. She soon became an habitué of one of the most elegant cafés in Otwock, meeting with other young people from wealthy families, chatting, joking, dancing, and socializing.

I was of course never admitted to that exclusive establishment, but as I walked past its doors, I could sometimes hear the sound of the orchestra playing, the guests conversing and laughing, the waiters serving food and drinks, and the kitchen help scurrying to prepare exotic dishes. It all seemed so interesting, so inviting. But what fascinated me most was the sign posted outside displaying in large letters some mysterious, unintelligible words which I read as "feeve otslotsk." Actually, they were English words, "five o'clock," and they were meant to convey that late in the afternoon there would be a tea dance. The use of English was intended simply to enhance the air of elegance and sophistication. But to me all the allure of the local high life was expressed in that spellbinding, mystical, wondrous, and incomprehensible "feeve otslotsk."

My aunt's involvement in the social life of Otwock's patriciate also served another important purpose besides having a good time. Like other affluent young women, she hoped that it would help her find suitable friends, admirers, and suitors, perhaps even a husband. She had recognized that she was unlikely to meet people of the right background in that amateur theatrical group of hers. To fulfill not only her social aspirations but her romantic hopes, she would have to start moving in the more elegant circles of Otwock society. Nor was she disappointed in her expectations, at least not at first. She did meet a number of young men of similar tastes, hopes, ambitions, and goals. Having seen some of them, I must admit that they seemed much more polished and self-assured than the shy, diffident devotees of Jewish culture who met at our house once a week to broaden their appreciation of the Yiddish theater.

One of Rivke's new friends impressed me particularly. He was tall, handsome, polished, and a little snobbish, but most important, he had travelled, or at least he claimed that he had travelled, throughout Europe and even beyond. To me that was fascinating. I would listen spellbound as he described some trip of his, to Istanbul, for example. I could see him wandering through the back streets and alleys of the Turkish metropolis, visiting the bazaars, admiring the sultan's palaces, and listening to the muezzins summoning the faithful to prayer in the mosque. How much more exciting than life in homely, dull Otwock. Or he would relate how he had learned to eat oysters on the half shell in Athens, or maybe it was in Marseilles or perhaps in Barcelona, by watching unobtrusively how the other guests in the restaurant consumed theirs. As far as I was concerned, he might as well have been talking about Cathay or Tierra del Fuego. It all sounded so exotic, so extraordinary. I ardently hoped that he would marry Rivke and become a member of our family, so that I could listen to his stories for the rest of my life.

Alas, it did not turn out that way. Rivke and her elegant suitor had a serious falling-out, after which they stopped seeing each other. As for the reason, I never did find out. I was too young to understand, they told me. Perhaps Rivke discovered that her friend was not entirely trustworthy, that his interest in her was inspired more by material calculation than romantic passion. Or perhaps he concluded that her financial future was not quite as rosy as he had been led to believe, especially because my parents would soon be returning from the United States to take me with them. Since their remittances would then stop, he might be better off seeking a suitable match elsewhere. The full story remains a mystery to me this day. I do recall, however, that there were weeks of tears and unhappiness in our household. My grandmother and my aunt would meet in long private conferences from which the former emerged even more stern and tight-lipped than usual, while the latter slowly followed, pale and red-eyed, looking profoundly unhappy. After about a month everything returned more or less to normal. But from that point on Rivke began to contemplate the possibility of finding a suitable marriage partner among the less polished but more upright young men who shared her cultural interests and activities.

My own life during those years was rather placid compared to that of my grandmother or my aunt. For me there were no dramatic ups and downs, no sudden ascent from privation to affluence, from obscurity to prominence. I was simply the pampered only child of a prosperous family. I could not remember a time when I did not have enough to eat, indeed, more than enough. I was always dressed in the latest fashion. My grandmother would take me every month or so to the barber, the tailor, the shoemaker, the doctor, or the dentist. To me such advantages seemed natural, almost preordained. I assumed that there would always be someone to help me wash and get dressed, to assist me with combing my hair and tying my shoelaces. There would always be someone to push the swing, pull the sled, cook the dinner, slice the chicken, clean the room, and make the bed. How could it be otherwise? Those assumptions of mine were the natural consequence of an affluent, privileged upbringing.

Yet there was also a price to pay for the advantages I enjoyed. They encouraged a certain lassitude, a certain indolence on my part. Without brothers or sisters, without the companionship of other children my age, I became withdrawn and introverted. I would sit on the steps of the veranda or swing in the hammock, meditating, contemplating, reflecting, and daydreaming. Those were not unhappy experiences. On the contrary, I often found them rewarding and satisfying, inducing a feeling of tranquillity, a soothing peace of mind. And yet even my grandmother recognized that I was too detached, too isolated. She tried to encourage me to become more active, more playful, even more mischievous, if need be. She would introduce me to the children of other well-to-do Jewish families. She would ask my aunt to get me more involved in outdoor activities, in running, jumping, climbing, or swimming. She would coax, admonish, urge, and plead. But nothing seemed to help. I remained an inveterate, incorrigible lotus-eater.

This persistent lassitude was not the only consequence of my unusual upbringing. There were other indications that beneath the placid surface of my childhood I suffered from fears, anxieties, and insecurities of which my family remained largely unaware. For one thing, it was at this period that my habit of biting my nails began, a habit I have never been able to shake. Another symptom of inner tension was my unconscious tendency in moments of preoccupation to twist or even pull out tufts of hair from the back of my head. And then there was the chronic constipation from which I suffered throughout my childhood. Interestingly, those symptoms of emotional stress began to abate after my reunion with my parents. To be sure, I remained an inveterate and incorrigible nail biter, but my hair pulling diminished and then ceased, while my digestive system began to function more or less normally around the age of ten. Clearly, the peculiar circumstances of my childhood, especially the separation from my parents, had a deeper psychological effect than might have been surmised from my tranquil outward appearance.

Shortly after my sixth birthday my grandmother decided that the time had come for me to begin my elementary education. Still, she hesitated to enroll me in a public school attended by many pupils of varying ages, experiences, and backgrounds. She was afraid of what all that yelling, pushing, roughhousing, and mischief-making might do to my delicate sensibilities. And so I was sent to a small private class of a dozen or so children from affluent Jewish families who met every weekday in the living room of Mrs. Szwagerowa to receive a genteel form of instruction appropriate to our social position. This was the start of what was to become a lifelong pursuit of formal learning.

Our teacher was a middle-aged lady distinguished in appearance, well-bred in manner, and elegant in speech. I have no recollection of ever seeing a Mr. Szwager, which is the masculine form of the family name in Polish. Perhaps our teacher was separated or divorced or widowed. Yet there must have been a Mr. Szwager at some point, because Mrs. Szwagerowa had a son about sixteen or seventeen years of age, a pleasant, jovial young fellow who wore the distinctive peaked cap of a *gimnazjum* student. Sometimes, after returning home early from the school he attended, he would tell us about the recondite subjects he was studying: French, Latin, history, literature, geography, and algebra. We listened in awe. For him they were a key which would unlock the door to some important position in Polish society. With their help he might perhaps become an academic or a professional or maybe even a government official. And what could be loftier than that? We mere beginners would cheer him on, assure him of our moral support, and wonder whether we too might not someday reach similar heights of eminence.

But first we had to master the alphabet. That was a long and tedious task, at least for me. Mrs. Szwagerowa was kind and patient, encouraging me in my struggle to learn what each of the letters looked like, what it was called, and how it sounded. And then one day it finally came to me. I am not sure how or why, but I suddenly realized that those strange and confusing letters could be put together to form a meaningful, intelligible word. I even remember the first one I ever deciphered. It was the word for wagon, which in Polish has only four letters. Once I grasped the underlying connection between alphabet and language, the rest was easy. I never became a star pupil, but after recognizing that connection, I learned to read very quickly. Not only did I turn out to be one of the best readers in our class, but soon I was spending a good deal of my leisure time poring over children's books of fables, anecdotes, short stories, and simple poems. My youthful appetite for reading began back there in Mrs. Szwagerowa's living room, where her calm, patient instruction introduced a small group of six-year-olds to the mysteries of the alphabet.

After class I would occasionally visit the home of some acquaintances of my family who lived across the street from my teacher's residence. I always thought of it as the home of Mrs. Pragerowa, although in this case there was also a Mr. Prager. But he was a retiring man, shy and not very affable, who seemed to spend almost all of his time alone in his study working. I am not sure what exactly his occupation was, but I have the impression that he was some kind of writer, a journalist perhaps or a novelist or a poet or maybe just a miscellaneous intellectual. In any event, the chief breadwinner and real head of the household was his wife, a bright, friendly, pleasant woman, always cheerful, always smiling, with short, frizzly blond hair, and always wearing a high-necked dress designed to conceal the large, purplish strawberry mark on her throat. A dentist by profession, she managed to support her family quite comfortably by drilling teeth and filling cavities with great skill. My grandmother, my aunt, and I were all at one time or another patients of hers.

The main purpose of my afterschool visits to the Prager home was to chat with the son of the family, a boy my own age whose name was Sewus. We resembled one another in many respects, though not in appearance. Whereas he was dark-skinned, I was fair; his eyes were brown, mine blue; his hair was black, while my hair was blond. In other regards, however, we were very much alike. Both of us were only children, both loners, both placid, both shy. We would sit side by side, intermittently exchanging opinions, comparing experiences, sometimes joking, sometimes complaining, and sometimes remaining silent for long periods of time. Each of us found it satisfying to know someone else whose temperament, outlook, and personality resembled his own so closely.

Even more enjoyable than my visits with Sewus were the solitary walks I used to take, especially in the fall, through the woods stretching behind Mrs. Szwagerowa's house. After a few minutes I would begin to feel completely detached from the rest of the world. No sign of a street or a building was to be seen, no sound of a human voice could be heard. All was serene, peaceful, restful. I would look up at the trees which seemed to stretch almost to the sky. I would listen to the dead leaves rustling under my feet as I wandered. Occasionally I would be startled by a crow's raucous caw or the sudden scurrying of a squirrel in the underbrush. But even that was not unpleasant. The everyday world with its pressures and demands seemed so far away. I found in those solitary walks a sort of liberation, a feeling of inner peace which I rarely experienced at home or in school. Even now I can remember the wide-eyed wonderment of a small boy meandering through the lonely woods, awed, a little apprehensive, and yet strangely free from the vague anxieties and insecurities which often assailed him when he was with other people.

I remained a pupil of Mrs. Szwagerowa not much more than a year. I have a dim recollection of subsequently attending for a few months another small, private class for the young sons and daughters of Otwock's patriciate. And then, when I was about eight years old, my grandmother enrolled me in the local public school for Jewish children. I am not sure why she decided to make the change. Could it have been that the private classes I had been attending accepted only beginning pupils? Or did my grandmother feel that the time had come for me to start mingling with children of different ages and diverse backgrounds? Perhaps she wanted me to see something of life on the other side of the railroad tracks. Or maybe she simply concluded that the value of a private education was not worth the cost.

In any case, I now entered a school with a much larger enrollment than I was used to, between a hundred and a hundred and fifty pupils, ranging in age from six to fourteen, some of them from middle-class families, others from the households of tradesmen and skilled workers, and quite a few from the ranks of the ghetto proletariat. Some were almost completely Polonized, others were halfway between orthodoxy and assimilation, and still others remained closely attached to the teachings and practices of traditional piety. Their social and cultural diversity reflected in miniature the social and cultural diversity of Polish Jewry as a whole.

While all the children in my new school were Jewish, not far away stood another public school exclusively for Polish children. I used to wonder sometimes why the two were so rigidly separated. After all, the curriculum in our school was purely secular; no religious instruction of any sort was included. The language used in the classroom, moreover, was exclusively Polish. Even the teachers, though mostly Jewish, included some Poles. My homeroom teacher, for example, Mrs. Kowalska, the wife of a local pharmacist, was a devout Catholic. Why then the need to segregate the town's schoolchildren by religion or ethnicity? Yet even while I was asking myself that question, I guessed or sensed what the answer was. The two communities were so sharply divided by mutual suspicions, resentments, and antagonisms that having their children sit in the classroom side by side would invite frictions, insults, fights, and animosities. Separation seemed the wisest course.

This does not mean that personal relations between Jews and Poles were invariably hostile. By no means. Mrs. Kowalska, for example, was kind, considerate, and friendly in dealing with her Jewish pupils. She never displayed any ethnic prejudice, or perhaps it would be more accurate to say that in her case ethnic prejudice had become transformed into social and cultural prejudice. I remember how one day, as we were both walking home after school, she engaged me in conversation, chiding me gently for not doing better in my classwork. Even some of the children from the "bazaar" district, she pointed out, were more attentive and diligent than I. Shamefacedly, I had to agree. For I too had come to assume, like Mrs. Kowalska, that I should be intellectually superior to the "bazaar" children because my family was more affluent than theirs, because I dressed better, spoke better, and looked better, because with my blue eyes and blond hair I could almost pass for a Pole. As for her, she was ready to accept Jews as equals, provided they did not talk, think, behave, or appear too obviously to be Jews. That attitude was not uncommon in liberal, tolerant circles of Polish society.

Yet in fact the "bazaar" children were just as bright, just as studious as those from well-to-do families, sometimes more so. Their clothes may have been a little shabby, their manners a little crude. Their inflections sounded at times faintly foreign; their features seemed occasionally somewhat alien. But they were eager to learn. To them education represented the only means of escaping the impoverished environment into which they had been born. Through learning they hoped to enter the ranks of the middle class, to become businessmen, professionals, intellectuals, artists. Anything might be possible. School was for them a means of liberation. Yet it would be unfair to ascribe their devotion to schooling solely to a desire for economic or social advancement. Many of them had a natural, a spontaneous interest in knowledge. They found the experience of education broadening and liberating. The traditional Jewish dedication to book learning had become transformed in their thinking from a quest for spiritual salvation into a hunger for secular knowledge. Their eagerness to study was inspired by more than self-interest. It derived ultimately from a recognition of the enlightening or liberating function of education. Many of them were taking the first hesitant steps to becoming true scholars.

I found their company quite congenial. My grandmother's fears that I might feel intimidated or out of place among so many children from lower-class families proved groundless. Actually, I rather enjoyed talking to some of them, especially those who were older. Although I was an indifferent student in such subjects as arithmetic, drawing, singing, and penmanship, I soon acquired a reputation for excellence in reading, history, and geography. That reputation gave me entrée to the company of pupils from the more advanced classes. They in turn were curious to find out how much that little upstart from the third grade really knew. Our conversations consisted therefore almost entirely of short quizzes, of questions and answers designed to determine the limits of my expertise. I remember with special satisfaction one such encounter with an older boy who felt confident that he could trip me up by asking where Chicago was. When I told him without hesitation that it was in the United States, he seemed genuinely impressed. As for me, I swaggered for at least a day or two afterward, overflowing with complacency and pride.

My precocious expertise in certain fields of knowledge was not gained solely in the classroom. It owed at least as much to Mr. Slawin's library. As in most small towns in Poland, Otwock had no public library. The cost would have been far too high, not to mention the danger of theft or vandalism. But Mr. Slawin, a genial, likable man, always smiling, always courteous, had established a private lending library in an unpretentious building near the railroad station. It consisted of two small rooms, one above the other, connected by a narrow, spiraling metal staircase. Their walls were lined with shelves displaying in neat order several hundred volumes, perhaps even as many as a thousand, almost all of them novels and short stories. By paying a modest monthly fee, subscribers could borrow two or three at a time to take home with them.

For me that library became a gold mine. My grandmother, though she paid the dues regularly, made little use of its resources. She was too busy with her household chores to do much reading beyond an occasional sentimental novel in Yiddish. My aunt was equally preoccupied with her amateur theatrical group and especially with the exciting café life of Otwock. But I more than made up for their cultural indifference. I would spend hours in the library under the approving supervision of Mr. Slawin. I would pull out one book, then another, then a third. I would flip the pages, browse, read a little, examine the illustrations, and study the tables of contents. It was fascinating. I thought that all the learning in the world, all the books that had ever been published, all works in all fields of knowledge, could be found crammed into those two rooms. More than that, if I only worked at it long enough and hard enough, I would succeed in reading all those volumes. And then I would become a polymath; I would achieve omniscience; I would gain world renown.

Still, the task of acquiring universal knowledge did not prove easy. Some of the books were rather dull or highly specialized or simply incomprehensible. But others were a delight. Among those I remember with the greatest pleasure were the novels of Henryk Sienkiewicz, especially *Quo Vadis?* I can still feel the excitement of that famous scene in the Roman arena where Ursus, the faithful slave, kills with his bare hands the wild bull to whose back the beautiful Lygia has been tied on Nero's orders. It seemed almost miraculous. And then there was another Sienkiewicz novel, *In Desert and Wilderness,* not as well-known as *Quo Vadis?* but equally interesting, about two Polish children in the Sudan who become separated from their parents during the Mahdist uprising. They wander alone through Central Africa, courageously facing dangers and enduring hardships, before finally being reunited with their parents. Reading that was great fun.

I also enjoyed books of another sort, those by the prominent educator Henryk Goldszmit writing under the pen name Janusz Korczak, who later died so courageously and tragically during the Holocaust. There was his affectionate account, both amusing and moving, of a camp for Jewish boys which he had directed, an account entitled in rough translation *Yossys, Moeys, and Izzys,* and a companion volume describing a similar camp for Polish boys, this one called *Joeys, Jimmys, and Frankies.* But even more enjoyable was Korczak's delightful novel about *King Matt the First,* the story of a young prince about my own age who unexpectedly ascends to the throne after the sudden death of his father. He can now do all the things and fulfill all the wishes which had previously been prohibited or denied. Whenever the royal councilors try to talk him out of something he wants, he simply stamps his foot, declaring in an imperious tone that he expects his subjects to obey the king's command without question. That always produces abject submission. I found vicarious satisfaction in this reversal of traditional roles, in this portrayal of a child who has the power to tell adults what to do. I only wished I had that power.

Among Mr. Slawin's books were also several designed to instill in the youth of Poland a sense of national pride and patriotic devotion. Though dealing with various periods and crises in the country's long history, they all taught one and the same lesson. Poland had always been the defender of Western civilization against successive barbarian hordes from the East. It had sacrificed the flower of its manhood and the substance of its wealth in this noble effort. And what had been its reward? Not only indifference on the part of those it had tried to protect, but participation by some of them in the cruel partition of their selfless protector. The fate of Jesus had in a sense been a prefiguration of the fate of Poland.

I believed all of that unquestioningly. I read with wide-eyed excitement those accounts of heroic Polish uhlans riding forth to do battle with the treacherous Tatars, who rode their horses backward so that while appearing to retreat, they could shoot their arrows with impunity, safely beyond the reach of their opponents. Then there were the heroic Polish hussars fighting the equally treacherous Turks to save Vienna, only to be repaid by the ungrateful Austrians with shameless spoliation a century later. And then there were the heroic Polish rebels fighting the most treacherous enemy of all, those awful "Muscovites," wicked, brutal, rapacious, and predatory. This nationalistic children's literature produced the desired result; it made of me an ardent Polish patriot. I came to feel that the enemies of Poland were my enemies, that its heroes were my heroes. The only vague doubt troubling me occasionally was that the few Poles I knew were not always as noble, heroic, chivalrous, and selfless as those I read about in Mr. Slawin's library.

I must admit, moreover, that the books I enjoyed most were not by patriotic Polish authors but by an enormously popular German writer whose works did not deal with history or warfare. Karl May's novels, though their setting is ostensibly North America and the Middle East, depict in actuality a never-never land which existed only in his own vivid imagination. My favorites, which I read in Polish translation, were those purporting to portray life in the Wild West. I used to lie in my hammock spellbound, reading about the adventures of "Old Shatterhand," scout, guide, pathfinder, and fighter for justice on the lawless frontier, two rifles slung across his back, one over each shoulder, a revolver at his side, and a long, sharp knife in his belt. So what if he never participated in a cattle drive or engaged in a fistfight with the town bully or walked slowly down Main Street for a shoot-out with the villain? What if he bore no resemblance, not the slightest, to Tom Mix or Hoot Gibson? Who cared? To me gently swaying on the veranda in Otwock, and to countless other young boys all over Europe, he was fascinating.

But Old Shatterhand was only one of the many colorful figures emerging from Karl May's pen. There was also his friend and companion, the

Apache chieftain Winnetou, educated, sophisticated, compassionate, sensitive, and benevolent, totally unlike those feathered and half-naked Indians portrayed in Hollywood films. Winnetou was familiar with the classical works of Western civilization, he pondered philosophical questions of justice and virtue, and he understood the thoughts and feelings of others, regardless of their ethnic origin or cultural background. He even converted to Christianity. In any comparison between him and Old Shatterhand, it is the white man who can more properly be described as the "noble savage" running "wild in woods." And besides those two remarkable protagonists, May portrayed dozens of other picturesque characters: Caucasians and Indians, Europeans and Arabs, Christians and Moslems, courageous heroes and cunning villains, adventurers, explorers, warriors, and sages. I could never get enough of them.

There was still another source of my childhood education, not as formal as the public school for Jewish children or as informative as Mr. Slawin's library, but very influential and most enjoyable. The movies in interwar Poland never became part of the popular culture to the same extent as in the United States. The cost of admission to a theater was so high that for the masses seeing a movie remained at best an occasional extravagance. But for me that was no problem; my family could afford the price of a ticket. The only question with which my grandmother and aunt had to grapple was whether a particular movie was suited to my delicate sensibility and guarded innocence. Fortunately, there were quite a few films which met even their rigorous standards. The fact that almost all of them were made in the United States did not present a serious obstacle to their enjoyment. Since they were silent anyway, there was no need to worry about subtitles or dubbing. That came later with the talkies. During most of the 1920s all that was required of the movie distributors was to substitute Polish for the English in the titles on the screen.

The films I saw were a source of unending delight. Especially those dealing with historical subjects seemed to me fascinating. I could observe right there on the screen, directly in front of me, what life was like centuries ago. I did not have to try to remember the names and dates which my schoolteachers monotonously recited in the classroom. I did not even have to visualize what the various characters in Mr. Slawin's books looked like. All I had to do was open my eyes, gaze straight ahead in the darkened theater, and see firsthand how people in ages past dressed, how they talked, how they behaved, and how they felt. I would be magically transported from sleepy Otwock to Camelot or Xanadu. For an hour or two I ceased to be a dreamy little boy and became a warrior, a pirate, a hunter, or even a prince.

Those visits to the movies were to me a means of liberation. They not only aroused my interest in the past; they also shaped my earliest historical impressions. My introduction to the ancient world, for example, came in the form of the memorable chariot race in which Ramon Novarro as Ben-Hur defeats the villainous Messala played by Francis X. Bushman. Could anyone ever forget that thrilling scene? I first became interested in the Middle Ages by watching handsome, acrobatic Douglas Fairbanks perform in *Robin Hood*, defending the cause of the rightful ruler of England, Richard the Lionheart, against his villainous brother, Prince John, and that wicked sheriff of Nottingham. And I owe my initial encounter with American history to William Boyd in *Yankee Clipper* as a bold sea captain racing the British to see who would be the first to reach Boston from China.

But the most interesting movies were those dealing with the First World War, at that time still a recent memory. I recall sitting entranced, while Victor McLaglen as Captain Flagg and Edmund Lowe as Sergeant Quirt fought the Germans and vied for the favor of the beautiful Charmaine played by Dolores Del Rio. The most moving film of all, however, was *The Big Parade* with John Gilbert, the story of a pleasant though shallow young man-about-town who achieves maturity and understanding through the cruel experiences of war. Watching those movies was just as enjoyable, just as exciting as reading the novels of Karl May, perhaps even more so.

These various cultural experiences of mine in the classroom, the library, and the theater shaped my decision regarding what I would do when I grew up. I resolved then and there to become either a sea captain or a historian, in that order of preference. As a sailor I would have an opportunity to see firsthand all those distant, exotic places I had read about in Mr. Slawin's books or observed on the screen in Otwock's movie house. I would be able to visit England and the Holy Land, I would travel to China and to the United States, I would walk over the battlegrounds of northern France and across the fields of Flanders. I would explore the remotest corners of the earth. I would become Douglas Fairbanks or William Boyd, bold, adventurous, dashing, and devil-may-care.

But if for some reason I could not be a sea dog, if unforeseen circumstances kept me from traveling around the world in search of adventure, then I would settle for second best. I would become a historian. In that way I would at least be able to continue pursuing the interests aroused by Mr. Slawin's library and by all those exciting movies. I would at least be able to meditate and daydream about the past. I would still try to understand and visualize what had happened a long time ago. I might find out more about it, perhaps even write about it. I might actually approach the scholarly and literary heights of Henryk Sienkiewicz or Karl May. It would not be as satisfying as sailing the seven seas, but it would certainly be better than such dull, plodding occupations as doctor, lawyer, dentist, or businessman.

My grandmother, however, had other ideas. She dismissed those early ambitions of mine as childish fantasies, a result of the sedentary life I was leading, the consequence of reading too many books and lying too long in the hammock. What I needed was more diversity in my interests, hobbies which were closer to everyday life, activities which were traditional, practical, and down-to-earth. That conviction helps account in part for her earlier efforts to make of me a pious believer or at least an expert bicyclist. My indifference to religious instruction and my lack of athletic talent did not discourage her. She kept on looking for some diversion which would get me away from those infernal books and out of that indolent hammock.

She found what she was looking for by accident, or at least she thought she found it. And I unwittingly misled her into thinking that. She had given me a toy violin on one occasion, as a birthday present, I believe. In my innocence, without an inkling of what it might lead to, I thrust the violin under my chin with a dramatic flourish and struck an artistic pose. That did it. My grandmother concluded on the spot that she had finally discovered where my true talent lay. Her misapprehension was understandable. The Jewish community of Eastern Europe was at that time sharing vicariously in the musical triumphs of child prodigies like Jascha Heifetz and Yehudi Menuhin. Why should I not turn out to be a *Wunderkind* as well? Just think of the praise and fame I might earn by my violin playing, not to mention the money. And all it would require would be a few years of lessons from a good music teacher. My grandmother knew right then and there what she had to do.

Unfortunately, my career as an artist turned out to be no more successful than my career as a theologian or an athlete. Placing the violin in position, grasping the bow, and assuming a soulful expression was not particularly difficult. Those endless scales and exercises, however, those scrapings and screechings, those futile efforts to coax a musical sound out of a stubborn instrument, they were most discouraging, not only to me but to my teachers as well. I remember one of them, an elderly gentleman with a bald head and a wrinkled forehead, vainly pleading with me not to be so "phlegmatic" in my playing. Even now the mere mention of that word arouses in me feelings of embarrassment and humiliation. Another one, a temperamental young man with a shock of black hair, a nervous twitch on his face, and a wild look in his eye, was even more critical. He would glare, threaten, rage, and yell, occasionally even tearing the bow out of my hand and hurling it to the ground. Nothing seemed to help. It became increasingly clear that I was simply not meant to be a great musician.

But my grandmother refused to recognize the obvious. She insisted that those boring, repetitive scales and exercises were primarily responsible for my lack of interest in the violin. If I just had something more interesting, more tuneful to play, my true musical talent would soon emerge. She therefore persuaded or coerced my instructor, despite his repeated objections, to try to teach me to play "Hatikvah," the hymn of hope of the Zionist movement. Still, I found that melody no more inspiring than the scales and exercises which had previously constituted my repertoire. The violin continued to scrape and screech, until even my grandmother was finally forced to face the hard, inescapable truth. After a little more than a year, my musical training came to an end. Jascha Heifetz and Yehudi Menuhin could now breathe more easily.

As for me, I returned to the placid, familiar routine of the classroom, the library, and the movie theater. My only diversions were the periodic visits from and to my relatives in Warsaw. Those were invariably very pleasant occasions, or rather the ones spent with my aunts were very pleasant. My uncles, on the other hand, appeared to me somewhat stern, aloof, and not too friendly. I felt a little uncomfortable in their presence. Perhaps that had something to do with my growing up in an environment which was almost exclusively female. Whatever the reason, at least the meetings with my aunts were always enjoyable and often delightful. They all seemed so likable, so cheerful, and so very kind.

On one of my birthdays, I remember, some of them came to Otwock to help me celebrate, bringing with them a golden crown made of pasteboard and a crepe-paper ermine robe. I strutted all day in my royal attire, pleased as Punch. A year later they even persuaded my grandmother to throw a birthday party for me and seven or eight other children from well-to-do families. At the conclusion of the festivities the youthful guests were driven home in an open limousine, escorted by their proud host. Admittedly, the limousine was slightly dented and worn. The chauffeur, moreover, who was also the owner of the vehicle, refused to pick us up at the house, because our street was unpaved and he was afraid of getting stuck in a rut or sandbank. We had to walk a block and a half to the nearest surfaced road for our luxurious means of transportation. But once we got into the limousine, the rest was sheer ecstasy. We rode through the streets of Otwock proud as peacocks, the cynosure of all eyes, an object of curiosity, admiration, and envy of every child we passed on the way. How could I or my guests ever forget that extraordinary experience?

My occasional visits to Warsaw were even more interesting. I would stand on the balcony of my grandparents' apartment looking down on the hustle and bustle of Gesia Street, the crowded sidewalks, the shops and pushcarts, the peddlers, the hustlers, the hawkers, the beggars. It was so much more exciting than Otwock. Across the street stood a grim prison which was surrounded by high walls topped with barbed wire. Peering from the balcony, I could see the courtyard with armed guards in uniform walking up and down, and sometimes a group of prisoners being marched to a work detail. There were even scary reports by my grandfather and my aunts about the sound of beatings and the cries of pain which could occasionally be heard at night from the other side of the prison walls. I would listen fascinated and a little frightened.

To the rear of the apartment building was a courtyard separating the more prosperous tenants from the mean lodgings of impoverished shopworkers and day laborers. I could see young boys about my own age playing down there, in skullcaps and earlocks, dressed in the somber clothing of orthodoxy, but laughing and roughhousing, appearing to have a wonderful time. I was often tempted to join them, to get to know them, perhaps take part in their games, perhaps share in the fun they were having. On one occasion I even tried it, but with disappointing results. When I descended to the courtyard, the others stopped playing and laughing. They eyed me suspiciously, recognizing by my clothes and my haircut that I was not one of them. When they began to approach me slowly, silently, and, it seemed to me, menacingly, I decided to beat a hasty retreat. I quickly reascended the staircase to my grandparents' apartment, resolving to resist hereafter any temptation to mingle with the pugnacious children of the Jewish proletariat.

That left the apartment's flushing toilet as the chief source of amusement during my visits to Warsaw. The toilet was not in the best working order, to be sure. The chain was a little rusty and the tank leaked. Nevertheless, if you pulled the handle, water would miraculously come rushing down into the ceramic bowl. To me that was a source of endless wonderment. I could not remember ever seeing anything like it before. All we had in Otwock were chamber pots and outhouses. And so I would spend long periods of time in the toilet, pulling the chain, watching the water flowing, listening to the tank refilling, and then pulling the chain again. It was rather relaxing and certainly safer than venturing into the courtyard.

Still, my visits to Warsaw were not all fun and games. Sometimes they required the fulfillment of solemn responsibilities and obligations. During Passover, for example, I as a grandson would be invited to participate in the *seder*, the festive family celebration of the holiday. Those occasions were memorable. All of us would gather in the evening around the long table in the dining room, my grandfather at the head, a gray-bearded patriarch in a black coat, a thick prayer book lying open in front of him. At the other end of the table was my grandmother in a satin dress, wearing the customary pious wig, pale, silent, and withdrawn, exhausted by long years of childbearing and child rearing. And on both sides sat their sons and daughters, all of them in secular attire, all talking in Polish, all confirmed freethinkers, none of them believing in the miraculous liberation of the Jews from Egyptian bondage, none believing in the long march through the desert to the promised land, none believing in the Bible, none even believing in God. But all of them were taking part in a solemn religious observance, partly out of filial duty, but partly also as an expression of loyalty, perhaps unconscious loyalty, to a culture, a history, a tradition, and a community.

My own role was to ask the prescribed "four questions" regarding the nature of the holiday we were celebrating. That was not easy, because the questions were all in incomprehensible Hebrew, and while the first few words of each one were the same, the rest was entirely different and had to be mastered by sheer memorization. Yet that was not the worst of it. The questions were followed by my grandfather's response in the form of a reading of the *Haggadah*, an interminable account of the Exodus in an unintelligible language. Everyone else around the table seemed to listen with interest to the familiar story of the cruel enslavement and divine liberation of our people. But for me it was terribly boring, since I could not understand a word of what was being said. I would grow drowsier and drowsier, finally falling into a deep sleep.

That might not have been altogether bad, except for one important drawback. Before each Passover I would firmly resolve to remain awake until the prophet Elijah joined us in the course of the evening, as I was solemnly assured he would. There was even a cup of wine placed in the middle of the table for his refreshment, in accordance with tradition. I had visions of a saintly graybeard in exotic Oriental dress entering the apartment, taking a sip of the wine, exchanging greetings with my grandparents, chatting with my aunts and uncles, and perhaps even approaching me with a kindly smile, patting me on the head, and asking how I was doing in school and whether I had been a good boy.

Yet not even that exciting prospect could overcome the soporific effect of the interminable, droning recital of the *Haggadah*. After an hour or two one of my aunts would wake me so I could wash my face, put on my nightshirt, and go to bed. She would tell me that our venerable guest had just left, that he had been very kind and gracious, and what a pity it was that I had not met him. I would vow that next time, no matter what, I would stay awake so that I could be introduced to him. But it was no use. Each year the reading of the *Haggadah* seemed to take longer and longer, the prophet's visit to Gesia Street began later and later, and my own drowsiness grew stronger and stronger. I never did get to meet Elijah.

Those childhood years of mine in Poland followed one another in uneventful, predictable succession, calm, pleasant, comfortable, and restful. Yet there was one bothersome, persistent concern which troubled our household's lotus-eating existence. All three of us, my grandmother, my aunt, and I, knew that our accustomed way of life was bound to come to an end, and we even knew when that would happen. As soon my parents became American citizens, they would return to Otwock to take me with them across the Atlantic. And this would mean a drastic change for each of us. My grandmother, who was barred by the immigration laws from accompanying us to the United States, would have to go to live with one of her other children. My aunt would have to give up the carefree existence of a small-town debutante and learn to support herself by her own efforts and accomplishments. And as for me, my childhood would be over, and I would start out on a new life in a strange, distant land altogether different in language, custom, and culture from the one I had known. The prospect was exciting, inviting, and challenging, and yet vaguely disturbing.

Chapter 5

On the Edge of the Volcano

As I look back in the twilight of life at the vanished world of my child-hood, I seem able to recall the events and experiences of three quarters of a century ago with greater clarity than ever before. Perhaps that happens to most people of advanced years, as their prospects for the future gradually become less inviting than their recollections of the past. But in my case there may have been a special reason for my previous inability or rather unwillingness to remember what had been. I may have recognized that remembering would not only bring back memories of a bygone age, some of them pleasant and heartwarming, others unpleasant or even painful. It would also raise questions in my mind about what happened eventually to those among whom I lived as a child, what happened after I left them, what happened when a few years later they had to face an unimaginable disaster. Maybe that was why I preferred not to think too much about my childhood.

But now that the passage of time has finally enabled me to look more closely at my life in interwar Poland, I find that I must grapple with unanswered and unanswerable questions, questions which I would prefer to avoid but which I seem unable to escape. What became of all those people—the men and the women, the adults and the children, the friends and the strangers—among whom I grew up? What happened to them after I left? What about Mrs. Szwagerowa, the kind, patient teacher in whose classroom I learned to read? And what about her son, the dashing *gimnazium* student so full of hope regarding the future? What happened to them? And how about Mrs. Pragerowa, the smiling, blond, blue-eyed dentist with that half-concealed strawberry mark on her throat? And her silent, withdrawn husband? And her silent, withdrawn son with whom I felt a certain indefinable kinship? What happened to them? And then there was Mr. Slawin, the genial, likable librarian whose books turned me into an avid reader. What became of him?

I wonder not only about those who were pleasant and kind. The same questions arise in my mind regarding those whom I remember with distaste or disapproval or fear. I do not recall ever meeting Mr. Gelbfisz, the quarrelsome co-owner of our house in Otwock, but what I heard about him from members of my family was invariably unpleasant. They described him as contentious, selfish, unprincipled, and greedy. There were apparently good reasons for disliking him. Nevertheless, I wonder sometimes what became of him after the German occupation of Poland. And what about that charming but faithless suitor of my aunt Rivke, the one who abandoned her to pursue more promising marriage possibilities? What happened to him? And what happened to that temperamental music teacher of mine who would shout and rage, threatening to break my screeching violin into pieces? And what about those tough little orthodox boys in the courtyard in Gesia Street who were preparing or appeared to be preparing to beat me up because I looked too elegant, too spoiled, and too worldly? What happened to them? Those are questions which continue to trouble me, questions from which I cannot free myself.

And yet there is more to it than that. To be quite honest, the questions troubling me are not really, What happened to so-and-so? What became of this one or that one? They are rather, How did so-and-so die? When and where was this one or that one killed? Was the end swift and merciful or slow and agonizing? Did he or she perish suddenly, unexpectedly, or were there months and years of growing privation, oppression, brutality, and suffering? In a few cases I know the answer. My grandfather was arrested, imprisoned, and shot, all in the space of a few days. One of my uncles was fatally wounded during the siege of Warsaw. An aunt of mine apparently died by poisoning, knowingly or unknowingly, I cannot be sure which. As for the others, especially those who were not members of my immediate family, I have no idea of how they met their end. But while wondering about them, I also continue to be disturbed by vague feelings of guilt for not having shared their fate.

Occasionally, I even try to imagine how they and the millions of other European Jews who perished in the Holocaust behaved in the face of death. Did they remain brave and defiant to the end? Were they composed and dignified? Or did they plead and grovel before the executioner? Did they weep and whimper, scream and lament? They probably were and they probably did all those things, depending on their particular character and situation. Yet it is perhaps presumptuous even to raise questions of that sort. Do the living have any right to ask the dead, especially the victims of an organized campaign of ethnic mass murder, whether they died heroically, defiantly, calmly, and steadfastly? No. To inquire would be an act of profound impiety. All those who perished, regardless of their conduct in the hour of final agony, should be treated with the same unintrusive respect by those who did not perish.

There are other questions, however, which may properly be asked of those who were not victims but witnesses of the Holocaust. How did they regard the decision of the Third Reich to settle the "Jewish question" once and for all? What was their attitude toward the policy of anti-Semitic genocide which National Socialism grimly described as the "final solution"? Such questions continue to confront all the nations of Europe, particularly those in the east, where the great bulk of European Jewry lived. How did the non-Jewish population of this region react to the extermination of the Jewish minority? The issue is so sensitive because anti-Semitism was widespread and deep-rooted among the peoples of Eastern Europe. Long before Hitler came to power, popular racist movements in Russia, Poland, the Ukraine, Romania, Lithuania, and Latvia were preaching that the Jews constituted not only a foreign but a corruptive and destructive element in national life. They would always remain fundamentally different from the native population, not only unassimilated but unassimilable.

Worse still, according to the anti-Semites, the Jews were not content to remain a separate and distinct minority within the nation which had magnanimously provided them with a place of refuge. They were trying, silently and insidiously, to gain dominance over those who had been their benefactors. They were repaying kindness with treachery, generosity with greed. Their rapacity could be seen on all sides. Economic control was the most powerful weapon in their campaign of conquest, a campaign which they were clearly winning. Just look at the names of those who held leading positions in commerce, business, and especially finance. Almost all of them Jews. But even that was not enough for them. They were also beginning to extend their control over the nation's culture. They were increasingly playing a dominant role in scholarship and education, in literature and philosophy, even in the fine arts. And on top of that, they were acquiring influence in politics, especially in the parties of the center and on the left. Their ultimate goal, whatever the ideology they ostensibly embraced, was to subvert traditional values and loyalties in state and society.

How were the machinations of this dangerous minority to be resisted? On this point the anti-Semitic movements of Eastern Europe were somewhat ambiguous. No one was as yet bold-faced or cold-blooded enough to advocate out-and-out extermination, at least not openly. But there was a great deal of talk about the urgent need to restrict the Jewish role in economics, politics, and culture. The means which were proposed usually boiled down to some form of segregation and expropriation, some system of legally enforced ghettoization. But even that was not enough for the more militant racists. They often spoke about the need for a wholesale expulsion of the Jews. Anything less would inevitably fail to protect the unsuspecting, guileless majority against a sly, cunning minority. As for the place of exile for the East European Jewish community, that was left rather vague. Palestine was mentioned most frequently, but occasionally there were also suggestions of some remote part of Africa or some distant region in South America. It did not really matter. The important thing was that the Jews leave, and the sooner, the better.

Thus when the Third Reich embarked on the conquest of Europe, its policies regarding the "Jewish question" could count on a measure of support in the occupied countries. The contention that those "treacherous aliens" must be deprived of their improper influence and ill-gotten wealth did not sound new or unreasonable to many of those living under the German occupation. They had heard similar views expressed by their own countrymen long before the war. Nor did it seem farfetched to maintain that the two communities, the Jewish and the non-Jewish, should be rigidly separated, each with its own law, its own economy, and its own culture. Ghettoization would mean that the Jews could live in accordance with their own unique racial character, while the non-Jews would finally be free of a pernicious foreign influence. Surely, that would be best for all concerned.

The ideological appeal of National Socialism's racist rhetoric was reinforced by important practical considerations. The expropriation of the Jewish community would enable the non-Jewish population to regain the possessions which had been stolen by Semitic guile and deceit. Not all of those reacquired possessions would be divided evenly, to be sure. The Germans would retain the lion's share. But some-thing—a bone at least, a scrap, a crumb—would be left for the native "Aryans." What had been a Jewish home would become a Polish or Lithuanian home. What had been a Jewish place of business would become a Ukrainian or Latvian or Slovak place of business. And that would not really be an expropriation or confiscation. It would be a form of restitution, an act of indemnification.

Such considerations help explain the success of the Third Reich in finding willing collaborators throughout occupied Europe, especially in the east. Not only in countries like Romania or Hungary, which were more or less willing allies of the Nazi regime, but even in those like Poland and Czechoslovakia, which had been its bitter enemies, the German authorities could count on significant popular support for their anti-Semitic policies. Indeed, of all the measures introduced by the Third Reich in the territories under its control, the ones which gained the widest approval, sometimes the only ones to win any approval, were those expropriating, segregating, and eventually "deporting" the Jews. Those who were themselves pitiful victims of Nazi brutality often remained indifferent to the fate of those who were even more pitiful victims.

This is not to deny that in all the occupied countries, including those where anti-Semitism had been strongest before the war, many people were horrified by the policy of mass murder. There were even some who risked their lives, and some who lost their lives, trying to help the doomed Jewish community. But others approved, justified, assisted, and profited from the "final solution." What the proportions were of those who supported, those who opposed, and those who chose to look the other way varied from country to country. Even for any par-ticular country no more than estimates and approximations are possi-ble. And yet it is clear that the effectiveness of the Nazi program of genocide depended to a large extent on the collaboration of the local population. Where public opinion generally disapproved of that pro-gram, as in Denmark, Bulgaria, and Italy, the Jewish community suf-fered relatively moderate losses. On the other hand, where hostility toward the Jews was widespread, as in most of Eastern Europe, the extermination measures achieved almost complete success. It seems clear in retrospect that at least in this region the Holocaust had all along been more than a possibility, more even than a probability. Sooner or later, in one form or another, it was almost bound to happen. It had become almost an inevitability.

Yet until the actual outbreak of hostilities, no one in Eastern Europe, neither the liberals nor the conservatives, neither the radicals nor the reactionaries, neither the devout Jews nor the rabid anti-Semites, anticipated what was about to take place. They all assumed that the ethnic struggle would go on as it had in the past, with more intensity perhaps, perhaps with greater bitterness, but with no significant change in weapons or tactics. The Jews continued to hope that they would little by little gain general acceptance. They would achieve the same status as the other minorities in Central and Eastern Europe, like the Ukrainians in Poland, for example, the Hungarians in Romania, or the Germans in Czechoslovakia, not quite trusted by the dominant majority, but at least recognized as a distinct community entitled to a measure of autonomy. Even more might be possible. A victory at the polls of the liberal parties would mean greater freedom for the Jewish community. A seizure of power by the far left would mean still more; it might lead to complete equality. There was thus no need for the Jews to despair.

What the anti-Semites expected was not drastically different. How could they have foreseen that the policy which they had been advocating for almost a century was about to be implemented by means more extreme than any they had imagined? They too assumed that the struggle against Jewish predominance would continue for a long time to come. They were therefore preparing to intensify their tactics, to become more aggressive, more militant. They began to organize boycotts of Jewish businesses, which in their view were the chief instruments of Jewish domination. They started agitating for restrictions on the admission of Jews to the universities, thereby seeking to limit their access to the learned professions. They loudly denounced members of the Jewish community who occupied important positions in scholarship, education, literature, and the arts. They even staged boisterous street demonstrations demanding the resettlement of the Jews, in Palestine or the United States or South America, anywhere except where they were now living. The anti-Semites assumed, however, that the struggle would be long and hard, that it would go on for the foreseeable future. Not even they could imagine how close they actually were to their goal.

During my childhood years in Poland, I was only dimly aware of the rising tide of ethnic bigotry. Although I learned of its existence from the conversations of the adult members of our family, my exposure to it remained indirect and infrequent. That was partly a result of my living almost exclusively within the Jewish community of Otwock. Most Jews in fact considered voluntary segregation to be the best protection against anti-Semitic prejudice. But equally important, the few Poles I did get to know were almost without exception from the lower classes, from the peasantry, as a rule. Some of them were employed by my grandmother; the livelihood of others depended partly at least on her patronage or good will. They could not therefore allow themselves to display any hostility they may have harbored against Jews. Such feelings had to be disguised. Expressing them openly might have had serious economic consequences.

Still, to put it that way would not be entirely fair. Whatever the attitude of lower-class Poles toward the Jewish community in general, they frequently maintained cordial or even friendly relations with individual Jews whom they had come to know as customers, co-workers, or neighbors. Their anti-Semitism, in other words, tended to be general or abstract rather than specific or personal. And this distinction had important social and psychological consequences.

The Poles whom I came to know well were first of all the successive live-in maids in our household. Here a word of explanation is in order. A live-in maid in Poland was not in any way a sign of her employer's wealth or social prominence. Even families of modest means could often afford to hire one. The rural masses lived in such abject poverty that the only compensation the head of a household needed to offer a servant was food and shelter. There were no fixed wages, no prescribed working hours, no holidays, no vacations. The maid, usually a young woman from a peasant family, timid, inexperienced, and submissive, would sleep on a simple cot in the pantry, scullery, or a corner of the kitchen. She would eat whatever was left over after the family's meal. On Sunday she might be given an hour or two off to go to church. Once or twice a month she might receive permission to visit her family for an afternoon. She would generally wear the hand-me-down clothes and shoes for which the rest of the household no longer had any use. On a few festive occasions celebrated by her employer, on holidays, weddings, or birthdays, for example, she might receive a coin or two. But that was all. Having a maid was no more extravagant than buying a radio or owning a gramophone.

I still remember three of our family's maids. The first was an agreeable young woman in her twenties or maybe early thirties whose name I have long since forgotten. She seemed hard-working and eager to please, though she tended to keep to herself. Perhaps she felt out of place in our home. What I recall most clearly, however, is the crisis which arose about a year after she came to work for us, a crisis culminating in her sudden departure. I remember overhearing Rivke one day telling my grandmother, in a lowered voice and with a knowing look, that during the previous night she had heard a soft knock on the kitchen door, then a strange male voice inside, and finally our maid talking quietly but animatedly with the mysterious visitor.

Once her suspicions were aroused, Rivke became increasingly observant, increasingly vigilant. There were more whispered conferences with my grandmother, more investigations, more reports, and more shocking surmises, while the expression on their faces became grimmer and grimmer. I think I may have even overheard something about our maid expecting a baby. In any case, the upshot was that she suddenly left our household, whether voluntarily or not remained a mystery, at least to me. I would have liked to ask why; indeed, I would have liked to know more about the entire affair. But I sensed somehow that it would be advisable to leave well enough alone. Too much inquisitiveness on my part would only lead to evasions and prevarications. It might in fact produce a sharp rebuke. I recognized even at that tender age that there were some things in life I was simply not meant to understand.

Our next maid was quite different from her predecessor. She was a young girl of about fourteen or fifteen named Kazia. Not much older than I, she soon became my companion and playmate rather than my mentor and protector. In fact, she turned into the older sister I never had. We used to play together, exchange stories, tell jokes, take walks, laugh, sing, and have fun. We grew quite fond of one another.

Indeed, Kazia came to feel that her duties were not confined to providing me with creature comforts. She also had a responsibility for my spiritual welfare, for my salvation in the afterlife. That feeling accounts no doubt for a decision on her part which could have had very serious consequences for both of us, especially for her. One day, while I was visiting her in her room, actually an unused pantry off the kitchen, she suddenly resolved to do something which she must have been contemplating for a long time. After looking carefully and apprehensively in all directions to make sure no one was watching, she removed the crucifix which hung on her wall and held it out to me to kiss.

Admittedly, that made me a little uneasy. I had no scruples about kissing the crucifix, but I sensed what the consequences would be if my grandmother ever found out what we had done. There would be a terrible scene. I would receive a major spanking for contemplating apostasy, while Kazia would be immediately fired for inciting it. Still, after a moment's hesitation, I summoned my courage and kissed the crucifix. Nothing happened. Indeed, it all turned out quite well. My grandmother, blissfully unaware of my brief lapse from our faith, went about her daily business as if nothing had occurred. I had the satisfaction of getting away with what I regarded as a naughty but harmless prank. And Kazia could feel that she had not only earned divine approbation for herself, but that she had probably made my life in the hereafter a little easier.

After that initial escape from the consequences of disobedience, Kazia and I became even bolder. We resolved to go on living dangerously. A few weeks later, having received permission from my grandmother to pay a brief visit to her family, but on the condition that she continue to look after me, Kazia took me with her to a remote part of Otwock where her parents were living. We came to a white wooden hut consisting of a single long room, one end of which was separated from the rest by a flimsy curtain. Those were the family's sleeping quarters. In the center of the room stood a big wooden table around which sat eight or ten men and women, all of them apparently Kazia's relatives, hungrily ladling and consuming some sort of stew from a large pot in the middle of the table. They seemed to be enjoying their lunch enormously. After warmly greeting Kazia, they invited her to sit down and join them for their simple meal. She accepted without hesitation, while I remained standing shyly on the side, feeling left out but too timid to approach the others without an invitation.

They must have sensed my dilemma. There was a brief whispered conference around the table, and then one of the men got up and looked cautiously out of each of the two small windows to make sure that none of the Jewish neighbors were around. They all knew what would happen if my grandmother ever found out what was about to take place. To her my eating *trefeh* food would have seemed almost as inexcusable as my kissing a crucifix. But after the lookout, having ascertained that the coast was clear, drew the curtains as an extra precaution, I was asked to join the company. I must admit that the stew was only so-so, but I had learned enough manners at home to assure my hosts that I found it delicious. Besides, the important thing was not the quality of the food but the satisfaction of once again defying with impunity my grandmother's stern injunctions.

My career as a secret rebel came to an end after two years, however, when Kazia, my co-conspirator, left our household. Her family concluded, and she apparently agreed, that the time had come for her to find a husband. Unfortunately, the life of a live-in maid did not offer much opportunity for meeting suitable marriage partners. It thus seemed best that she seek some new employment in which she would be more likely to encounter eligible young men. She departed, partly sad at leaving a family to which she had grown attached, but partly also elated at the prospect of new and exciting experiences. I regretted her departure much more, saddened by the loss of someone who was not only a playmate of mine and a fellow mischief-maker, but a make-believe sister as well.

Kazia's successor was altogether different, far more different than her two predecessors had been from one another. For one thing, she was not even Polish but Russian. Her name was Katia. While I am not sure why she had left Russia, I do recall hearing some talk about her emigrating to Poland during the chaos which followed the Bolshevik seizure of power. She still had a son in Russia who wrote her letters from time to time, although I never found out exactly where he lived, what his occupation was, and whether his father or any of their other relatives were still alive. During the two or three years that Katia spent with us, we were her only family.

There was another important difference between Katia and the previous maids, namely, religious faith. While they had both been devout Roman Catholics, she was a devout Eastern Orthodox Christian. That meant that instead of a crucifix hanging from the wall of her tiny bedroom, she had an icon placed in one of the corners. Here she would kneel down every morning and two or three times later in the day, cross herself, and pray ardently in some strange language. I used to watch her secretly from the kitchen, puzzled, curious, and faintly awed. What deity was she addressing? Which god was she entreating? The kneeling woman, so far from home, bowing down before a sacred image, reminded me in some ways of my grandmother blessing the candles on Friday night. Both of them, each in her own fashion, seemed in communion with some mysterious, supernatural force which controlled the destiny of us all.

The curious resemblance between those two women suggests another important difference between Katia and our other maids. The latter had been quite young. The first one I can remember, the one who left us suddenly under mysterious circumstances, was about the age of some of my aunts. I regarded her in fact not very differently from the way I regarded Rivke or Jadzia or Hala. Kazia, on the other hand, was my chum and playmate. She did not seem to me to be really an adult. She was just a child, a little older than I, to be sure, but very much like me in outlook, personality, and temperament. That was why I found it such fun to be with her. But there could be no pretending that Katia was my sisterly companion or even my aunt. She was already well in her fifties when she became a member of our household, gray-haired, stoop-shouldered, and grim-faced. She was in age and appearance another grandmother of mine.

There were indeed striking similarities between the two elderly women who looked after me, despite their obvious though superficial differences. Both had grown up in poverty, both had received a very limited education, both had been widowed in middle age, both had become separated from their children, and both were now living in an alien, uncongenial environment. No wonder they resembled each other. Katia, like my grandmother, looked glum and cross much of the time. She rarely smiled, she rarely said more than was absolutely necessary, and she almost never engaged in banter or gossip. And yet, again like my grandmother, she was capable of unexpected kindness and affection, emotions which a hard life had forced her to suppress. She too would sometimes display toward me a loving concern which she had been unable to express toward her own children. She too would make sure I was washed, combed, and dressed. She too would take me for walks, push the swing, and pull the sled. Katia became my second elderly surrogate parent.

What I learned about Polish lower-class life came from still another source. Besides a live-in maid, my grandmother employed a caretaker who lived with his family in a small wooden hut a short distance behind the main building. His name was Jan, I believe, and his job was to protect the house and property against thieves, take care of essential maintenance work, and repair any minor structural damage which might occur. He was a tall, strapping fellow, hard-working, experienced, skillful, and on the whole reliable. In dealing with members of our household he was always friendly and courteous, almost deferential. We were after all his employers. But I still felt vaguely uneasy in his presence. There was something hard or even mean in his expression, a look which suggested suppressed resentment, underlying hostility. I wondered sometimes whether he was not really like some of those awful *pogrom-tshiks* my grandmother used to talk about, those lower-class anti-Semitic rioters who would periodically attack Jewish life and property in the towns and villages of Eastern Europe. I even wonder now occasionally about what he might have been doing a decade or so later.

Jan's family consisted of his wife, who was quite ill and slowly getting worse, a daughter about fourteen or fifteen years old, and a son who could not have been more than ten. I got to know them fairly well because our maid Kazia became a good friend of the daughter. The two were of approximately the same age, the same background, the same education or rather lack of education, and with the same bleak prospects for the future. Thanks to this friendship between the two girls, I frequently visited the caretaker's drab, one-room hut, where he and his family slept, ate, dressed, washed, and attended to various bodily needs and functions.

Those visits gave me an insight into the harsh, impoverished existence of the Polish masses. More than that, they taught me something about the brutality to which this existence could lead. On one occasion when Kazia and I went to visit her friend, we found the poor girl standing in a corner in tears, frightened and whimpering. Her father, quite unconcerned, told us in passing that she had disobeyed or disregarded his instructions, and that she therefore had to be punished. Pointing to a stool still moist with what looked like water, he said, smiling grimly, that he had placed her over the stool, taken off his belt, and beaten her so severely that she had wet herself. And then, after telling us about what he apparently regarded as only a minor incident, he engaged Kazia in a whispered conversation, giving her knowing looks, making naughty comments, and confessing to amorous inclinations. Kazia, hardly older than the daughter he had just beaten, seemed interested, pleased, and flattered.

This brutality bred by brutalization, this callousness nurtured by impoverishment, could be seen in other ways as well. At the same time that our caretaker was flirting with his daughter's teen-age friend, his wife was lying in bed only a few feet away, slowly dying of tuberculosis. She had fought the disease courageously, continuing to perform her many strenuous household chores and duties for as long as possible. But by now she could barely get up. The members of her family and indeed she herself knew that the end was not far-off. Yet almost the only form of medical care she received was an occasional bottle of cough syrup that her husband would grudgingly purchase out of his meager earnings. Only when the disease reached its final stage was a doctor summoned to examine the dying patient. But by then all he could do was prescribe some other futile medication. About a week later she was dead.

Then, after a simple funeral and a brief period of mourning, Jan began looking for a new wife. After all, someone had to take care of the housekeeping, the cooking, the sewing, and the gardening. His children were visibly frightened of what might happen to them with a step-mother in the family, but their fears concerned him very little. He soon found a willing partner, a widow about the same age as his recently deceased wife, hard-working, tough-minded, and conveniently without children of her own. Either she had had none or they had been sent to live with relatives in unpaid drudgery. The match seemed mutually advantageous.

On Jan's wedding day a traditional Polish social ritual was observed, though in a somewhat incongruous form. The groom, dressed in his best Sunday suit, called on his patroness, kissed her hand, and humbly asked for her approval and blessing for his marriage. The custom went back to the days of serfdom, I suppose, when the peasant was expected to seek permission to marry from the lord of the manor. In this case the lord of the manor happened to be a short, stout, nearsighted, gray-haired woman who came from a distant Lithuanian ghetto. But she did her best to live up to the grave responsibility which had been thrust upon her. She assured Jan in her best broken Polish that she approved of his decision to remarry, and as a token of her good will, she slipped a few zlotys into his expectant hand. Since that was probably the chief purpose of the ceremonial anyway, both parties could be pleased with the outcome, he with the modest financial gift he had received, and she with the graciousness she had displayed toward a humble dependent.

For Jan's children, however, his remarriage had very unfortunate consequences. Their fears of what might happen once a stepmother entered their lives proved fully justified. She had no intention of spending her time looking after another woman's offspring. To her they were simply a burden, a nuisance. Nor did their father quarrel with her views. Within a few months after his remarriage, the children were sent away to live with distant friends or relatives as unpaid hired hands, to look after the domestic animals, to work in the fields, and to perform various menial household chores. They would now live the rest of their lives in hardship and privation, their minds impoverished and their spirits crushed, in an unending struggle for survival. Like so many children of the rural masses, they would grow up bitter, angry, and callous. The cruelty of their existence would make them cruel as well.

The poverty in which the Polish peasants lived helped shape and define their anti-Semitic prejudices. To many of them, perhaps to most, the Jews were not only infidels responsible for the crucifixion of the Son of God, cursed for all time because of their unpardonable crime.

They were not only outsiders who did not even as a rule speak proper Polish, interlopers who had outlandish customs, manners, tastes, and beliefs. They were greedy and cunning schemers who had managed to enrich themselves at the expense of honest, trusting Poles. This perception remained unaffected by the obvious fact that most Jews lived in a poverty almost as desperate as that of the Polish masses. The hungry, oppressed peasant wanted to believe, indeed, he had to believe, that the hardships he was forced to endure had been caused by demonic alien forces embodied in Jewry. This view provided him with an explanation of his hopeless poverty. More important, it seemed to point to a solution for that poverty, although the full implications of the solution did not become apparent for about another decade.

Belonging to a prosperous and privileged family, living the high life of Otwock, I remained largely protected against Polish ethnic prejudice. That was in part a result of living almost entirely within the Jewish community. Besides, the few Poles I did know never displayed any hostility toward Jews. They could not afford to. Yet their friendliness should not be ascribed solely to caution or expediency. Not all Poles were anti-Semitic, not even all Polish peasants. That too became apparent a decade later. Still, though enjoying a sheltered life, I would catch glimpses here and there of the widespread ethnic bigotry of the rural masses. That was a harsh reality of which not even a pampered child could remain unaware.

I remember on one occasion, while on a walk with Katia, seeing three or four Polish boys about my own age, barefoot and ragged, taunting a Jewish youngster in a skullcap and an *arba kanfoth*, the fringed, rectangular half apron worn by orthodox believers under their outer garments. The little fellow, a few years younger than his tormentors, seemed terrified of something which they kept poking at him amid loud laughter. I could see that they were holding in their hands small pieces of meat, obviously pork, which they were attempting to push in his face, while he was covering his eyes with his hands, trying desperately to avoid looking at those loathsome morsels. He had been taught in his *heder*, his religious school, that pork was not only an unclean food but a symbol of everything corrupt and sinful. And now he was terribly frightened of becoming contaminated, maybe even damned, by contact with that unspeakable evil.

The little game of torment and terror came to an end when an elderly Jew, perhaps a relative of the diminutive victim, suddenly appeared and, grasping the situation, scattered the bullies by threatening them with his walking stick amid a stream of Yiddish imprecations. They ran away still laughing, still enjoying the little prank they had played, eager to tell their chums about the fun they had tormenting their captive. As for the captive himself, he slowly walked in the opposite direction under the protective arm of his orthodox liberator, still sniffling, still whimpering, still trying to recover from the shock of his close encounter with hateful, defiling pork. The incident reflected in miniature the bitter tensions of the Polish-Jewish relationship.

There were other incidents as well, like the annual athletic contests between pupils from the Jewish school and those from the nearby Polish school, contests by which some well-meaning but overoptimistic educators hoped to encourage closer contact between the two. The result was usually the reverse; the competition merely aggravated their mutual dislike and hostility. The young spectators would gather on opposite sides of the running track, the Jews in one group, the Poles in another, each cheering the runners from its own school, each jeering at those from the other. What had been intended to foster greater understanding only revealed their underlying mistrust and resentment.

Worse still, the athletic contests sometimes led to displays of hostility more graphic even than cheers and jeers. There were also epithets and insults and occasional blows. I remember how at one of those competitions a little Polish boy made the mistake of standing on the Jewish side of the track. Trying to encourage the runners from his school, he urged them loudly to show those "mangy Jews" who the real athletes were. That had unfortunate consequences for him. On the other side of the racecourse his remark would have gone unnoticed; indeed, there it could be heard over and over again. But on this side it brought swift reprisal. An older girl who had overheard his exhortation, outraged, berated him angrily, underscoring her disapproval with a sharp blow to the back of his head. The little fellow seemed startled; he was not even aware that he had said anything improper. He had probably heard remarks of that sort at home so often that he could not understand why anyone would object to them. He lowered his head, tears came to his eyes, and sobbing softly he crossed over to the opposite side. There he undoubtedly found a more sympathetic audience.

My most vivid memory of lower-class Polish anti-Semitism, however, is associated with an incident which may never have actually taken place. One day in school I heard a rumor which aroused not only great interest but considerable apprehension among the pupils. The story quickly spreading throughout the building was that a group of boys from the Polish school, twenty of them or thirty or maybe even fifty, armed with sticks and penknives, had marched on our school in order to "kill a few of those dirty little Jew boys." But the janitor of the building, himself a Pole, scattered the youthful would-be *pogromtshiks* with a few blows from his shovel. They ran away, vowing to return at a more opportune moment to carry out their bloodthirsty design. As for their intended victims, we felt sure that it was only a matter of time before we would have to face a new assault.

How accurate was this story, which continued to trouble us for days afterward? Had there really been an anti-Semitic plot to assault the pupils from our school? Had its purpose been to kill or beat up or simply frighten us? Had there been twenty or thirty or fifty would-be assailants, or had there been only two or three? In fact, had there been any at all? Could the entire story have been concocted by one of the Jewish pupils with a vivid imagination and a hunger for attention? Who knows? What matters is that the rumor appeared quite plausible; it seemed to reflect the hostility by which the Jewish community felt perpetually confronted and threatened. Its factual accuracy is less important than its revelation of the state of mind of a profoundly disliked ethnic minority living on the edge of the volcano.

The anti-Semitism which I myself encountered occasionally in Otwock was almost entirely of this crude variety common among the masses. Its roots were primarily religious and economic. That is, it expressed hostility toward Jews because they rejected the Christian faith and because they were trying to enrich themselves at the expense of honest, hard-working, good-natured but gullible Poles. There was also another kind of anti-Semitism, however, genteel and highbrow in tone, essentially cultural and ideological in emphasis, which was prevalent mostly among the Polish patriciate. It derived from a concern that the unique spirit and special character of the nation, its historic values, beliefs, and loyalties, were being undermined by foreign minorities, especially the Jews. The dangers Poland faced had an economic and political aspect as well, according to this view, but they were essentially spiritual and moral rather than material in nature.

This fear of insidious alien influence was reinforced by the fact that the Polish state did include several national minorities which together constituted almost a third of the total population. In addition to the Jews, there were Ukrainians, Belorussians, and Germans, each of them numbering over a million. Still more serious, each of them was dissatisfied with Polish rule, each regarded the established government as alien, each sought to achieve greater autonomy or even outright separation. The Polish nationalists, knowing all this, regarded them as threats, as potential sources of subversion. The conflict between Poles and non-Poles thus became a central feature of political and cultural life in interwar Poland.

But of all the various minorities, the one which aroused the greatest suspicion on the part of the dominant majority was the Jewish community. At first glance, that may seem strange. The others were after all secretly and sometimes openly secessionist. Their ultimate purpose was to rejoin their compatriots on the other side of the frontier. They may have ostensibly demanded nothing more than self-government, but what they actually hoped for was separation. The Jews, on the other hand, had no secessionist ambitions, no separatist goals. They had no sympathetic countrymen just beyond the boundaries of Poland whom they wanted to join or rejoin. Their future was tied, for better or worse, to the future of the Polish state. Essentially, what they wanted was a measure of autonomy within the established order, a limited degree of self-determination with regard to religion, language, education, and culture. Other than that, most of them were willing to accept the territorial and political status quo.

Yet despite this willingness, the Jews were widely regarded as the most subversive of the ethnic minorities. The others were at least Christian like the Poles, even if some were Eastern Orthodox and others Protestant. Most of them, moreover, spoke a Slavic language resembling Polish, while those who did not, the Germans, for example, spoke one which was at least well-established in East European history and culture. Above all, they were concentrated in only a few regions of the country, the Ukrainians in the southeast corner, the Belorussians in the northeast, and the Germans scattered in the north and west. The bulk of the Polish population, living at some distance from those minorities, did not feel directly threatened by them.

The Jews were different, different in faith, in culture, and in their relationship to the Poles. Their religion was not only alien but hostile, rejecting the central teachings of Christianity. The language most of them spoke was alien as well, a strange Germanic "jargon" which even the Germans had trouble understanding. But worst of all, they could be found throughout the country, closely involved in national life, directly influencing the national economy and the national culture. And yet they remained alien to the national mentality and character. What concerned the upper-class anti-Semites most was the perceived corruption or subversion of the uniquely Polish spirit by cunning, sinister Jewry.

Not all educated Poles shared this view, of course. There were some, perhaps even many, who believed in the basic equality of the various peoples living in Poland regardless of their ethnic origin or cultural heritage. An attitude of tolerance could be found especially in the arts and letters, among the Polish intelligentsia, among the supporters of various liberal political parties, and in the radical movements of the far left. But there were other Poles, much more numerous, who shared the fear common among the well-to-do classes that the soul of the nation was being threatened by the "Jewish" forces of revolution and materialism. They regarded with alarm the disproportionate number of Jews occupying important positions in economic life, especially in finance and commerce. They expressed concern about Jewish influence in the professions, the many Jewish doctors, dentists, lawyers, brokers, and accountants. And then there was the growing role of Jews in the cultural life of the nation, in publishing and journalism, in education and scholarship, in literature and the fine arts. Where would it all end?

These highbrow anti-Semites did not see themselves as bigoted or arrogant or oppressive. Not at all. They were simply defending the national heritage. They were the ones who were being threatened with aggression, with the usurpation of what was rightfully theirs. They were not victimizers but victims, not instigators but targets of discrimination. They were merely trying to protect themselves against alien invaders, just as their brave ancestors had done in fighting the Tatars, the Turks, the Muscovites, or the Teutonic Knights. The struggle was essentially the same. It was being waged, now as before, in defense of the nation's honor, the nation's culture, the nation's soul. To suggest that the Poles, fighting to preserve their distinctive ethnic character, were anti-Jewish would be utterly false. Rather, the Jews trying to subvert that character were anti-Polish. The battle would have to go on until the forces threatening Poland's historic legacy were defeated once and for all. There was no other way.

My own encounters with this kind of upper-class anti-Semitism were rare. The bigotry common in Otwock was almost entirely of the coarse, lowbrow variety. But during my occasional visits to Warsaw I discovered that expressions of hostility toward Jews were not confined to illiterate peasants who had drunk too much vodka. They could also be found among educated Poles who would never dream of using the vulgar curses common among the rural masses, preferring to express their prejudices in elegant, upper-class locutions. The discovery that bigotry was not incompatible with learning and breeding, that status and education affected not the substance but merely the form of discrimination, came to me as something of a surprise. It seemed to challenge my youthful assumption that knowledge was bound to have a salutary effect on character and conduct.

On one of those visits, while I was walking with my aunt Hala near my grandfather's house, a Polish lady, elegantly dressed and haughtily aloof, passed us, making loud disparaging remarks to her companion about the Jewish riffraff she saw around her. What had aroused her scorn or anger was not clear. Perhaps someone had jostled her or said something she did not like or tried to cheat her. Nor do I recall precisely what the anti-Semitic sentiments were which she was expressing with such obvious disdain. But Hala heard them, and they drove her into a rage. Though usually so kind and jovial, she now suddenly seemed beside herself. She began to follow the snobbish interloper, loudly scolding her for her arrogant behavior. Who did she think she was? What was she doing anyway in the Jewish quarter, which she considered so far beneath her? Why didn't she go back to her Polish neighborhood, where her bigotry would no doubt find a sympathetic hearing? Didn't the Jews have enough trouble without visits from haughty, self-important bigots like her? All of Hala's pent-up resentment against pervasive anti-Semitic prejudice came pouring out in a long, bitter tirade.

The Polish lady, realizing now that she had provoked greater hostility than had been intended, walked on, looking straight ahead, tight-lipped and grim-faced, with Hala in close pursuit, hurling one imprecation after another. The encounter came to an end when we finally arrived at an intersection with another street which led away from the Jewish quarter. Here the discomfited intruder turned in relief toward the more congenial Polish neighborhood where she lived, eager no doubt to tell commiserating friends what had happened to her among those coarse, awful people on the other side of the city. Hala, nearly exhausted, returned home as well, describing to her parents and siblings the confrontation with that insufferable Polish anti-Semite. As for me, I found the incident not only puzzling but disturbing. How did it start? What did it mean? How could two intelligent, educated people have been drawn into such a bitter dispute? Their confrontation provided me with my first real insight into the tragic nature of Polish-Jewish relations.

I saw an even more graphic display of ethnic animosity about a year later, again in Warsaw. This time I was walking with another one of my aunts, Jadzia, I think, when we saw a large crowd gathered in a circle at the street corner ahead, excitedly watching some sort of disturbance or commotion. As we approached, we suddenly saw a scene which would have warmed the heart of any ardent, red-blooded anti-Semite. A fight was going on between a Pole and some Jews. It was easy to guess which was which, because the appearance of the combatants was stereotypical. In the center stood the Pole, tall, muscular, blue-eyed, and blond-haired, neatly dressed, a university student perhaps or a bank teller or maybe a junior clerk in some business establishment. He had removed his belt and was flailing away with it at his assailants. Surrounding him were three young Jews, short and thin, dark-haired and dark-complexioned, trying to get in close enough to land a few hard blows. There was no telling what had started the fight, but it was clear that the Pole was holding his own. He was striking out with his belt now at one of his attackers, now at another, now at the third, managing to keep them all at bay. Some of the Poles in the crowd may have even been reminded of their courageous ancestors resisting the superior forces of other swarthy, alien invaders from the East.

Who would emerge victorious in this battle never became known, because suddenly a Polish policeman in the familiar dark-blue uniform appeared. In an imperious tone he ordered the onlookers to disperse. Reluctantly and grumblingly, they obeyed. Then he turned to the combatants themselves to determine responsibility for the disturbance of the peace. As each of them told his side of the story, the policeman wrote copiously in his notebook. And then, after issuing a few summonses to appear in court, he turned and walked away, while the adversaries, sullen and disgruntled, slowly went their separate ways. The incident was over. I never found out what the final outcome was. Who was eventually charged with starting the fight? Who was found guilty of assault and battery? Who had to pay a hefty fine or perhaps even spend a few days in jail? Though I never found out, I think I can make a pretty good guess.

Most of what I learned about the effects of ethnic bigotry, however, came not from what I saw but what I heard. The conversations of members and friends of our family would often mention, almost casually or matter-of-factly, instances of anti-Semitic prejudice. So-and-so had been denied admission to the university, despite his strong academic record, allegedly because of some scholarly deficiency, but actually because of his ethnic background. Someone else had been turned down for a job, in the theater or with an orchestra or in publishing or at a school, because he was Jewish. And then there would be the case of someone who did manage to find employment with a Polish cultural institution or business firm, but who was then denied advancement, while others with a less solid record but more acceptable background moved ahead. Some of those stories were undoubtedly exaggerated. The claim of ethnic victimization can be used to disguise personal shortcomings and inadequacies. And yet incidents of unmistakable bigotry were so frequent that the Jewish community, struggling in an alien, hostile environment, began seeing enemies on all sides, some imaginary, some magnified, but some only too real.

My awareness of ethnic prejudice derived from still another source. I found it repeatedly in the books I used to read, books borrowed from the library of Jewish Mr. Slawin. Especially those dealing with the heroic deeds of Polish warriors and patriots would often contain a disparaging portrayal of Jews which contrasted sharply with the valiant character of the Poles. While the latter were invariably chivalrous, generous, selfless, and courageous, the former were often cringing, fawning, calculating, and grasping. I remember in particular stories about idealistic Polish rebels who, after the partition of their country in the eighteenth century, would meet secretly to plan an uprising against czarist tyranny. At the end they would all be arrested by the Russian secret police and sent to Siberia for life. And who would betray them to the cruel oppressor? Almost always some Moishek or Itzik or Yankel or Leibl. Reading those books was nearly enough to turn even me into a little anti-Semite.

Yet there was also another aspect to this tragic story of bigotry, an aspect which cannot and should not be ignored. Hostility bred hostility; prejudice on one side fostered prejudice on the other. Many Jews regarded the Poles with the same resentment which many Poles displayed toward the Jews. This resentment was partly rooted in religious exclusiveness or intolerance. Pious believers in each community regarded members of the other as infidels, as enemies of the true faith who deserved scorn and reprobation. The refusal of those stubborn unbelievers to recognize divine truth had led to their spiritual decline and moral corruption. Devout Poles often regarded the Jews as devious, cunning, and unprincipled, while devout Jews reciprocated by characterizing the Poles as ignorant, coarse, and dissolute. Hateful stereotypes on each side poisoned relations between them. Forced to live side by side, often dependent on each other economically, they managed as a rule to maintain at least minimal civility in dealing with one another. But inwardly they often shared a profound mutual hostility.

Their antagonism was reflected in language even more clearly than in behavior. The Polish word "zyd," meaning a Jew, did not simply define a religious identity or affiliation. It also carried connotations of cringing sycophancy and sly dishonesty. Ethnic prejudice could be found just as easily in Yiddish, the everyday language of the Jewish masses. The word "goy," for example, meant more than a gentile. It carried overtones of ignorance, vulgarity, dissipation, and mindless pugnacity. To describe a Pole who did not conform to this stereotype, some modifying adjective would generally be added. That is, so-and-so was a "decent goy" or an "educated goy" or a "tolerant goy" or sometimes simply a "Christian," a term which had no serious pejorative overtones.

Similarly, "shikse" had implications extending beyond its literal meaning of a young woman who was not Jewish. It carried a suggestion of immodesty or coarseness, even promiscuity. Thus the term was often applied to Jewish girls who failed to display sufficient diffidence or reserve, who seemed too bold or assertive or mischievous. By the same token, "shegetz" meant more than simply a boy who happened to be gentile. It also had connotations of rudeness, belligerence, and dissipation, so that a young Jew who was insufficiently pious or modest could be described as a "shegetz" as well. Polish-Jewish hostility was thus as common in daily speech as in daily conduct.

It could even be found in popular humor, in the jokes and stories which circulated among the Jewish as well as the Polish masses. Those directed against the Jews generally made fun of their greed, servility, and cunning. Those making fun of the Poles focused on their obtuseness or dissoluteness or combativeness. Sometimes the humor was relatively harmless, but more often it revealed a deep underlying antipathy. I remember some of the pupils in my school singing a bitter parody of the opening lines of the Polish national anthem: instead of "Poland is not yet lost,/As long as we live," a derisive "Poland is not yet lost,/But it soon will be." This too was in a way a protest against the cruelty of ethnic bigotry.

What could the Jewish community do to oppose the forces of anti-Semitism? To the pious believers the answer seemed obvious. The hardships they had to endure were providentially ordained, decreed by the divine will. Only God could end them. The Jews would have to accept their fate until the Messiah came to lead them back to the promised land. In the meantime, they must find strength in prayer and in their sense of solidarity. And besides, isolation and ghettoization were more than symptoms of oppression; they were also a source of faith, a reinforcement of religious identity. Jews and Poles were so different, so far apart, that the only contacts between them should remain impersonal, confined to economic transactions and governmental affairs. Segregation was not only unavoidable but desirable.

This was the view of only a minority, however, a large and influential minority, but a minority nevertheless. Most Jews in Poland, and throughout Eastern Europe for that matter, were not willing to wait for the Messiah to free them from bigotry. Increasingly secular in outlook, they hoped to achieve the liberation of their community by means which were this-worldly. They differed, sometimes sharply, regarding the means to be used in gaining social and political equality. But they were at least in agreement that faith in divine providence was not enough.

Of the various secular movements seeking to achieve Jewish emancipation, the one which resembled the orthodox position most closely was Zionism. At first glance that may seem paradoxical. The Zionist ideology was after all nonreligious in its origin; it was based on the doctrines of modern nationalism, not the teaching of the Old Testament. Nor did its followers assign special importance to traditional Judaism in the state which they hoped to establish in Palestine. And yet they resembled the devout believers in their conviction that Poles and Jews would never be able to coexist in a relationship of equality. Separation was the only solution. The major difference was that the orthodox favored internal separation within the boundaries of the existing state, while the Zionists insisted that separation must be external, achieved by mass emigration from Europe to the Middle East.

Curiously, this latter view was also shared by anti-Semitic Poles, who rejected as illusory all proposals for Jewish integration. The signs which they carried in their parades and demonstrations proclaimed defiantly, in large letters, that "the Jews must go to Palestine." All three movements, the orthodox, the Zionist, and the anti-Semitic, were thus in agreement on at least one point: the essential irreconcilability of the differences between the Polish and the Jewish community. They had to remain segregated. There was simply no other way.

Yet for most secular Jews ghettoization in whatever form was not the answer. They continued to believe that sometime, somehow, they would gain acceptance under a more tolerant government in a more compassionate society. Admittedly, that would not be easy. It would demand firm resolve and tireless effort. It would require a determination by the liberal and humane forces in both communities to work together for the creation of a system of authority under which peoples of diverse origins and cultures could live in harmony. The task would undoubtedly prove arduous, but the goal was worth the effort.

The small assimilationist movement was the one most firmly committed to the integration of Poles and Jews. It maintained, without saying it in so many words, that the "Jewish question" would disappear once Jews ceased to be Jews. That meant that the Jews should learn to speak, look, think, and behave like the Poles. Indistinguishability was the key to acceptability. The Jews might still retain their traditional faith, if they were so inclined. But in every other regard they should become completely Polonized. The assimilationists accepted at face value the anti-Semitic contention that what made Jewry so objectionable was its clannishness, its stubborn attachment to an alien tradition and a separate culture. The implication was that once the Jews abandoned their special identity, once they became indistinguishable from the Poles except for religious belief, they would find acceptance and equality.

Yet overcoming anti-Semitism was more complicated than that. Those Jews who tried assimilation, most of them from a small, affluent, and acculturated minority, soon discovered that becoming Polish was by no means as easy as they had been led to believe. Talking, dressing, and behaving like Poles was not enough. There was always something about them which was not quite authentic, something which was alien or spurious or suspicious. Some of them did manage to win positions of prominence in Polish society and culture. But even they were always aware of whispered and sometimes loud complaints about their foreignness or pushiness or shiftiness. As it turned out, ceasing to be a Jew was almost as difficult as being one.

Most secularized members of the Jewish community preferred therefore to avoid the extremes of either Zionism or assimilation. They sought rather to achieve emancipation by an alliance with those political movements in Poland which advocated a system of government under which the national minorities could enjoy civic equality while retaining their distinctive culture. That meant that most Jews supported parties which were left of center: the democrats, the socialists, and the communists.

Yet this resolve to change the established system of authority left the Jewish community open to charges of disloyalty and subversion. In addition to the old, familiar accusations of greed, cunning, and untrustworthiness, the Jews were now also portrayed as trying to undermine the devotion of Polish society to state, religion, and tradition. By exacerbating economic resentments and class antagonisms, they were hoping to achieve dominance over the Poles. The disproportionate number of Jews in the Communist Party aroused special fear and anger among the anti-Semites. In their eyes, communism and capitalism were both simply weapons by which the Jewish community was seeking to gain power. The seeming contradiction between the two ideologies was only a clever deception designed to disguise their common goal. Each was a different aspect of the same conspiracy. Their common purpose was the subjection of simple, trusting, good-natured, and unsuspecting Poles to Jewish rule.

It did little good to point out the illogical nature of this argument, since it was based not on logic but psychological need. It was useless to talk about the weakness of the Communist Party, whose membership never rose above 20,000 and whose share of the popular vote in parliamentary elections, gained mostly through various front organizations, remained below 7 percent. The anti-Semites continued to insist that the Jewish community was a Trojan horse serving the designs of the Russians, the traditional enemies of Poland. The danger confronting the nation, they maintained, had only increased since the Bolshevik overthrow of czarism, because now the Poles faced a double threat. They had to be prepared to fight aggression from abroad and at the same time fight subversion from within. Their success in defending their independence would depend on a recognition of who the internal as well as the external enemy was.

The anti-Semitic prejudices of the Poles reinforced the radical sympathies of the Jews, while the radicalization of the Jewish political outlook increased the intensity of Polish anti-Semitism. One fed the other. Yet both performed essentially the same psychological function. At a time of growing class tensions, in a nation torn between the prescriptions of social tradition and the demands of economic progress, radicalism as well as nativism seemed to offer uncomplicated answers to complicated questions. They identified the problem, they described its cause, they defined its remedy, and they predicted its outcome. They presented a way out of the complexities of political reconstruction and industrial modernization. Each was a cry of anguish expressing a yearning for simplicity.

I have only a few personal recollections of the "communist menace" in Poland for which the Jewish community paid such a heavy price. I can remember seeing every week or so a little red flag, attached by a string to a pebble or a metal weight, hanging down from the telegraph wires overhead. Sometimes the flag would display a barely legible slogan exhorting resistance against capitalistic tyranny. This was the way the Communist Party, which had been outlawed and forced to go underground, would make its existence known. Its demonstration of defiance seemed to produce little effect, however. A few passersby would glance up briefly and try to decipher the message on the flag. Most would simply walk on without so much as a look. After about an hour a policeman would come carrying a ladder, he would climb up to remove the dangerous incitement to revolution, and then he would walk away with the heavy ladder and the little flag, all the time muttering to himself. A few days later the scene would be repeated: another red flag hanging down from the telegraph wires, another display of public indifference, another disgruntled policeman cursing under his breath, and another victory for law and order over the forces of subversion.

It all seemed senseless to me. What is the fuss all about? I used to wonder. Why the secretive rebelliousness on one side and the grim repression on the other? Why could not the two simply ignore each other, tacitly agreeing to live and let live? Would that not be better for all concerned? To find an answer to those perplexing questions, I once asked my grandfather during an afternoon stroll to explain to me what communism was. I had heard the word used from time to time, but I had no idea of what it meant. I remember that he stopped, looked around cautiously to make sure no one could hear him, and then half whispered in fluent, faultless Polish that communism advocated the public ownership of the means of production and transportation. I was greatly impressed. Not that I understood a word of what he had said, but I sensed intellectual profundity and stylistic elegance in the way he had said it. The elderly man walking beside me, dressed in the traditional garb of orthodoxy, with his long beard and black coat, apparently knew a great deal not only about personal salvation in the next world but about social conflict in this one. I began to regard him with new respect.

Still, the most tragic consequences of the bigotry which the Jewish community in Poland had to endure were not the obstacles to political, social, economic, or cultural equality. They were rather the serious psychological wounds and disabilities inflicted on its victims: the lack of self-esteem, the feeling of inadequacy, and the secret sense of inferiority. Like many scorned minorities, the Jews often felt that the criticisms directed against them were not entirely without foundation. They would never admit that publicly, to be sure, because to do so would mean capitulation to the enemy. But privately, in moments of solitary soul-searching or confidential conversation, they would sometimes concede that the common charges raised against the Jews were at least partly justified. The Jews were in fact not as bold or self-confident as the Poles; they were more humble and servile. Not only that, they could sometimes be greedy or shifty or devious. And as for the complaint that they were crude and uncultured or even dirty and smelly, anyone who had ever visited a small-town ghetto could attest that the allegation had some basis in fact. The most destructive result of anti-Semitism was that so many of its victims, while vehemently disagreeing with their victimizers in public, agreed or half agreed with them in private.

This psychological surrender to a powerful adversary was not restricted to qualities of character or behavior. It also extended to physical appearance. Not only did there seem to be a clear difference between Jewish and Polish features, but many Jews would concede in confidence that the latter were indeed more attractive and desirable than the former. Blue eyes were better than brown eyes, blond hair was more attractive than black hair, and there could be no doubt that a fair complexion was superior to a dark one. It was important to "look good"—a common euphemism among secularized Jews for not looking Jewish—partly because "looking good" was socially advantageous, but partly also because it was aesthetically more pleasing than "looking bad."

Such self-disparagement helps explain the strenuous efforts of many Jews to appear and behave like Poles. I remember once hearing my aunt Felka declare during a heated family discussion of the ethnic problem that if only there were fewer Jewish hooknoses and protruding ears, there would be less discrimination against Jews. It was an example of a phenomenon common among all oppressed minorities. The victims of prejudice, isolated and insecure, come to feel that they themselves are at least partly responsible for the injustices they have to endure. If only they were better, handsomer, braver, more polite, or more sophisticated, they would be treated with greater respect. They half convince themselves that they actually help bring on the misfortunes of which they complain so bitterly.

The propensity to self-deprecation in the Jewish community of Eastern Europe, sometimes bordering on self-condemnation or self-resentment, could even be found in popular speech and popular humor. The same ethnic slurs which the Jews indignantly condemned when expressed by Poles were sometimes heard when they themselves felt outraged by something a fellow Jew had said or done. Then they too might mutter about "Jewish" greed or "Jewish" cunning or "Jewish" aggressiveness. They themselves would often tell "Jewish" jokes, not very different from those heard in anti-Semitic Polish circles, about the crudeness, shrewdness, or unscrupulousness of the Jews. The most tragic consequence of the ethnic prejudices so deep-rooted in Eastern Europe was that the victims often saw themselves in the same light as the victimizers. They tacitly accepted many of the accusations directed against them. They frequently succumbed to feelings of inferiority and guilt. Even while opposing the forces of anti-Semitism, they too would sometimes become anti-Semites.

Was there then no answer to the "Jewish question" in Poland? The Jews tried tirelessly and desperately to find one, but without much success. The orthodox among them acknowledged the hopelessness of the situation by proclaiming that only the coming of the Messiah could bring about their emancipation. Thereby they conceded that a solution to the problems their community faced was beyond human intelligence. Only God could solve them. The Zionists had greater faith in organized political activity, but the program they embraced did not seem much more practical. After all, the Arabs were uncompromisingly hostile to Jewish migration to the Middle East, the British were strongly opposed as well, and the Jews themselves were generally reluctant to leave the lands where they and their ancestors had lived for centuries in order to start a new life in some distant, alien region.

The opposite contention that assimilation was the only way to end anti-Semitism seemed equally unpersuasive. Most members of the Jewish community were unwilling to renounce their distinctive customs, beliefs, and traditions. Those who were willing often lacked the social pliability or educational background essential for successful adaptation. And as for the Poles themselves, though they often criticized Jewish "clannishness," most did not really favor the mass Polonization of those they regarded as intrinsically and incorrigibly foreign. To many secularized Jews, therefore, the best strategy seemed to be an alliance with the forces in Polish political life which favored self-determination for the minority nationalities. But were those forces—weak, divided, and isolated—ever likely to come to power? Not really. There simply seemed to be no way out.

Yet in fact there was a solution to the "Jewish question," a clear, simple, and final solution, too clear, in fact, too simple and final, to be advanced openly. But though unspeakable, it was not unthinkable. Indeed, it could be heard occasionally in muttered curses and whispered threats. It lurked behind tall fences and locked gates. It was concealed by curtained windows and closed doors. It lay hidden in back rooms and neighborhood taverns, under card tables and inside vodka bottles. But it was there all the time, waiting quietly and patiently, preparing with an inexorable logic for the right moment.

A photograph of of me and my aunt Rivke taken in 1924 while we were living in Kückelheim, Germany.

A photograph of me taken in Otwock around 1925.

A photograph of me and our dog Lulu in Otwock taken around 1926.

Photograph, around 1926, taken in Otwock, with my aunt Rivke
on the right and my aunt Nacia on the left.

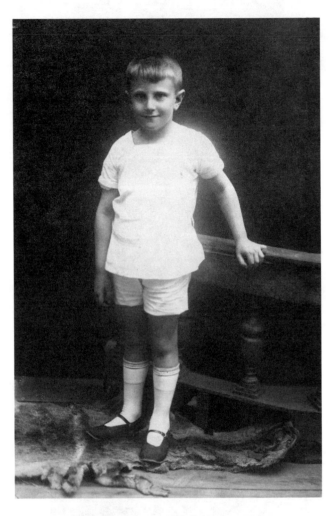

A photograph of me taken in Otwock around 1927.

Photograph around 1928 in Otwock, with my grandmother in the center,
my aunt Nacia on the left, and my aunt Rivke on the right.

A photograph of me taken in 1928 in Otwock, Poland.

Photograph taken in 1928 at the entrance of one of the hotels in Otwock. My grandmother is the elderly woman sitting in the center, my aunt Rivke is the second from the right in the front row, and I am at the far right in the front row.

A photograph taken in the summer of 1930 in Paris, while we were on our way to New York. I am on the left, while my cousin Thomas, the son of Esther, is on the right. I don't know who the boy in the center is.

My maternal grandfather, Getzl Rubinlicht, in Warsaw in the late 1930s, at the age of about eighty.

Photograph taken in 1944, near Otwock, my uncle Leon on the left in the Polish military uniform, a member of the Polish army which was part of the Soviet armed forces, and on the right my uncle Henick, who survived by living on the "Aryan" side.

Chapter 6

A Reunion at Arm's Length

My growing awareness of the prevalence of ethnic prejudice in Polish society did not cause me any serious concern about my own future. I felt confident that I would always be protected against the discriminations and injustices which were such a frequent topic of discussion in our family. There was nothing for me to worry about. First of all, there were those monthly remittances which kept coming from the New World, large enough to provide me with a very comfortable standard of living. They had a highly soothing effect on my perception of the future. But even more important was the knowledge that my life in Poland would soon come to an end, that I would exchange the placid, pleasantly dull existence of Otwock for interesting, exciting, and challenging experiences on the other side of the ocean. I would become Douglas Fairbanks or Tom Mix or maybe even Old Shatterhand. Why then should I be concerned about the bigotries of the Old World? Before long I would be enjoying all the advantages of the New. That was what mattered.

My realization of the vast difference between what awaited me and what awaited my relatives and friends helped shape my attitude toward them. I was still fond of them; I still had a genuine interest in their welfare. And yet in the back of my mind there was always the thought that soon our paths would diverge. I even knew almost exactly when that would happen. As soon as my parents became American citizens, they would return to Poland and everything would change. There would then be another crossing of the Atlantic, this time westward. And then another home, another school, another language, another way of life. Old acquaintances in Otwock would be replaced by new acquaintances in New York. Familiar ways of doing things would give way to unfamiliar ways. Before me rose the challenge of a complete transformation, a drastic change in habits, customs, attitudes, and expectations. I was both excited and uneasy. How could I, how could anyone have remained indifferent?

Actually, my customary existence began to change even before my parents' return as the result of developments which were unforeseen, unforeseeable, and disastrous. Their immediate consequence was that the members of my family ceased to be proud landed proprietors and homeowners, becoming instead mere tenants and renters. And all that was ultimately the fault of my grandmother's gallstones. Those gallstones had been making the poor woman's life progressively more miserable until someone, a relative or an acquaintance, suggested that she might find relief in a health resort, unpronounceable in English, called Ciechocinek. Its mineral waters were supposed to have remarkable curative properties, especially for gallstones. The spa was only about a hundred miles northwest of Warsaw, and the clientele was largely Jewish. Thus traveling there would not prove too strenuous for my grandmother, while the milieu would be both familiar and congenial. After some hesitation, she decided to take a chance and spend a few weeks in Ciechocinek. I in the meantime was to remain in Otwock under the vigilant care of Rivke and Katia.

That first experience my grandmother had of life in a popular health resort turned out to be an unqualified success. To begin with, her gallstones became much less troublesome. They did not disappear altogether, as became only too apparent a few months later, but they retreated, waiting insidiously for an opportune moment to reappear. She was delighted. More than that, my grandmother found the social ambiance of Ciechocinek quite pleasant. She got to know several people of roughly the same age, the same background, the same faith, and the same general outlook on life. Though usually shy and reserved, she learned to enjoy her daily meetings with fellow sufferers from gallstones and other ailments, the opportunity to chat, gossip, commiserate, and philosophize. It was a welcome change from the lonely existence she led in Otwock. And when she returned home after about a month, she found me just as healthy, placid, and seemingly contented as before. There had really been no reason for her to feel uneasy about taking a short vacation from her household duties and responsibilities.

She therefore decided that the following year she would return to Ciechocinek, especially since her gallstones soon began reemerging from their hiding place. But this time she would take me and Rivke with her. Why should we be denied a chance to enjoy the salubrious mineral water and stimulating social milieu of a nice, pleasant spa? It would be good for all of us to spend a vacation together. Our ties to one another would be strengthened; we would become closer and fonder, more understanding, more affectionate. And so in the summer of 1928 the three of us set out from Otwock to spend a few relaxing and healthful weeks in Ciechocinek.

But it did not turn out that way. Not at all. What had been intended to be a restful vacation became a disaster. There were warnings and portents almost from the outset. The three of us having to share a single room proved to be an inconvenience, at times in fact an annoyance and nuisance. Then there was the problem with Rivke, whose morose disposition seemed to grow even gloomier away from her friends and from the high life of Otwock. She found the company of elderly sufferers from gallstones unexciting. She yearned to be with young people who shared her tastes, interests, and pastimes. And I myself only added to the mounting disgruntlement. The mineral waters of Ciechocinek, which had such a beneficial effect on my grandmother's gallbladder, produced a catastrophic upheaval in my digestive system. It is best not to dwell on the details of my condition. Suffice it to say that it was a source of profound embarrassment for me and an occasion for some of the more disagreeable chores of child rearing for my grandmother and my aunt. Why elaborate?

Yet all those annoyances and disappointments came to seem insignificant by comparison with the terrible calamity which occurred two or three weeks after our arrival. We were having lunch on the veranda of the hotel where we were staying, when a guest at one of the neighboring tables who was reading a newspaper turned to us and asked casually whether we were from Otwock. He thought he had heard that we were. We answered that yes, we did come from Otwock. He then told us, still quite matter-of-factly, that there was a story in his paper about a fire which had just occurred there, seriously damaging or even destroying an entire building. We asked, now with growing interest, what the address was. After checking the story, he reported that the fire had taken place at 4 Jagiellonska Street. A moment of stunned silence followed, and then gasps, cries, sobs, and lamentations. That was our address.

My recollections of what happened next are confused. I do remember, however, that there was a feverish packing of personal belongings, a hurried settling of hotel accounts, and a long, miserable train ride back to Otwock. There it turned out that the newspaper story which our lunch neighbor in Ciechocinek had reported was only too true. There had indeed been a terrible, devastating fire which destroyed our home completely. Nothing was left. As for the cause, that emerged only gradually, in little bits and pieces. It had to do with my grandmother's decision a few months earlier to install electric lighting in the part of the building in which we lived. We had until then relied exclusively on candles and oil lamps. But the back of the house, the part where the summer renters lived, continued to be illuminated in the old way. My grandmother felt that she could not afford to pay for the electrification of the entire building, at least not all at once. This commendable caution of hers proved to be the indirect cause of the catastrophe which followed.

It seems that one of the renters in the rear of the house, incensed at a decision which he considered blatantly unfair, decided to do something about it. Why should the wealthy landlady enjoy the benefits of electricity, while he, the poor, hard-working tenant, had to strain his eyesight by relying on candlelight or lamplight? Our vacation in Ciechocinek seemed to offer the perfect opportunity for rectifying a glaring social injustice. The rebellious renter decided to install electricity in his room on his own. It seemed simple enough. Just extend an ordinary wire from the electric line running outside the building to a bulb hanging from the ceiling of the room. Unfortunately, his plan miscarried, with tragic results. At some point in the delicate operation something went wrong. Sparks began to fly, then a small fire started, then the flames spread, and soon the entire room was ablaze. Now the rebellious tenant lost his nerve. Grabbing his belongings, he rushed to the railroad station and took the next train back to Warsaw. As for the house, within a few minutes it became the scene of a vast conflagration.

Since we were away in Ciechocinek, it took a long time for the fire brigade to be summoned. But even if we had been there, even if we had called for help immediately, the outcome would not have been much different. The firemen of Otwock had never been noted for their skill or efficiency, the wooden building was bone-dry in the middle of summer, and the water for fighting the flames had to be hand-carried from wells and pumps. There were no outdoor hydrants. Not only the house but most of our belongings were completely destroyed. And the few which were rescued quickly disappeared. The conflagration had attracted a large crowd of curious peasants, some of them simply onlookers, others amateur fire fighters, and quite a few eager scavengers. The sight of household furnishings, kitchen utensils, articles of clothing, and wall ornaments and decorations lying about on the ground unattended was too much of a temptation. Hungry and impoverished, they began to grab whatever they could. And who can blame them? To them the fire was a stroke of good luck, almost a godsend. But to us it meant the end of our social eminence as proud landed proprietors.

The aftermath of that terrible summer day dragged on for almost twenty years. There was first of all the task of selling the property on which the house had stood and paying off the mortgage with which it had been burdened. Then there were problems with the insurance policy which was supposed to cover at least part of the loss, problems much too complicated for my innocent childish understanding. The greatest source of difficulty, however, was that invisible but omnipresent Mr. Gelbfisz, whose earlier differences with my family were only aggravated by the disaster we had both suffered. First my grandmother attempted, timidly and ineffectually, to deal with the financial complexities arising out of the fire. Then a year later, after my parents arrived from the United States, my father tried his hand at it, but without much greater success. His talent as a businessman proved almost as feeble as my grandmother's. And so a year after that, when my parents sailed back to America, my grandfather was entrusted with the task of carrying on the fight. He, the experienced real-estate broker, the time-tested litigant, seemed ideally suited to the task of standing up to the formidable Mr. Gelbfisz.

The struggle of those two wily antagonists continued for almost a decade, from 1930 to 1939, with neither one able to prevail against the other. I am not sure whether they were so evenly matched or whether the legal issues were so complicated or whether the judicial system of Poland was so intricate and convoluted. What is clear is that the victories of the German army in the first few weeks of the Second World War quickly settled the controversy which had been dragging on endlessly through the Polish courts. Not only were the property rights of Jewish litigants peremptorily abrogated, but the litigants themselves were gotten rid of as well, once and for all. Although the defeat of the Third Reich six years later led to a reopening of the case, by then it had almost ceased to matter. The new Polish government, hoping to gain the good will of the United States, agreed to offer compensation to

American citizens who had a legitimate claim to property in Poland. And so, some two decades after that catastrophic fire, a modest check made out to my father arrived in New York from the authorities in Warsaw. That seemed to put an end at last to the long, sad story.

But not quite. There was to be yet another epilogue, equally anticlimactic. In 1986, more than half a century after our family left Poland, I returned for about two weeks as a tourist. I spent part of the time in Warsaw, but then traveled on to Cracow and then to Gdansk and then back to Warsaw, still unable to decide whether to visit Otwock. On the one hand, I was curious to see once again the scene of my pleasant, placid childhood. But on the other, I felt a vague uneasiness about arousing perhaps painful memories or bitter reflections on the tragic events of long ago. In the end I resolved to take a chance. I bought a round-trip ticket at the Warsaw railroad station and left on the next train to Otwock.

The trip was quite short, even shorter than I had remembered, only half an hour or so. Almost everything else, however, had become completely altered with the passage of time. The passengers were no longer chiefly businessmen and professionals, most of them Jewish, leaving the big city to join their families vacationing in a suburban summer resort. Now they were almost all workers returning home from a hard day in the factory or mill, hungry and tired. Some of them stared vacantly into space, others nodded or dozed, and a few were obviously drunk. The station in Otwock, which once seemed to soar majestically into space in architectural splendor, now looked small, drab, grimy, and badly in need of paint. As for the main street not far from the railroad tracks, which had once been filled with restaurants, stores, shops, and the movie house where I used to watch in wide-eyed fascination Douglas Fairbanks playing Robin Hood, now it was rutted and dirty, its gloominess only intensified by a few dreary, run-down taverns.

Deciding that it would be best to go on as quickly as possible to where we had once lived, I entered one of those taverns to ask in my rusty Polish how to get to Jagiellonska Street. The middle-aged woman behind the bar looked me over carefully, even distrustfully, I thought, before replying that she was not sure where it was. Could she have decided that it would be best not to say anything to a stranger from abroad? Could she have suspected that I was one of "those people" who had been "deported" during the war, coming back now to file a claim or make some bitter accusation? Could she have concluded that non-involvement was probably the best policy? Or did she really not know where Jagiellonska Street was? I can only speculate.

It might have been better in fact if I had decided at that moment
to turn around, walk back to the station, and take the first train to
Warsaw. It would have saved me considerable disappointment. But I
resolved instead to continue in the direction where I thought our
house had once stood. Not long after leaving the tavern, I came across
a friendly young man repairing a bicycle in his front yard who, in
reply to my inquiry, informed me reassuringly that Jagiellonska Street
was only a few blocks away. All I had to do was keep going straight
ahead; I could not miss it. He was right. About a quarter of an hour
later I arrived at a corner which a sign proclaimed to be the start of
Jagiellonska Street, and there, a few buildings from the corner, stood
number 4. I had at last arrived at my destination.

But actually I never got there. What I saw was so very strange, so
completely different from what I remembered. Even the street, though
still as dusty and unpaved as in the old days, seemed to run north to
south rather than east to west. And what had happened to the property
on which our home had stood? Where were the trees and bushes in
front of the building, the green meadow, and the stretch of white sand
which had once been my playground? Now there was nothing but a
thin cover of sickly, pale-green grass. And as for the new house in the
center of the lot, it was a squat, wooden, two-story structure divided
into small, cheerless apartments. Some of the residents, seeing an
unusual visitor staring at their dwelling place, engaged me in casual
conversation. They were quite cordial, especially after learning that
sixty years earlier I had lived at the same address. One of them, an elderly widow, even invited me to see her apartment, which consisted of a
small, sparsely furnished living room, a familiar crucifix hanging from
its wall, and an even smaller adjoining kitchen. I found it all so depressing that I left as soon as I could without offending my genial hosts.

Yet even that was not the end of it. As if to intensify my feeling of
strangeness, of permanent and irreparable loss, a woman began to follow me, a gypsy, I think, judging by how she was dressed. Recognizing
that I was a foreigner, probably an American, she persisted in pleading
with me in a piteous voice to give her a dollar or perhaps two, if at all
possible. I would be richly rewarded for my generosity, I would be
blessed, I would find happiness in the hereafter, and I would father
many, many children. But I remained unmoved. I marched on as fast
as I could, silently and grimly, in the direction of the railroad station.
The poor supplicant, realizing finally that her appeals would prove
unavailing, resumed walking to wherever she had originally intended to

go, while I caught the next train to Warsaw. That brief visit to Otwock forced me to recognize at last the futility of trying to recapture what had once been. The past was dead, dead beyond recall.

Half a century earlier, however, when the past was still the present, I found the changes in my life caused by that calamitous fire on Jagiellonska Street not unwelcome. It gave me my first taste of the normal experiences of growing up. It put an end, at least partly, to the solitary, placid, overprotected, and oversupervised existence I had been leading. I now had an opportunity to meet with other children day after day, to play with them, have fun with them, exchange confidences with them, quarrel with them, even fight with them occasionally, and then make up again as if nothing had happened. I never became outgoing and uninhibited; I always remained a little shy and ill at ease. Yet those last years in Poland were as close as I ever came to an ordinary, playful, lighthearted, mischievous childhood.

For the adult members of my family, however, what happened that terrible summer was an unmitigated disaster. My grandmother in particular never got over the feeling that she had failed to meet her responsibility to those close and dear to her. She never said it in so many words, but she must have suffered terribly under a burden of guilt. Since she had been entrusted with the care of her son's property, its destruction had been her fault, at least to some extent, she kept telling herself. If only she had not gone on that ill-fated vacation in Ciechocinek, if only she had left someone reliable in charge of the house, if only she had not installed electric lighting in one part of the building, or if she had installed it in both parts, that awful tragedy would not have occurred. Those terrible ifs continued to haunt her for a long time, probably for the rest of her life.

My aunt Rivke did not suffer quite as much. Having been too young to be entrusted with the supervision of our property, she did not have to assume responsibility for its destruction. But she too had to pay a price. She could no longer hold those weekly meetings of her amateur theatrical group in our living room. She could no longer play the generous patroness of art and culture. Worst of all, her position in Otwock's *haut monde* declined precipitously. She was no longer a proud landed proprietor and house owner. She was now just an ordinary tenant, like almost everyone else in town. She could still attend the afternoon tea dances at her favorite café, she could still chit-chat, gossip, smile, and flirt. Yet it was no longer the same thing. That all-consuming fire meant a humiliating demotion for her in the hierarchy of local high society.

My parents, however, were the ones most painfully affected by the calamity, especially my father. There was, to begin with, the serious financial loss. I am not sure how much they had invested in the purchase of the property in Otwock, but it must have been a considerable amount. Not only that, the chances of recouping even part of the loss by selling the land and collecting the insurance were seriously jeopardized by their unending controversy with Mr. Gelbfisz. As long as the differences between them remained unresolved, there could not even be an accurate assessment of the full extent of the catastrophe. Most painful, however, were not the economic but the emotional and psychological consequences of that disaster. To my parents their house had been a visible sign of artistic success, palpable evidence that the bohemian existence they had been leading could produce just as much affluence as more respectable bourgeois pursuits. My father in particular regarded his property in Otwock as a measure of how far he had come since his impoverished childhood in Kovnata and that grim apprenticeship in Vilna. And now it was all gone, burned and destroyed. For him that was a terrible tragedy.

But for me it was a new beginning full of excitement and adventure. Not that I had been unhappy in our old home. Quite the contrary. I had felt sheltered and protected, secure, contented, and sometimes even loved. Yet I also sensed that I was different from other children, that I lacked the companionship, the playfulness, the mischievousness, and especially the freedom which they were enjoying. Now that would change. I would become like the others, running, jumping, playing, yelling, and savoring life. For that matter, I might now and then go beyond the acceptable bounds of childish sportiveness; I might occasionally be reprimanded or scolded for too much frolicking and prankishness. I might even receive on rare occasions a gentle slap on the backside for too much ebullience. But that would be a cheap price to pay for my emancipation from overregulation and oversupervision.

As it turned out, my expectations were never fully realized. Even after those terrible, liberating flames had destroyed our house, my grandmother and aunt remained vigilant and protective. Yet my life did become less isolated and reclusive, more independent, more venturesome. I began to move, hesitantly and fitfully, toward greater gregariousness. As for the material comforts to which I had become accustomed, they remained unaffected by the loss our family had suffered. Immediately afterward we moved to a small house of which we were the sole occupants, but which was surrounded at a short distance by four or five larger buildings, most of them with several apartments. The living quarters here were not quite as spacious as before, but they were more than adequate. There was even room to accommodate Katia, for whom a curtain was spread across a corner of the kitchen behind which stood her simple cot, her few belongings, and her Orthodox icon. All in all, it was not an uncomfortable arrangement. Then, about a year later, anticipating my parents' return from America, we moved again, this time to an apartment on the second floor of a large building not far from where our old home had stood. Here we remained until we left Poland in the summer of 1930.

It was during this period that I began to enjoy for the first time some of the ordinary experiences of childhood. I found a few friends, especially a Polish boy named Andrzej who lived in one of the apartment buildings nearby. He became in fact the only Polish friend I ever had during my years in Poland. I used to wonder why his parents, who were seemingly educated and well-to-do, chose to live in a Jewish section of Otwock. Very few other middle-class Poles did. Perhaps Andrzej's parents were free of the ethnic prejudices common in Polish society. Still, when he introduced me to them, I thought they were a little cool and standoffish. Maybe they were that way with most people, or maybe I just imagined that they were somewhat aloof. In any case, there could be no doubt about the genuineness of Andrzej's own friendliness and affection. He and I would meet day after day, we would tell stories and swap jokes, we would stroll or jog or sometimes run, and we would plan various pranks, tricks, adventures, and excursions. Being with Andrzej was great fun.

Occasionally we would do more than walk and talk. We would mount broomsticks, which had been borrowed from our respective kitchens and become magically transformed into fiery steeds, galloping at full speed through the neighborhood to determine which of us could complete the racecourse first. At other times the broomsticks turned into swords with which we would duel to the death, Andrzej a Polish uhlan and I a Russian Cossack, or, reversing our roles, I a Polish hussar and he a Turkish janissary.

And then there were the exciting contests to decide which one of us was the faster sprinter. I still carry a permanent reminder of those competitions. One evening, after it was quite dark, we agreed to run around the house in opposite directions to see who would return to the starting point first. We never actually found out because midway, rounding a corner, the two of us ran into each other with full force.

Andrzej staggered home with a black eye which took about a week to heal, while I, whimpering and in tears, shuffled into our house to be comforted by my grandmother and aunt. To this day I think I can feel a slight bump in my forehead reminding me of the painful outcome of my athletic rivalry with Andrzej.

After we moved the second time, I missed my old companions very much for at least a week or two, maybe even longer. But then I found new friends, just as likable, just as congenial as the old ones. Directly below us, on the ground floor of our apartment building, lived a family conforming to the usual, the traditional pattern: a father, a mother, a son roughly my age, and a daughter a few years younger. I never got to see much of the father, a shopowner or small businessman in Warsaw who seemed to be away most of the time. Perhaps he commuted by train from Otwock, leaving early each morning and returning late at night. Or perhaps he stayed in Warsaw during the week, rejoining his family only on weekends. But as for the other members of the household, I came to know them quite well. I used to visit them almost every day, observing with keen interest how the children talked to one another, how they were treated by their parents, how they were sometimes praised, sometimes scolded, now petted and then reprimanded, first supervised and later ignored, and all that in rapid succession. I would look and listen to what was going on, occasionally with a touch of envy.

Even more interesting were the times spent outdoors in the company of my young neighbor downstairs and another boy our age who lived in the same apartment building. The three of us would race, jump, push, jostle, and wrestle. That too was a new experience for me. What I remember most vividly, however, are the expeditions on which we would sometimes embark, extending as far as a mile or two, for the purpose of exploring the environs of Otwock. Often we would march eastward, toward a luxuriant pine forest reputed to provide protection against all sorts of pulmonary illnesses. At other times we would proceed to the west, to a narrow stream which, despite its strong current and cold temperature, used to attract many swimmers in the summertime. Sometimes we would decide to see how the other half lived by visiting the "bazaar" neighborhood, inspecting the marketplace, scrutinizing the shops, and sniffing at the goods and foodstuffs displayed on the pushcarts. And when we felt a little lazy, we would stay in our own part of town, comparing other streets and buildings with ours. It was all so adventurous and enjoyable.

That terrible yet serendipitous fire on Jagiellonska Street provided me not only with interesting new friends. There were also interesting new neighbors. We had previously lived among poor Polish peasants, some of them agricultural laborers, others working as gardeners and caretakers, and a few employed as servants. We had been the only well-to-do family in the neighborhood. But that changed after we were forced to move. Now we resided among people, mostly Jews, who were generally lower-middle-class: tradesmen, shopkeepers, bookkeepers, office managers, clerical workers, and salesmen. But we also had some unusual neighbors who used to gather next door to the apartment building to which we moved not long after the destruction of our old home. I could see them almost every day on the other side of a wooden rail fence, visiting a house which either belonged to or was rented by a prominent Hasidic rabbi.

That alone would have made the house something out of the ordinary in my eyes. Almost all the Jews I knew were secular in dress, locution, and belief. Even the few who were devout, my grandfather, for example, were unobtrusive, almost subdued, in their religiousness. But there was nothing restrained about the devotion displayed by the rabbi's followers, who would gather in his house every Friday evening to begin their celebration of the Sabbath. I used to watch them in fascination from one of the windows in our apartment or through a chink in the fence. They appeared to me almost as strange, almost as exotic, as the whirling dervishes of Turkey I had read about or the frenzied worshippers of Jagannath in India. I felt that an invisible but insurmountable barrier separated me from them. They and I seemed to belong to two totally different social and cultural worlds.

I cannot recall ever seeing women entering the rabbi's house. Perhaps they were admitted by a rear door and directed to some back room, where they could observe, silently and invisibly, what was going on in the main hall. But there were no such restrictions on the young sons of the Hasidim, those little boys who would gather in the front yard to chat, joke, play, and sometimes quarrel and yell at one another. They were miniature copies of their pious fathers, wearing the same black hats and long coats, the same earlocks and the same fringed half aprons. They even prayed in the same singsong intonation and with the same rocking motion. They were being brought up to be unquestionably loyal to the faith in which their ancestors had lived and for which some of them had died.

Although I would observe them with lively interest, I never made an effort to join them. I had a pretty good idea of what might happen if I

did. Those boys would immediately recognize by my clothing, my haircut, my speech, and my general bearing that I was not one of them.
Indeed, to them I would appear worse than a "shegetz." After all, a
"shegetz" could not help being a "shegetz." He had simply not been
taught the right religion; that was not really his fault. But I, I had been
born into the true faith, the faith which I had then abandoned and
betrayed. That made me worse than an infidel; it made me a renegade,
a traitor. For me and for others like me there could be no forgiveness,
no mercy, either in this world or the next. Knowing how they felt, I was
very careful to remain on my side of the fence.

Yet my caution did not diminish my curiosity. Glued to my window or peeking from behind a tree, I would observe in fascination
the extraordinary activities next door. Even more interesting than
what the little boys were doing in the front yard was what the grown
men were doing inside the house. First there would be the sound of
Friday evening prayer. Then the Hasidim would begin singing some
nigun, a wordless chant or melody expressing their rising devotional
fervor, first softly and then louder and louder. Finally, they would
form a circle, link arms, and begin to dance. I could see them going
around and around, ever more rapidly, their heads raised heaven-
ward. I could hear their feet stamping on the floor, their voices rising little by little to shouts and cries. Their religious ardor was often
reinforced by a generous consumption of alcohol. But this form of
inebriation, they would have insisted, was altogether different from
that of the Polish farm hands and day laborers. The drunkenness of
the goyim merely aroused their lasciviousness; it revealed their
coarseness and pugnacity. But the intoxication of the Hasidim produced a feeling of pious ecstasy, a sense of devoutness and spiritual-
ity, a more intense and selfless love of God. There could be no
comparison between the two.

I used to watch the proceedings next door in openmouthed astonishment. My neighbors, though living close-by, seemed to me so
strange, so alien. It would have sounded preposterous to me to suggest
that they and I were part of the same community or even that there
was some vague similarity in our views and beliefs. We existed in two
completely separate worlds. Their life was inspired by a religious passion which could verge at times on obsession or even fanaticism. My
family and I, on the other hand, moved in the society of nonreligious
Jewry, the society of fashionable cafés and tea dances, in an environment of worldly thought and culture, in a milieu of secular literature,

dramaturgy, art, and learning. The two were completely apart; they had nothing in common except an unforeseeable, imminent doom.

Those last years in Otwock taught me something else beside the pleasure of youthful comradeship and the multiformity of spiritual faith. They also revealed to me for the first time the darker side of human nature. As long as we had lived on Jagiellonska Street, I continued to assume in my sheltered innocence that most people were like my grandmother or my aunt, a little severe at times, a little stern perhaps, but basically fair and honorable. I did learn from the books I read that there were also occasional rascals and scoundrels in life, individuals without principles, without a sense of right and wrong. But they were relatively rare, and sooner or later their villainy would be discovered and punished by an implacable decree of providential justice. My experiences after the destruction of our house, however, began to shake that confidence in the essential goodness of people, whether children or adults. Indeed, by the time I left Poland, I had already embarked on the long road to a more Calvinistic view of human character and behavior.

For one thing, I discovered that not all young boys engaging in athletic competition observed the same strict rules of fair play which I had learned by reading Karl May. Perhaps they had been reading the wrong books. I learned this lesson very painfully one day when I challenged another youngster, roughly my own age and size, to a test of strength to be decided by which of us could throw the other to the ground. My intention was to follow a strategy of pushing and pulling, aided perhaps by a little deceptive though permissible tripping. My opponent, however, had a better idea of how such contests had actually been conducted in the days of the Wild West. While we were grappling, neither of us able to budge the other, he suddenly raised his knee and hit me square in the groin. I don't know where he had learned that technique. Karl May had certainly never mentioned it in any of his stories. But its effect was devastating. I felt a sudden sharp pain and fell writhing to the ground, unable even to cry out. When I had challenged my opponent to hand-to-hand combat, I never imagined it would end like this.

Even he seemed to be taken aback. He hesitated for a moment, unable to decide whether to exult in the extent of his victory or attempt to evade its likely consequence. Finally, concluding that discretion was the better part of valor, he turned tail and ran off as quickly as he could. His escape came just in the nick of time. By then I had begun to recover from my initial surprise and pain. My grandmother, hearing me moaning, groaning, and sobbing in the front yard, came rushing out of the house to see what had happened. She and my aunt carried me inside, they tried to soothe and comfort me, they applied warm compresses to the injured area, and they chided me gently for being so trustful in dealing with youthful ruffians. Within an hour or so I had achieved an almost complete recovery. Still, from that point on I was much more careful about whom I challenged to a wrestling match.

I also learned at about the same time that emotional or psychological blows could be even more painful than a knee to the groin. That lesson was impressed on me by the affair of the "Anglasy." But to understand it requires a few words of explanation. The Anglas Company was a well-known Polish manufacturer of candies and confections whose most popular product was a thin piece of chocolate, wrapped in tinfoil and a white paper casing, which children could purchase for a few small coins. Its chief appeal lay not in the quality of the chocolate, which was only mediocre, but in the small pictures, inserted between the tinfoil and the outside cover, portraying various national, ethnic, and racial types in their distinctive native dress. Most of the pictures showed ordinary, run-of-the-mill Europeans: Englishmen, Frenchmen, Germans, and Russians. But a few displayed exotic specimens from distant regions and continents: Indian tribes in North America, Mongols and Tartars in Asia, Zulus and Tuaregs in Africa, Maoris in New Zealand, and Fijis in Melanesia. These strange, outlandish figures had the greatest appeal for those of us who had become avid collectors of "Anglasy," the pictures accompanying the chocolates. And of all those avid collectors, no one was more avid than I.

I was also one of the most successful. Soon I began to look down on mere Britons in derby hats or Frenchmen in berets and kepis or even Austrians in short leather pants and feathered hats. The minimum requirement for acceptance into my collection was a fez or a turban or a burnoose. There were very few white faces among my pictures; dark skins and non-Caucasian features were the dominant characteristics. My accumulation of "Anglasy" soon became an object of admiration and jealousy among all the children in the neighborhood, puffing me up with pride at the treasures I had amassed by my tireless collector's zeal. It helped make up for my lack of athletic talent and my unimpressive performance in games and sports. Here was one field of endeavor in which I clearly excelled. It provided me with even greater satisfaction than the contents of Mr. Slawin's library.

To tell the truth, my success as a collector was not due entirely to sound judgment or aesthetic perceptiveness. It depended to a large extent on an unwritten agreement I had concluded with a shopkeeper living in our apartment building. He was an elderly Jew, quiet and retiring, who occupied two small rooms somewhere in the rear. The first room was his place of business, furnished with a few wooden shelves which were mostly bare. Here and there a modest loaf of bread could be recognized or a package of tea or a bag of sugar. But there were also always a few boxes of Anglas chocolates, which were for me the chief attractions of the place. A bell attached to the front door would ring whenever a customer entered, although I cannot remember ever seeing anyone else there while I was shopping for my "Anglasy." The owner would then come shuffling out of the rear room, which served him and his wife as a living room, dining room, bedroom, and bathroom, all in one. I would make my modest purchase, give him the few coins I had managed to save up, and leave again by the front door, while he shuffled back to his living quarters. How the poor man made a living is still a mystery to me.

After I had become a more or less regular customer of his, an idea crossed my mind. Why not make a deal with the shopkeeper, a deal which would benefit him as well as me without really hurting anyone, at least not directly? I hesitated for a while before suggesting it. I have never had much business sense; wheeling and dealing has not been one of my strong suits. But finally, summoning my courage, I outlined the plan. If he would let me examine all his Anglas chocolates before I made my purchases, specifically, if he would let me extract the pictures so that I could buy those which were interesting while carefully replacing those which were not, I would try to cajole and wheedle my grandmother into giving me a little more change, change which would then end up in the shopkeeper's till. The arrangement seemed so logical, so obviously sensible. Everyone would win, nobody would lose.

The shopkeeper agreed, and for a while we both seemed to prosper. I managed to amass the finest collection of "Anglasy" in the neighborhood, while he succeeded in avoiding or at least postponing bankruptcy, thanks in part no doubt to my patronage. But then our cozy little arrangement fell apart, with serious financial consequences for him and heartbreaking emotional pangs for me. What led to this collapse was basically my growing reputation as a successful collector. It attracted the attention of other youthful connoisseurs and devotees, who would approach me from time to time with proposals for

consultations, loans, trades, or even purchases. I would usually agree to
meet with them, flattered by their unspoken acknowledgment that here
was one area of endeavor in which I excelled. It helped make up for the
indifference I usually encountered in the more common forms of
youthful competition. It made me feel that even if I was not much of
a sprinter or soccer player, no one could beat me when it came to accu-
mulating "Anglasy."

And then tragedy struck. It appeared in the form of a boy I had never
met before who suggested a business meeting for the purpose of comparing our respective collections and perhaps doing a little bartering. I
agreed without much hesitation. After all, I had previously taken part
in a number of similar commercial negotiations, sometimes with very
satisfactory results. Why not now? Afterward it seemed to me that right
from the outset there had been something fishy about this unknown
young entrepreneur, something cunning in his look, something devious
in his manner. But perhaps I only imagined that in retrospect. At the
time I suspected nothing. Dishonesty was something I had read about
in books, but had never actually encountered in real life. And so I went
upstairs, gathered my priceless collection of "Anglasy," returned to the
front yard for the business meeting, and began showing off my accumulation of Uzbeks, Bantus, Sikhs, and Lapps.

That was when it happened. The boy I was dealing with turned out
not to be a collector at all. He was a thief. While I was proudly displaying my paper treasures, he suddenly reached out, grabbed the
"Anglasy" I was holding in my hand, quickly turned around, and in the
twinkling of an eye he was gone. I remained stunned for a moment,
unable to realize what had happened. By the time I finally began chasing the little crook, he was already rounding the corner. And when I
myself reached that corner, there was no one in sight. That was when it
really hit me. I had been deceived, cheated, robbed of my most precious
possessions by a heartless, unscrupulous villain. I let out a piercing howl
of rage and pain, and then slowly returned to our apartment, sobbing
and whimpering, utterly inconsolable. It was my first direct encounter
with the dark, sinister undercurrents of human nature. As for that juve-
nile criminal, I never saw him again. I suppose that about a decade later
he received his due punishment and probably much worse.

My recovery from the shock of this terrible incident was slow and
painful, yet it would have been even slower without the other exciting
events of that memorable summer. For that was when my parents
finally became citizens of the United States. Now they were free to

return to Poland for a reunion with their son. Moreover, after making arrangements for the support of my grandmother and my aunt, they planned to take me back with them to America. The knowledge that a new chapter in my life was about to begin, much more colorful, interesting, and challenging than the old, helped me cope with the loss of my cherished "Anglasy." As for my grandmother and aunt, I am not sure how they felt about the imminent return of my parents, but I suspect that they were more apprehensive than I. For them it would mean another migration, another beginning, another adjustment, another source of financial support, and another position on the social ladder, probably much farther down than the present one. They had good reason to feel uneasy.

For that matter, I myself had mixed feelings. On one side was the spell of the New World about which I had read so much, that half-mythical land of adventure, challenge, excitement, and boundless opportunity. What young boy would not have been exhilarated at the prospect of seeing it firsthand? But there were also nagging questions in my mind which would not go away. I had only very vague recollections of how my parents had looked and how they had behaved. Now that we were about to be reunited, I could not help wondering whether we would get along, whether I would live up to their expectations and they to mine. I had become accustomed to life with my grandmother and aunt. I had learned to read their shifting moods and tastes, their likes and dislikes, their inclinations and their aversions. I knew what to expect of them. But my parents? How would I know what they wanted me to do? How would I find out whether they were pleased with me or displeased? How would I tell whether the time was right to ask them for some favor or whether it would be better to keep quiet for the time being? Those were troubling questions.

There was one point, however, about which I had no doubt. My parents would bring me presents from the other side of the ocean, many presents, rare presents, valuable presents. They would bring me more, much more, than the sweet chocolates or tin soldiers or illustrated books I usually got on my birthday. Their gifts would exceed anything which any boy in Otwock had ever gotten, perhaps any boy in Poland. Yet what precisely those gifts would be continued to elude me for a long time, until suddenly one day I had a brainstorm, a vision. My parents would bring me a motorcycle.

I can no longer explain how I got that idea. I had never met anyone who owned a motorcycle, and I would not have known what to do if one had actually been given to me. I could barely manage to stay on top of a bicycle. But a motorcycle came to represent the sort of extraordinary gift which loving parents from America could be expected to present to their only son after a separation of so many years. I even told some of my playmates that before long I would not only have the same kind of family they had, a family with a father and a mother, but more impressive, I would have a motorcycle. They all seemed to believe me; no one voiced any doubt. Perhaps they were being polite.

About a week before the scheduled return of my parents, the three of us—my grandmother, my aunt, and I—took the train to Warsaw to wait in my grandfather's apartment on Gesia Street for the fateful day of our reunion. On the long anticipated morning more than a dozen of us, the Hamerows from Otwock and eight or nine Rubinlichts with a few of their friends, rode in a procession of taxicabs to the main railroad station. The prevailing mood was one of rising excitement. As the international express began to pull into the depot, there was a brief but intense competition to see who would be the first to recognize the returnees among the many faces leaning out of compartment windows. The winner was my grandfather. He picked out my parents from all the other passengers who were shouting, laughing, and waving handkerchiefs. As the car in which they were riding continued to move forward beyond the point where we stood, he began to run after it with unexpected agility, crying at the top of his lungs, "There they are! There they are!" It was a strange sight: an elderly Jew in a long coat and black hat rushing down the platform, his coattails flapping behind him, yelling, waving, pointing with his cane, and exhorting the rest of us to follow.

The next ten or fifteen minutes were total chaos. As my parents descended from their compartment, there were shouts, screams, shrieks, sobs, tears, and hysterical laughter. There were hugs, kisses, caresses, cries, incoherent questions, and incomprehensible answers. While all this outpour of emotion was going on, I stood shyly on the side, watching the others with interest but also a certain detachment. My parents appeared to me to be strangers, vaguely familiar strangers, but strangers nevertheless. After our initial embrace, in which I displayed some reserve or even uneasiness, they turned to their relatives and friends, talking excitedly about what had been and what would be, about how they had missed them, how they had waited for this day so longingly, and how glad they were to see them all again.

Do you still remember that wonderful trip ten years ago to Cracow, or maybe it was Lublin or maybe Bialystok, and what fun we all had?

Do you recall that lovely party at so-and-so's which we all enjoyed so much? And whatever happened to that nice fellow or that charming girl who had once been such a devoted friend of ours? While they were all laughing and crying, reminiscing and storytelling, I became slightly bored and a little impatient. What did all that excited conversation have to do with me? Who were all those people they were talking about with such pleasure and animation? I wished they would get it over with, so we could all return home.

My wish was granted after about a quarter of an hour, although it seemed much longer than that. Little by little the hubbub began to subside, the tone became quieter, the voices grew calmer and more sub- dued. Another procession of taxicabs took us back to my grandfather's apartment, and there the celebration of the wanderers' return contin- ued around the long wooden table in the dining room. The center of attention was, as usual, my mother. It was almost as if she had never been away. She picked up where she had left off five years before, jok- ing, teasing, laughing, charming, telling funny stories, and describing, probably with some embellishment, various interesting experiences she had had. The role of the entertaining raconteuse was the one she liked best, whether on or off the stage. And the others seemed to like it as well. They smiled, they nodded, they laughed at the right moments, and they shook their heads in sympathy or surprise or amusement. They were captivated.

As for my father, he sat quietly at one corner of the table, impassive, reserved, and taciturn, as if nothing unusual had been happening. He had decided, probably from force of habit, to avoid any display of emo- tion. But then his feelings got the better of him. The chatter and laugh- ter around the table, which had been stimulated by my mother's skill as a storyteller, suddenly began to subside. Family members started to nudge one another, to point as unobtrusively as possible in the direc- tion of the corner chair, and to look at each other meaningfully, raising their eyebrows as a sign that something unusual was taking place. That something was the spectacle of my father succumbing at last to the real- ization that his long separation from his family, especially from his only son, was now over. The strange, introverted man had tried so hard to hold back, to appear unmoved or even indifferent to what was going on. The struggle against himself proved too much, however. He finally had to give up. He took out his handkerchief, dabbed his eyes with it, and began to cry softly. The animated conversation around the table became subdued or ceased altogether. No one had ever seen him cry before. It was a rare peek behind the curtain of impassivity with which he usually disguised his emotions.

As for me, this initial encounter with my parents was something of a revelation. It showed me how different they were from one another, in personality, character, temperament, and outlook. She, the pretty, lively, mischievous, outgoing charmer, always eager for attention and praise, seemed the exact opposite of the silent, aloof, withdrawn, and stern loner who never felt comfortable with people, who was often critical of others and always dissatisfied with himself. The only thing the two of them had in common was their interest in culture, especially the theater.

That interest was what had brought them together in the first place, and it remained almost the only topic of serious conversation between them. They used to talk quite often about the people they had met in their profession, the writers, dramatists, directors, and actors with whom they had associated and worked. Yet their discussions did not deal solely with problems and experiences they had encountered in the theater. They would also exchange views regarding broader questions of artistic merit, the achievements, for example, of such and such an author or poet or playwright, non-Jewish as well as Jewish. Here there was a frequent meeting of minds. But otherwise they had almost nothing in common; they remained diametrically dissimilar in their tastes and habits. What saved their marriage from disintegration was their recognition of the differences separating them and their willingness to accept and live with those differences.

There was something else about my parents which I began to sense almost immediately after their return. I had assumed that once we were reunited, I would become the apple of their eye, the chief object of their interests and concerns, perhaps the only object. They would be asking me constantly how I felt, how I was doing in school, whether I was hungry or thirsty or tired, and whether I wanted to go outside and play or stay inside and read. Those had been the usual subjects of my grandmother's inquiries. Only my parents would be less gruff and crabby; they would display their affection for me more openly. They would hug me and stroke me and kiss me and tell me how much they loved me. Life with them would not be very different from what it had been before, but it would be nicer and cozier.

I soon discovered, however, that those expectations had been unrealistic. Not that my parents were mean or surly. On the contrary, they were always kind and often affectionate, especially my mother. Not only did they scold me very rarely, but they never used spanking, even

gentle spanking, as a form of discipline. That was against their principles. In fact, they instructed my grandmother, who had fewer scruples
in this regard, not to employ physical force as a means of punishment.
Still, while I appreciated their enlightened views on child rearing, I was
also disappointed to discover that my welfare and happiness was not
their only concern. They had other interests as well, interests which
were almost equally important to them.

For example, they would talk constantly about theater engagements,
about new plays being written or old plays being revived, about friends
currently appearing on the stage, and about rivals who were enjoying
greater success than they really deserved. Occasionally I would even
meet some of the people they had been talking about, mostly actors or
directors or playwrights. I would be introduced to our guests, I would
say how glad I was to meet them, as I had been taught to do, my parents would say a few nice things about me, that I was bright perhaps or
cute or well-bred, and then I was expected to withdraw so that the
adults could continue to engage in serious conversation. The day-to-day
supervision of my activities was left, now as before, to my grandmother.

In short, almost immediately after the reunion with my parents I
began to sense that my earlier assumptions regarding what my future
life would be like were mistaken. Not only did I recognize intuitively
that my parents were mismatched and that their professional aspirations outweighed their domestic interests. I also received soon after
their return concrete confirmation of what had at first been only a
vague suspicion or surmise. I had previously imagined that they would
shower me with gifts far rarer and richer than any I had ever received.
I had even boasted to my chums, and had almost convinced myself,
that they would bring me a motorcycle, although I would have been
willing to settle for something a little less cumbersome. Actually, what
I received was rather modest. A few days after our reunion, while my
parents were still unpacking the huge steamer trunk they had brought
with them, they presented me with a pair of roller skates and a small
picture or sketch which, when viewed fixedly and unblinkingly, was
supposed to produce the image of a famous American aviator. I had
been taught enough manners to know that I should thank them for
their generosity. And yet I cannot deny that I felt a little disappointed.
What had ever happened to that motorcycle I had been expecting?

To make matters worse, I learned a little later, in the course of a conversation between my parents, that they had acquired those presents for
me quite incidentally, almost as an afterthought. The cigarettes my

father used to smoke in America—Chesterfields, I believe—were sold with a coupon attached to each pack. The smoker who accumulated a certain number of those coupons could exchange them for some unpretentious gift, a decorative vase, for example, a kitchen utensil, a children's toy, or a household appliance. That was how I happened to become the owner of the only pair of roller skates in Otwock. To be sure, my knowledge of how they were obtained did not interfere with my enjoyment of them. Although I never became an expert skater, I did manage to weave, wobble, sway, and teeter on my skates, while the other children on the block watched in wonderment and envy. That was satisfying. And yet my pleasure was diminished by the realization that the process by which I had gotten that gift had been so commonplace.

This realization also affected my view of the second present, even more modest and less impressive than the first. I owed that present as well to my father's smoking habit and his assiduous collecting of Chesterfield coupons. It consisted of a picture of a man's face in black and white, but with the usual pattern of colors reversed. That is, the face itself was black, while the eyes, the hair, and the outlines of the features were white. The identity of the subject was unrecognizable. But if an observer gazed intently for about a minute, without blinking, at the three white dots in the middle of the subject's nose and then looked at some white surface, a ceiling, for example, or a whitewashed wall, he would, at least according to the statement on the back of the picture, see the face of Charles A. Lindbergh in conventional black and white.

The brave young aviator, who two years earlier had become the first man to complete a solo flight across the Atlantic, was not as famous in Poland as in America, but his remarkable achievement was generally known throughout the Continent. What mattered to me, however, was not what Lindbergh had achieved, but whether I could see his face on the ceiling after looking long and hard at the nose in the picture. Here I met nothing but frustration. I would look from the picture to the ceiling and then back to the picture and then back again to the ceiling. To no avail. All I could see was the same unidentifiable face with the three dots on its nose. Some of my friends insisted that they had been able to recognize "Lucky Lindy" in clear outline. Others said that they thought they had seen him, although they did not sound very sure. And still others, I suspect, merely pretended to have seen him. But as for me, it was no use. No matter how hard I tried, all I could see were the same smiling, familiar, and yet unrecognizable dark features. It was just another of several disappointments I experienced after the reunion with my parents.

Still, I must not exaggerate the extent of those disappointments. My grandmother explained to me—and I accepted her explanation, though not without some inner reservations—that my parents would love to spend more time with me. But they were so busy, they had to work, they had to earn a living in order to support me and the rest of our family. And they did in fact become involved in several theatrical projects and ventures almost immediately after their return. My father in particular, acting as business agent for both of them, was away from Otwock a great deal of the time, planning, discussing, investigating, and negotiating. He was constantly in touch with various people in his profession, with actors, dramatists, directors, and producers, usually in Warsaw, but sometimes also elsewhere in Poland, and occasionally even in one of the other countries of Eastern Europe.

I remember in particular his account at the family table of a trip he had recently taken to Romania, either to perform there or to make arrangements for some future engagement. He spoke disparagingly about the artistic tastes of the theatergoers in Bucharest, Jews as well as non-Jews. Many of them were coarse or even vulgar. What they were looking for on the stage was little more than an off-color skit, a risqué story. They also seemed to enjoy musical reviews displaying a bit of flesh, like those in Paris, but without the Parisian charm or piquancy. As for the loftier aspirations of dramatic art, they appeared to have little appreciation of those. I listened attentively to my father's indictment of the Romanians, curious, disapproving, but faintly titillated.

During his brief stays in Otwock he would rarely display affection toward me, and almost never when others were present. He was as reserved with his son as he was with his wife, his mother, or his sister. Aloofness had become a deep-rooted part of his character. And as for playing ball with his son, engaging in athletic competition with me, participating in my games, or joining in my pranks, that was simply unthinkable. At that time it would not even have occurred to most fathers in Europe. Egalitarian chumminess between parent and child was still an almost exclusively American phenomenon.

Nevertheless, when friends or colleagues were present, he would sometimes praise me, though with restraint, or even boast of my precocious academic learning. On one occasion, for example, he asked me to demonstrate to some visitors how much I knew by naming all the czars of Russia beginning with Catherine the Great. That was no problem for me. Proud as peacock, I rattled off the names, each in proper order. But then my luck and my knowledge ran out. Someone asked me which Russian ruler had freed the serfs. This posed a serious dilemma. I could of course have admitted that I did not know, but it might have diminished the admiration I had just earned by naming all those Romanovs. Deciding to live dangerously, I blurted out with my fingers crossed that it was Czar Paul who had been the liberator of the Russian peasantry.

As soon as I said it, I could see that my gamble was not going to pay off. There was a brief, embarrassed silence in the room, and my father began to look a little crestfallen. Then everyone seemed to recover, the guests started to smile once again, a few of them even made friendly, reassuring comments, and I was gently informed that the right answer was Alexander II. I did manage to regain some of the lost ground by correctly identifying the commander of the victorious Russian army in the war against Napoleon in 1812 as Field Marshal Kutuzov. But from that day on I was less cocky regarding the breadth of my learning, while my father became more cautious about showing off his child prodigy.

My relationship with my mother was entirely different. She, unlike my father, had no difficulty displaying her emotions. Indeed, she liked to display them, preferably in the presence of others. To her the line separating the theater from life was very thin; sometimes it disappeared altogether. She embraced her new role as mother with the same intensity, the same feeling of personal involvement and identification, with which she performed on the stage. She would hold and hug and caress and kiss me, in public as well as in private, perhaps even more in public, repeating over and over again how hard it had been for her to be separated from her only child, how she had longed to be reunited with me, and how happy she was now that we were together at last. Those witnessing these displays of motherly love seemed genuinely moved.

As for me, I was of course delighted to have suddenly become the object of such lavish affection. No one had ever shown so much love for me before, neither my grandmother nor my aunt and certainly not my father. It was a completely new experience, a joyful, a delightful experience. I began to feel more like the other children I knew. I was getting at last as much attention from my mother as they were getting from theirs, perhaps more.

Yet I could not overcome a vague feeling of uneasiness, a certain sense of insecurity. Some of it may have been simply the result of being unaccustomed to effusive displays of affection. Not even my playmates received such frequent or such ardent assurances and reassurances of maternal love. But there was more to it than that. I sensed almost from the outset that I was not the only object of interest and concern in the life of my parents. They had other pursuits, other goals and ambitions, in which I played no part. Those other pursuits, moreover, were very important to them, almost as important as I was, maybe just as important, maybe—and that was the most troubling thought—more important. That my father was generally preoccupied with his professional problems more than with his domestic responsibilities had become clear to me quite early. I had almost come to accept it as an unalterable reality, a fact of life. But I could not become reconciled to the seeming contradiction between my mother's constant declarations of love for me and what I sensed was her persistent longing to be with other grown-ups, to amuse, attract, perform, and bask in the limelight. I found that disturbing. Perhaps my feeling was nothing more than childish jealousy or possessiveness, but I believe even now that it was probably not without some basis in fact.

I can still remember one evening in Otwock when a group of visitors from Warsaw—friends, colleagues, and relatives, most of them actors, directors or playwrights—gathered on our veranda for snacks, drinks, stimulating conversation, and a good time. I was of course banished to the interior of the house so as not to interfere with the fun which the adults were going to have, but I could catch glimpses of them out there, talking, laughing, nibbling at the cookies, and sipping their drinks. They seemed to be enjoying themselves enormously. And there in the middle of it all was my mother, pretty, charming, vivacious, and coquettish, the center of attraction, as usual.

When bedtime came, my grandmother helped me undress, wash, and climb into bed. And then she beckoned unobtrusively to my mother on the veranda to come and lull me to sleep, as she used to do almost every evening when in Otwock. She came into the room a little breathless, a little flushed, bright-eyed and radiant. Performing before an audience at a party was almost as exciting for her as performing on the stage. She hugged me, she kissed me, she told me an amusing little children's story, she even hummed Brahms's lullaby to help me fall asleep. And yet I was unable to shake off the feeling that she was anxious to get back to the gathering on the veranda, get back to charming her guests, to winning their attention and their admiration. I closed my eyes and began to breathe heavily, as if in slumber. I heard my mother get up softly and tiptoe out of the room. A few minutes later her voice reached me from the outside, joking, laughing, teasing, and captivating. I remained awake for a long time, not really sad or unhappy, but reflecting uneasily on my relationship with my newfound parents and wondering what my future life with them would be like.

Some of those vague disappointments which had begun to trouble me were no doubt inevitable. My hopes and expectations had been so inflated, so unrealistic, that no parents could have lived up to them. In my imagination the loneliness and isolation I had previously experienced would now be compensated by a wonderful new life in a never-never land in which I would be the sole object of the attention, admiration, and love of my parents. Such wishful anticipation was bound to end in sobering disenchantment. Even in a family more conventional than mine, the everyday realities of earning a living, running a household, shopping, cooking, cleaning, and enjoying an occasional moment of rest or recreation would have made the realization of my expectations impossible. That roaring motorcycle from America was never more than a childish dream. A pair of roller skates or something like it was really as much as I could reasonably expect.

The reunion with my parents, moreover, even if it did not live up to all my exaggerated hopes, had a clearly beneficial effect on me. Once I recognized and came to terms with the realities of our relationship, I began to emerge from the self-absorption in which I had spent so much of my childhood. I never became outgoing or assertive. I never became a leader in the games and escapades of the children in our neighborhood. But at least now I was ready to take part in them. Now I felt more like my playmates, who had been raised by their mothers and fathers, not their grandmothers and aunts. I grew a little more confident, a little more secure. I soon overcame the habit of twisting and pulling my hair in moments of preoccupation. And as for my digestion, so sluggish and unpredictable for almost five years, suddenly it became more or less regular. Those were all signs, some obvious, others indirect or disguised, that the return of my parents had helped me overcome, in part at least, a previous state of vague but persistent tension.

Most important, however, was the feeling that even if the reunion with my father and mother was not everything I had hoped for, a great change was about to take place, a change for the better. In a few months, in a year at most, they would take me to America. And there I would have a new start. Everything would be much, much nicer. My grandmother would not be there to take me to school or to the barber for a haircut or to the tailor for a jacket and a pair of short pants. Katia would no longer be around to help me tie my shoelaces or make sure my underwear was clean. All of that would become the exclusive responsibility of my parents, especially my mother. It would bring us closer together, strengthen our relationship, make us more of a family. In that fabled land of boundless opportunity, we too would become transformed and uplifted. All the expectations which had remained unfulfilled in Poland would be realized in America. It all seemed so exciting. I could hardly wait to get started on that great journey to the legendary, fascinating West.

Chapter 7

Leaving the Titanic

That year which elapsed between my reunion with my parents and our departure for the United States, the last year of my childhood in interwar Poland, seemed to me to drag on endlessly. Almost as soon as they arrived, I began to look forward to packing my belongings—my toys, my books, my tin soldiers, and my newly acquired roller skates—and sailing across the Atlantic. But they appeared to be in no hurry. And so, while they were lingering and dawdling, the days turned into weeks and the weeks into months. I just could not understand it. What was taking so long? What were my mother and father waiting for? Why couldn't we just buy three tickets, take the train from Otwock to Warsaw, from Warsaw to Paris, from Paris to Cherbourg or Le Havre, and then an ocean liner to New York? It was so simple. I even asked them once or twice why we couldn't hurry up, but they sounded vague, evasive, or faintly annoyed at my importunacy. I concluded that it would probably be best to restrain my impatience.

Actually, there were good reasons why my parents were so slow about returning to the United States. The reunion with me had not been the sole purpose of their visit to Poland. They had also planned to undertake a few theatrical tours like those in which they had participated years before with the Vilna Company. That was why they were away from Otwock so much of the time. I am not sure where in Eastern Europe they appeared or what their repertoire was. But the delay in our trip back to the United States was partly a result of their desire to perform one more time, for the last time, as it turned out, in the cultural environment which had shaped their careers as actors.

Their tours did not prove an unqualified success, however. They coincided with the great Wall Street crash of 1929. And while the economic depression which followed did not have the same disastrous effect on the Yiddish theater in Europe as in America, its consequences were serious enough. The brilliant flowering of secular Jewish dramaturgy was now coming to an end. People who found it difficult to pay for necessities like food and rent became increasingly reluctant to spend their money on tickets to a play. My parents were thus among the first to feel the onset of hard times. I know little about the details of any financial reverses they may have suffered, but I remember hearing my mother complain later that while they had been able to afford cabin-class accommodations on their trip to Europe in the summer of 1929, on their return trip to America a year later they were forced to travel tourist-class. It was the beginning of a bitter decade of hardships and disappointments for them.

Ill-fated theatrical ventures, however, were not the only reason I had to wait so long in Otwock for that exciting crossing of the Atlantic. There were also important decisions to be made regarding the future of the other members of our household. First of all, what should be done about my grandmother? The poor woman had already been forced to go through three major migrations in barely ten years: from Lithuania to Poland, then from Poland to Germany, and then from Germany back again to Poland. Where was she to go now? That was not an easy question.

My parents would probably have been willing to take her with them to the New World. There she would have been able to continue playing the role of surrogate mother. She would have seen to it that I got up on time, washed and dressed, had a healthy, nourishing breakfast, and got to school before the bell rang. Those were duties with which she was quite familiar. My parents, on the other hand, recognized very early that leading an actor's life had not prepared them for the burdens of child rearing. They rarely went to bed before two or three in the morning, and they almost never got up before ten or eleven. During a theater engagement they really had no choice. The performance would usually end close to midnight, and then they would need two hours, sometimes more, to remove the makeup, wash up, change clothes, chat, relax, enjoy a glass of tea, and maybe occasionally have something a little stronger. But even during the off-season, when they had more leisure and greater flexibility, their schedule remained pretty much the same, simply out of habit. How then could they suddenly be expected to assume full responsibility for the care of a young boy who was barely ten? The obvious answer seemed to be my grandmother.

Unfortunately, the American immigration authorities did not see it that way. They insisted that the laws regarding naturalized citizens were perfectly clear. I as a minor child had become a citizen of the United States at the same time as my parents, before even setting foot on American soil. But the provisions pertaining to the parents of naturalized citizens were not nearly as generous. My grandmother would have to add her name to the long list of would-be emigrants from Poland and then patiently wait her turn. That might take years, perhaps even a decade, perhaps more. Obviously, some other solution had to be found.

What about my uncle Max? He was living in the Soviet Union, in Moscow, I believe, gainfully employed, seemingly contented, exchanging letters occasionally with his mother, and even sending her a few rubles from time to time as a token of his enduring affection. Could he not be asked to take her in and look after her in her old age? His brothers and sisters, and that meant mostly my father, would surely be willing to contribute something toward her support. But that idea too was eventually rejected. Life in Stalin's Russia seemed too unpredictable, too precarious. Who knew what the future might bring? There might be economic crises, political upheavals, domestic uprisings, or international conflicts. And besides, how would my grandmother feel about living with Max? He seemed to have become completely assimilated, without any attachment to the Jewish community. His wife was in fact Russian, and that meant that their son could not, according to the orthodox religious law which my grandmother scrupulously observed, be considered a Jew. Would she not feel isolated, alienated from her new environment, even more so than in Berlin or Kückelheim? No, a resettlement in the Soviet Union would not work.

That left only Paris, not a bad option, all things considered. To start with, two of her daughters already lived there, having emigrated from Lithuania in the early 1920s. Rivke planned to move there as well, even before my parents and I left for the United States. My grandmother would thus be cared for by members of her family, by people willing to look after her, willing to offer her help, encouragement, comfort, and support. More than that, a sizable colony of East European Jews had settled in Paris after the First World War, concentrated in a few neighborhoods which she would find quite congenial. There she could meet people very much like her, with similar experiences, views, attitudes and beliefs. She would find an environment not very different from that of Otwock. And then there was the appeal of Paris itself, a glamorous, fascinating city, tolerant, sophisticated, and fun-loving. How could anyone feel bored there? It seemed an ideal place for spending the last golden years of life.

My grandmother agreed to this arrangement, though not without some qualms. She recognized that her new social position, whatever the attractions of the French capital, would be far below her previous one. In provincial Otwock she had been a member of the patriciate, despite her lowly origin. She had been a houseowner, a landed proprietor; she had been the employer of a maid and a handyman; she had been able to play the generous benefactor and gracious philanthropist. Most important, she had enjoyed a princely income of a hundred dollars a month. So what if she had never received a formal education? What if she spoke only broken Polish? Who cared that she did not dress in the latest fashion? Who cared that her manners were not always the most polished? The important thing was that the economic resources she commanded had won for her a place in a small-town elite.

Now all that would change, and she knew it. She would become just another elderly retiree dependent on the support of the younger members of her family. It would not be a life of hardship, but it would be an empty, a purposeless life, without direction or goal. There would no longer be a household to manage, a rent to collect, a servant to supervise, or a grandson to care for. Instead, she would get up in the morning, wash, dress, eat breakfast, go for a walk, sit on a park bench, and occasionally converse and commiserate with fellow superannuates. The prospect was bleak and discouraging.

Yet my grandmother did not grumble, she did not complain. She remained to the end the self-possessed, tight-lipped, impassive matron. She felt that it would be beneath her dignity to bemoan her fate, whine and whimper, or indeed display any emotion at all. She left for Paris shortly before our departure for the United States, still seemingly calm, seemingly unruffled. She must have found saying good-bye to me very difficult, however. After all, she had really my mother almost from the time I was born. She had nursed and nurtured, fed and clothed me. She had seen me grow from a helpless infant into a lively, thriving schoolboy, almost an adolescent. And now it was over. We were about to part, perhaps never to see each other again. How could she not have been saddened? But she kept her feelings to herself. Our parting was quite brief, almost perfunctory. She left for her exile still proud and composed, her head held high. There was something remarkable, almost heroic, about that stoical old woman resolutely clinging to her independence, no matter what.

For Rivke the imminent change in her life was not as difficult. She was still young, barely twenty, energetic, ambitious, and adaptable. For her a new existence in Paris had its attractions. She would be reunited with her two older sisters whom she had not seen in ten years. Her mother would be there as well, still offering advice and guidance which Rivke would now be free to ignore. Even more important, there would be new friends, new associations, new interests, new attachments. She would find a job, acquire a skill, learn to support herself, in short, she would become independent. That prospect was a little disturbing, but also challenging and appealing. And then there was always the spell of Paris, the city of light, elegance, and gaiety. A young woman could face moving there more readily than an elderly widow.

Still, Rivke must have recognized that her new life would present serious difficulties as well. She had never acquired much schooling. When she was a child, her parents could not afford to provide her with formal instruction, and when she became an adolescent and could afford it, she found it tedious and distracting. There were, to be sure, private tutors who would come to the house from time to time, yet the knowledge they imparted was intermittent and unfocused, mostly a hodgepodge. Rivke had acquired little academic learning and even less occupational skill. That made no difference as long as she lived in Otwock. There her position in high society did not depend on intellectual accomplishment. But once she had to start thinking about migrating to Paris, the problem of how she would support herself became serious.

Little by little she learned to accept the decline in social status which she now had to face. In fact, her position in the *haut monde* of Otwock had been diminishing for almost two years prior to her departure from Poland. First there had been that awful fire which not only destroyed our home but reduced our prominence as well. Yet more damaging still was the general knowledge that before long my parents would be returning from the United States. Once that happened, their financial support for my grandmother would be decreased, perhaps even withdrawn. And that meant that Rivke's charms began to pale. She was no longer welcomed with the same cordiality into the company of the daughters of well-to-do families. She was no longer regarded with the same interest by the fashionable young men-about-town. The worldly, sophisticated bachelors who had traveled or said they had traveled to Turkey, Greece, France, and Spain started to find her less attractive. She ceased going to her favorite cafés as frequently as before. She ceased looking forward to the afternoon tea dances with the same eager anticipation. Her world was now beginning to change.

Rivke tried to adapt to her altered circumstances by returning to her earlier cultural interests. She could no longer provide a suitable meeting place for amateur theatrical groups dedicated to Yiddish dramaturgy. The modest size of our apartment made that impossible. She did, however, renew her friendship with some of the young men and women whose artistic ideals she had once shared, but whom she had then neglected in her search for more distinguished company. They came generally from a lower-middle-class or even working-class background. Yet most of them had managed to acquire a fairly broad education, partly by attending evening classes, partly by studying on their own. There could be no doubt about the genuineness of their commitment to learning and culture. What they lacked in social elegance they made up by their sincere devotion to intellectual pursuits.

Rivke found among them more than companionship and understanding. She also found a suitor. He was a far cry from those superior young men who had once shown an interest in her and in whom she in turn had been quite interested. Her new friend was a person of simple background, a tailor by occupation, I believe, but well-read, well-educated, and deeply interested in both Polish politics and Yiddish culture. He and Rivke had first met a few years before, when he attended the meetings of a dramatic club over which she presided. At that time a closer relationship between them had been out of the question. Their social differences had been too great. But now, in her new straitened circumstances, the two of them came to know each other much better. There were frequent meetings, long walks, frank conversations, whispered confidences, and eventually declarations of love. Shortly before Rivke was to leave for Paris, they announced their engagement. They had decided to travel from Poland together and get married as soon as they got to France. They would face the future side by side, as husband and wife.

This plan was put into effect almost at once. My recollections of the good-bye to Rivke are even vaguer than of the good-bye to my grandmother. The relationship between the two of us had never been very close. She regarded me as a usurper, I suspect, as an ingratiating little rascal who had stolen her mother's love. I in turn sensed her resentment; it made me feel vaguely uncomfortable in her presence. Thus our separation did not cause either of us any profound sorrow. On the contrary, the truth is that we were both secretly relieved.

As for Rivke's life after she left Poland, I learned about it only in bits and pieces, through casual remarks by relatives and friends of the family or through occasional allusions in the conversation of my parents. Apparently she and her fiancé got married almost as soon as they arrived in Paris. When I visited my grandmother fifteen years later on a three-day pass from the army shortly after the war in Europe ended, she told me in considerable detail, without any prompting on my part, about the circumstances of Rivke's marriage. It seems that she had warned her daughter in the strictest terms against "going to the hotel" until the wedding ceremony had taken place. But that advice had been ignored. The young couple had in fact anticipated their marriage by "going to the hotel" a few days before its solemnization. That still evoked bitter condemnation on the part of the widowed mother.

I was a little puzzled by her persisting outrage at a transgression which had occurred so long ago, a transgression which had been rectified almost as soon as it had been committed. Did it really matter now, more than a decade later, that the young couple had "gone to the hotel" shortly before getting married instead of waiting? After all, the important thing was that they did get married. But to my grandmother what Rivke did was a violation of a strict religious commandment; it was sinful and immoral. Yet could there have been more to it than that? Could she, a widow for such a long time, have been secretly or subconsciously expressing a vague feeling of envy toward a daughter who was about to enter the state of matrimony? Perhaps.

I know even less about Rivke's life after her marriage. Apparently both she and her husband found employment in the clothing industry, she as a dressmaker, he as a tailor. It was not an easy existence. They earned enough between them to live in modest comfort, but they had to be very careful with their expenditures. There was no room for any extravagance. For Rivke the experience of proletarianization must have been hard, psychologically even more than economically. Only a few years earlier she had been an elegant young lady mingling with the high society of Otwock. Now she was an ordinary seamstress living in a lower-class district of Paris, working in a crowded shop, performing common household chores, and carefully counting her pennies. It was quite a comedown. She soon became even more stern, sullen, and disgruntled than in Poland.

Not only that, Rivke quickly developed a radical social conscience. Previously, as member of a small-town patriciate, she had felt no qualms about having a maid to make the bed and a gardener to mow the lawn. That had seemed to her part of the natural order of things, providentially ordained and immutable. Nothing could be or should be done about it. But once she herself became part of the working class, she changed her mind. All her bitterness, all her resentment at the precipitous decline in her social position turned against the class system which she held responsible for that decline. Why should the capitalists rake in the profits, while the workers toiled for a pittance day after day? Why should the rich live in luxury, while the poor hungered and suffered? Was that fair? Rivke moved farther and farther to the left; she became increasingly vehement, increasingly aggressive, increasing militant. She ended up an ardent supporter of the Communist Party.

But the member of our household who had to face the greatest hardship was Katia. Rivke after all had two older sisters to help her adjust to her new situation. She had a husband to share her troubles and disappointments. She had her mother with whom to reminisce about the years of poverty in Lithuania and of prosperity in Poland. She was not alone. Nor did my grandmother have reason to feel abandoned. She may no longer have been the well-to-do matron of Otwock. She may no longer have enjoyed the social prestige of houseownership and landlordism. But at least she knew that her future was secure, that her children would support her, that she could spend her last years in tranquility. For Katia there was no such assurance. For her our departure was an unmitigated disaster. She would now be all alone. She knew little Polish and no Yiddish; she was neither Catholic nor Jewish; she belonged neither to the national majority in Poland nor to any of the organized ethnic minorities. To whom then could she turn for help? What charitable organization would offer assistance to an alien, an outsider, a total stranger? Katia faced a catastrophe.

She did have a son somewhere in Russia, but he had never been in close touch with her. Even if he had wanted to help, there was not much he could do. That left only God. Katia had been taught by bitter experience that it was futile to cry, lament, plead, or beseech. It would do no good. Instead, as the dreaded day approached, she began to retire behind the curtain in the corner of the kitchen even more frequently than before, kneeling before her icon and praying ardently, almost desperately. Perhaps that helped a little. Shortly before we left, my parents gave Katia a bonus or going-away present of a few hundred zlotys, about thirty dollars. That was all the assistance she ever received. There were no mandatory old-age pensions in interwar Poland, no social security checks, no government welfare payments. Our farewell was brief and rather perfunctory, without embraces or tears. But I still think of Katia from time to time, wondering what happened to her. I think of her with almost the same sudden pang of sorrow with which I remember those others about whose fate I am better informed.

There was one member of our household, however, who viewed its approaching dissolution not with fear or regret but eager anticipation. To me what was about to happen seemed so inviting, so enticing. I knew that I should be sad about my imminent separation from my grandmother and my aunt, who had cared for me since I was a baby. I knew that I should feel mournful about having to say good-bye to relatives and friends I might never see again. I even knew that the future would not be all rosy, that there might be times when I would feel lonely or bewildered or homesick or out-of-place. But it was no use. No matter how hard I tried, I could not make myself suffer the grief which adults assumed I was suffering and which I told myself I should suffer. Cheerfulness kept breaking in.

I did experience now and again a vague uneasiness at the thought of leaving the comfortable, indolent existence I had led in Otwock. But those momentary doubts were quickly overcome by the knowledge that in a few months, and then in a few weeks, I would be crossing the ocean, I would be arriving in one of the great cities of the world, I would be starting a new life full of excitement, adventure, and fun. How could any boy of nine or ten have remained sad for very long with a prospect like that?

Before we left Poland, I tried to prepare myself for what was to come by learning as much as I could about the New World. I had acquired some information from my visits to Mr. Slawin's library, especially from reading Karl May. But as the day of our departure drew closer, I began to feel increasingly that I should know more. What was life really like on the other side of the Atlantic? And what were the people over there like? What were their customs, tastes, interests, attitudes, and beliefs? I realized that knowing all about Old Shatterhand and Winnetou would not be quite enough. I needed to learn more about the ordinary, every-day experiences of living in the United States. And so I began to seek information from those who knew something about America, preferably through direct observation, by having lived there. And that meant that my chief mentors in this process of extraterritorial Americanization were, in ascending order of importance, my father, my mother, and Boris Auerbach.

Perhaps that is not quite fair to my father. He did in fact answer to the best of his ability almost all of my endless questions, directly and correctly as a rule. But he never elaborated, never embroidered, never digressed. He was brief and businesslike, always to the point. When asked, he would tell me that it took about a week to cross the ocean, that the Wild West was no longer as wild as in the old days, and that New York was much bigger than Warsaw, although he was not quite sure by how much. And then, after succinctly providing me with the information I was seeking, he would return to the more pressing business at hand: a new play in which he was planning to appear or a theatrical tour he was hoping to organize or a meeting he had arranged with some director or impresario. As for me, although I appreciated his summary descriptions of life in the United States, I was also a little disappointed. What he had to say sounded rather ordinary, even drab. Was that really all there was beyond the Atlantic? No, I refused to believe it. There had to be more.

My mother made up for my father's stubborn matter-of-factness. She more than made up for it. To her, talking about her experiences in New York was even more gratifying than talking about her experiences in Berlin or Paris or London. Impressing others, amusing them, surprising them, captivating them, that was of far greater importance than mere dry, factual accuracy. And so she would improvise, decorate, dramatize, and glamorize. In her depictions America became a land of boundless opportunity and limitless wealth, a land of allure, challenge, novelty, and adventure. Those of us living in Eastern Europe could not possibly imagine what life beyond the ocean was like. We were too much the creatures of custom and tradition. As my mother's audience became more and more enraptured, the contrast between New-World marvelousness and Old World stodginess would widen and deepen.

One incident in particular stands out in my mind. It was inspired by the sight of my grandmother one day darning some socks which I had worn out. To me that was just an ordinary occurrence. I had often seen her or Katia mending old clothing: shirts, pants, socks, gloves, coats, and underwear. But to my mother here was an opportunity to return to one of her favorite themes. In the United States, she declared with a touch of superiority, no one ever darned socks. Old socks which had holes in them were simply thrown away and new ones were promptly purchased to replace them. This information impressed all of us, especially me. In every family I knew, even in well-to-do house-holds, old clothes were routinely repaired, sometimes over and over again. That in the United States socks were thrown away as soon as they developed a single hole seemed an extraordinary extravagance, a sign of boundless riches. I marveled at such a display of wealth.

In short, while my father's America was simple and ordinary, rather like the small town in Lithuania in which he had grown up, only bigger, my mother's America sparkled and glittered, infinitely exciting, challenging, and enticing. It was an Eldorado, a never-never land; it was the Shakespearean "other Eden, demi-paradise." And then there was still a third America I encountered long before I actually landed there, an America quite different from the other two. That was the America of Boris Auerbach.

I met Boris Auerbach for the first time about a month or two after my parents returned from the United States. I remember one morning hearing my father tell my mother, with an unmistakable hint of irritation in his voice, that he had just received a letter or telegram from that "crazy" Auerbach announcing that he had arrived in Poland and that he would be visiting us shortly. My mother received this news quite casually, almost with indifference. "Is that so?" she said, or something like that, calmly continuing with whatever she had been doing, as if the information did not really interest her very much. But something in her manner and her voice suggested that the nonchalance was at least partly feigned.

A few days later a droshky drove up in front of our house, one of those horse-drawn carriages for hire which served as the chief means of transportation for well-to-do residents of Otwock, since taxis were not only few and very expensive, but they would generally refuse to travel on unpaved streets for fear of getting stuck in the mud or between ruts. In the back of this particular droshky sat a tall man about forty years of age, neatly dressed, in a suit, coat, fedora, and spats, with a kind and friendly expression on his face, his dark hair carefully combed from one side over the top of the head to the other side, so as to cover a balding spot in the middle. He leaned out of his seat, looked at me with a warm smile, shook my hand, and said in good Polish, though with a slightly foreign accent: "I am Uncle Boris and I am very glad to meet you." That was my introduction to a man who was to remain close to me and my parents for the next thirty years, sometimes as a frequent visitor, sometimes as a member of our household, and always as almost a blood relative. And we in turn were to become his surrogate family.

Boris Auerbach was an actor on the Yiddish stage, like my parents. Yet he and they were entirely different, not only in their professional skills and ambitions, but in their personal backgrounds and experiences. I never learned much about his family or childhood. He did not like to talk about his early years. Although I gathered that he had been born in Odessa, I do not remember ever hearing him mention his parents. I surmise from occasional remarks by my mother, who knew much more about him than either I or my father, that he had been abandoned by them while still very small. I doubt whether he ever knew who his father was, and as for his mother, she either died or left him early in his childhood. He was apparently raised by relatives or in an orphanage or perhaps simply on the street. It was a grim start in life for someone who, despite his upbringing or lack of upbringing, always remained kind, genial, and surprisingly cheerful.

Shortly before the First World War, when he must have been about twenty, Auerbach came to the United States. I never found out what he had been doing before he left Russia, what had made him decide to emigrate, where he had gotten the money to pay for his passage, and what sort of job he had found upon his arrival. But it is clear that not long after crossing the Atlantic he went through two important formative experiences, one of which determined his attitude toward his new homeland, and the other his choice of an occupation.

The first was his service in the United States navy during the war. When hostilities between America and Germany broke out in the spring of 1917, Auerbach was drafted, sworn in as a member of the armed forces, and trained to become a sailor. He was suddenly taken out of the familiar, cozy environment of the Lower East Side of Manhattan to which he had by then become accustomed. Now he had to live among strangers, almost none of them Jews, almost all of them native-born, many of them contemptuous of greenhorns, and quite a few of them anti-Semitic. The change must have been very unsettling for the recently arrived young immigrant.

The year or two Auerbach spent in the navy had a lasting effect on the way he regarded the United States. He soon learned to stand up to the "tough guys" he encountered in the service, the rowdies, bullies, brawlers, and blusterers. They were not really very different from the "hooligans" and "bandits" he had often met on the mean streets of Odessa. But dealing with them also led him to conclude that to be a real, red-blooded American you had to learn the manly art of self-defense, you had to be quick on the draw. America was no country for mama's boys, for the timid and squeamish, for those who read or meditated or spent too much time in a hammock. In America you had to be tough.

The second decisive influence in Auerbach's new life was the Yiddish theater. As a young man in Russia he had not been much interested in the stage. Even if he had been, he was far too poor to do anything about it. But that changed after he arrived in New York. Here he became a devoted theatergoer, then an amateur performer, and finally a professional actor. Still, he was never a devotee of the new "serious" Yiddish dramaturgy which my parents found so appealing. He never aspired to perform in the plays of Asch or Hirschbein or Ansky. He was basically a song-and-dance man; he had no desire to be anything more. Tall, handsome, ingratiating, and endowed with a pleasant tenor voice, he felt most at home in musicals and operettas. Even here he never received any formal training. Although he would sometimes appear in solo performances holding a musical text in his hand and glancing at it from time to time as if to refresh his memory, my mother once confided to me that actually he had never learned to read notes. His strong points were a nice voice, an agreeable manner, good looks, charm, humor, and affability. For an actor such assets can be of considerable importance.

I don't know how my parents first met Auerbach. Perhaps they were introduced by some director or playwright in the Café Royal. Or perhaps they became acquainted while appearing in neighboring theaters on Second Avenue. Or maybe they got to know each other at one of the meetings of the Hebrew Actors Union, to which almost all performers on the Yiddish stage in New York belonged. In any case, Auerbach soon became a frequent visitor to my parents' apartment, then a close friend, and eventually an intermittent member of our household. He had no relatives in the United States, no acquaintances from the Old World, no family of his own. He did get married during a theatrical tour of South America to a young woman who had also emigrated from Russia and had settled down with her mother in Rio de Janeiro. But the union was not a happy one. The two were quite incompatible in their tastes, temperaments, and aspirations. That was probably why they never had any children. Not long after their marriage they separated but remained reluctant to get a divorce. For the next thirty years there were periodic reconciliations and renewed attempts at marital coexistence, each followed by another lengthy separation. Thus for Auerbach my parents became a surrogate family, a substitute for the domestic life he had never really known.

When they returned to Poland in the summer of 1929, he promptly followed. The ostensible reason was a contemplated theatrical tour of Eastern Europe, but I strongly suspect that he was also driven by a need to be close to my parents, especially my mother. He found a small furnished apartment in Warsaw or perhaps even in Otwock, I forget which. But I do recall that he spent a great deal of time with us. He soon developed, moreover, a genuine interest in me, in my education, and especially in my readiness to face the profound changes which were about to take place in my life. Maybe he saw in me the son he had never had. He would tell me stories about America and Americans, what they were like, what they thought, what they did, and above all, what they would expect from a young newcomer to their country. I listened in rapt attention. Except for the novels of Karl May and the movies starring Douglas Fairbanks and William Boyd, Boris Auerbach became the most powerful single influence in the process of Americanization which I underwent before ever leaving Poland.

Still, he was not content merely to describe to me the wonders of the New World. He felt that he must also prepare me for its demands and challenges. Specifically, I would have to be taught to confront the bullies in American schoolyards and playgrounds with the same boldness which he had displayed when confronting the bullies in the American navy. And that meant that I had to master the fine art of boxing. I eagerly agreed. Why should I not learn to subdue villains, just like those daring heroes I had read about in books or seen on the silver screen? And so, two or three times a week Auerbach and I would square off in the living room of our home for a test of strength and skill.

We would start by warily circling one another for a few moments, and then Auerbach would take the offensive. He would weave and bob, he would jab with his left, and then deliver a gentle uppercut with his right. He would tap me on the nose or the cheek or the chin or the chest. And all the time he would be exhorting, challenging, urging, and encouraging me. But I could do nothing except flail wildly with both arms in a determined though futile effort to strike at my opponent. I simply lacked the timing and the cool, calculating craftiness required for success in the ring. It soon became apparent that my career as a pugilist would end like my career as a violinist or a Talmudist. I was just not cut out to be a Jack Dempsey any more than a Jascha Heifetz or a Maimonides.

The denouement came only a few weeks after my boxing instruction began. We were going through a typical lesson, Auerbach bouncing back and forth, challenging me to try to hit him, and I vainly attempting to land a blow, becoming more and more frustrated. And then it happened. Hoping to provoke me to greater pugilistic ardor, he hit me on the nose a little harder than usual. The pain was not very severe, but in combination with my growing feeling of futility it led to a most unathletic display of emotion. I burst into tears. As for my opponent, he appeared quite disconcerted by this sudden TKO. He had never expected our sparring session to end like this.

But worse was still to come. My mother in the next room, hearing me sobbing, rushed in and, seeing what had happened, tried to comfort me with gentle hugs and soothing words. Then she turned to Auerbach, who was by then completely crestfallen, and told him calmly but firmly that there were to be no more boxing lessons. He readily agreed. As for me, this tacit acknowledgment of my pugilistic limitations came as both a disappointment and a source of relief. It did represent an admission that I might not be able after all to stand up to the youthful rowdies on the sidewalks of New York. But at the same time it freed me from the burden of trying to acquire an athletic skill for which I clearly had little talent.

Still, if I could not achieve Americanization by my own efforts, I could at least bask in the reflected glory of those who did. I would therefore accompany my mother and Auerbach on their frequent evening walks along the main streets of Otwock. My father, always the loner, never comfortable with people, preferred to stay home reading or writing or meditating. But for my mother, being with others, even with strangers, even in a crowd, was almost a necessity. She could not stand being alone for very long. And so she and Auerbach, who acted as her more or less permanent escort, would saunter through the fashionable part of town talking animatedly in English, while I walked a few paces ahead of them, puffed up with pride at being in such distinguished and glamorous company.

The three of us would attract a great deal of attention, not only from well-dressed strollers, shoppers, and patrons of outdoor cafés, but from bedraggled vagrants, beggars, tramps, and drunkards along the way. They would all look with curiosity at that elegant, foreign-looking couple conversing in a strange language and at that smiling, strutting little boy who was their companion. They would stare, whisper, point, and sometimes even turn around to gaze at the unusual sight. And I loved it. To be the center of attention, the cynosure of all eyes, gave me a feeling of importance which I otherwise rarely experienced. It was almost as good as being a champion boxer, maybe better.

I know now that those evening walks which my mother used to take with Auerbach, and especially those lively conversations in English, were designed primarily to impress the natives, to create an air of sophistication and exoticism. Actually, she and my father almost never spoke English in the United States. Their command of it always remained limited. And that still continues to puzzle me. They had after all mastered several other languages without difficulty. My father could speak, in addition to Yiddish, fluent Russian and passable Polish and German. My mother's linguistic accomplishments were even more extensive. She felt most comfortable in Polish, more comfortable in fact than in Yiddish. But she had also been required to learn Russian in school, she had acquired German in the war years during the occupation of Warsaw, and she had been taught French in the *gimnazjum* she attended. Why then did my parents find it so difficult to learn English?

The only explanation I can think of is that they never really felt at home in the New World. They found the way of life there strange and alien. They saw themselves as intruders, as outsiders, except perhaps on Second Avenue. They remained to the end stubbornly, incorrigibly, ineradicably European. Their inability or unwillingness to master the language of America probably reflected a feeling of profound estrangement from American life.

All of that was of course unknown to me during those evening walks through the streets of Otwock. I knew only that we were the center of attention, that we excited wonder and respect. I did not find it strange that my mother should be conversing in English. After all, she had lived in the United States for five years. What could be more natural than her speaking in the language of her adopted country? I did not even find it surprising that her escort on those walks was not my father but Auerbach. If her husband did not enjoy sauntering, chatting, looking into store windows, and sipping wine or liqueur in a café, why should she not choose someone to accompany her who did? It all seemed to me quite understandable.

But not everyone was as broad-minded as I. Some people, especially family members and close friends, began to wonder, to speculate, to whisper, and to gossip. Why did Bella spend so much time with that Auerbach? Why didn't Shneyer object to his frequent visits to our home? Was there perhaps something improper in their relationship? Could it be that Shneyer was unaware that an intrigue might be going on behind his back? And if he was unaware, shouldn't someone tell him? The rumors and suspicions grew and multiplied,

I later learned, until they came to be widely accepted as probabilities or even certainties.

Shneyer, however, refused to listen. He knew about the rumors which were circulating, about the conjectures and speculations. Yet he was too proud and too upright to lend them any credence, at least not openly. Still, he must have had his moments of doubt; he must have wondered occasionally whether all those conjectures were entirely baseless. His behavior toward Auerbach, though courteous and correct, was always cool. Auerbach in turn, sensing that my father was not entirely free of suspicion, remained polite but distant. The two had little to do with one another. They never engaged in casual chitchat; their infrequent conversations focused almost exclusively on professional concerns and problems. Each was basically uncomfortable in the other's presence, one because of a vague jealousy, the other because of a vague guilt. They tried to avoid each other as much as possible.

Many years later my father told me that his mother had asked him one day, in a low voice and with a knowing look, whether he knew that Auerbach was visiting his wife almost daily. Was that really prudent? What would people say? Shouldn't he perhaps talk to Bella about the frequency of those visits? But he rejected her suggestion indignantly. He could not bring himself to say anything to my mother which might imply that he distrusted her. That would be demeaning to both of them. A marriage had to be based on mutual confidence and respect. To admit that he had suspicions about her loyalty would be unworthy of him and insulting to her. No, he refused to question her conduct, even cautiously, even indirectly. There was something righteous and honorable, something almost noble, about that strange, lonely, silent introvert.

And yet, was there in fact an intimate relationship between my mother and Auerbach? I can't be sure, but I doubt it. Admittedly, the two of them must have found each other's company comforting. They were both gregarious and outgoing, both eager to mingle and socialize, both dissatisfied with their marriages. My mother must have recognized very early that she and my father were altogether different in their tastes and temperaments. To be sure, thanks to him she was able to realize her most cherished ambition, she was able to enter the world of the theater. But otherwise they had very little in common.

My father certainly did not share my mother's hunger for the life of the artist, for glamor, excitement, freedom, and bohemianism. This discovery must have been very hard for her to accept. She had thought

that being married to one of the stars of the Vilna Company would be
an unending adventure, a perpetual succession of performances, recep-
tions, celebrations, and parties. It would be so different from the predictable, uneventful existence in her parents' home on Gesia Street.
Instead, she found that her husband was in his own way just as staid,
just as sober and conventional, as her father and mother. She began to
feel that life had tricked her.

Auerbach's situation was similar. He too had sought in marriage an
escape from an existence which he found lonely and unsatisfying. But
his wife was as different from him as my father was from my mother.
She was not interested in the theater, not even the unpretentious musical stage on which he appeared. She felt uncomfortable and out of place
in the company of actors, playwrights, and directors. The two became
increasingly dissatisfied with their marriage, increasingly dissatisfied
with the incompatibility of their personalities and outlooks. Soon there
was a separation, then a brief reconciliation, then another separation,
then another brief reconciliation, and so it went for more than thirty
years. They never divorced. They both continued to hope that maybe
someday they would learn to get along, to understand one another, to
help and support one another. Yet though that hope was never realized,
neither was willing to abandon it. In the meantime, during the long
periods of living apart, each tried to find companionship and understanding elsewhere.

That was how my mother and Auerbach became friends. They each
wanted someone to talk to, to walk with, to gossip, reminisce, joke,
and visit the Café Royal with. But could there have been more to it
than that? Could their friendship have turned into mutual attraction
and eventually into physical intimacy? Probably not. They may have
experienced moments of covert or suppressed desire, an occasional
longing or craving which was more than platonic. But I don't think
there was any infidelity in the strict sense. What Auerbach wanted
most was a sense of closeness, a feeling of belonging, rather than
amorous fulfillment. And my mother, though lively and flirtatious,
would probably have been reluctant to betray her husband in his own
home, almost in his presence. I don't believe therefore that there was
ever any improper relationship between them. But that is admittedly
only a guess on my part.

In any event, all the rumors and speculations were soon silenced by
the piecemeal dissolution of our household. The approaching departure of my parents for America meant that those who had been part of

it would now have to start a new life elsewhere. The first to leave was Auerbach, who had by then become almost a member of the family. His return to the United States, however, did not mean a permanent separation. Far from it. He had simply decided that, since we were about to leave anyway, and since his theatrical tour of Poland had not proved very successful, he would go back to New York earlier than planned and wait for us there. In fact, once we were reunited, he resumed his familiar role in that strange tricornered relationship which constituted nearly, though not quite, a *ménage à trois*.

The next to go was my grandmother. The arrangement which had been worked out was that she would move to Paris, where two of her daughters, Esther and Hanke, were already living, and where she would soon be joined by a third daughter, Rivke. She therefore left for France about six weeks before we left for America. I have only vague recollections of our parting. But there were no tears or lamentations, no endless kisses or lingering embraces. It was all quite brief, almost casual.

In my case that was perhaps understandable. I was about to embark on a glorious adventure, on a new existence full of challenge and novelty. How could I then be expected to shed tears or assume a sorrowful expression? My grandmother's situation was different. She was about to lose a grandson who had become her son. She was about to be deprived of the duties and responsibilities which had given her life a sense of direction. She would henceforth be an elderly widow in retirement, enjoying a measure of financial security, surrounded by children interested in her welfare, but living without purpose or vocation, sitting on some park bench, waiting for the end. She knew all that, and yet she refused to show any emotion, she refused to voice her concern or bewail her fate. She remained impassive, as always. There was a brief farewell, a quick kiss, a word or two of advice and admonition, and she was on her way.

Then it was Rivke's turn. A month after my grandmother's departure, she and her fiancé left Otwock for a new beginning in Paris. Our good-byes were even more perfunctory than those a few weeks earlier. Rivke never really liked me, and I in turn sensed her resentment and reciprocated her dislike. But at least she could face the future with greater confidence than my grandmother. She was still young, her life was just starting. She would surely find a job in Paris, she would get married, she would have a family, she would form new friendships and associations, she would embrace new beliefs and convictions. Her future was by no means grim.

Indeed, even before leaving Poland, she had almost completed her transformation from a fashionable, well-to-do young lady of high society into a class-conscious, militant member of the proletariat. She now complained more and more about the excesses of capitalism, the exploitation of the workers by the bourgeoisie, and the unending, rapacious pursuit of wealth by the propertied classes. She was only a step or two away from becoming an ardent Marxist. And those last few steps were taken shortly after she arrived in Paris. Yet that same rebelliousness of hers, that militancy and assertiveness, helped her later survive two years in Auschwitz and live to be almost ninety.

The last member of our household to leave was Katia. For her the future was much more ominous than for the rest of us. My grandmother would at least live out her remaining years among people who cared for her. Rivke was young enough and strong enough to adjust to a new, alien environment. As for me, what could be more exciting than discovering the New World, just like Christopher Columbus? But for Katia there was nothing; she was all alone. To make matters worse, she had no illusions about what awaited her. Yet, like my grandmother, she showed little emotion as the day of our departure approached, except perhaps by praying before her icon even more fervently than usual. When the time came to say good-bye, she dabbed at her eyes once or twice, there was a faint sniffle, a shy, cautious embrace, and then it was over. Although I never saw or heard of her again, I still think of her from time to time. Like the others left behind, she must have suffered a great deal in the years following our departure.

As for my parents and me, shortly before sailing for America we took the train to Warsaw for the last time. I have no recollection of my farewells to friends and acquaintances in Otwock, whether children or adults. I was probably too excited by the wonders waiting for me beyond the ocean to think much about personal ties which were about to be severed. I simply couldn't wait to set out on that great journey. I do remember my last meetings with relatives and friends in Warsaw, though in most cases only faintly. Three of those good-byes, however, are still fresh in my memory even after seventy years.

First, I recall my parting from a young boy my own age whom I had gotten to know rather casually in the course of my visits to my grandparents' home. His name was Jurek Gabinet. His mother, a pleasant, attractive, but tense and nervous woman, was a good friend of one of my aunts. Her husband, whom I never met, worked as a traveling salesman or business representative, so that he was almost always on the road. At least that is what I was told. Perhaps he and his wife were really separated, which would help account for her chronic nervousness. As for Jurek, he had been brought up to be or at least to behave like a little Polish aristocrat. He would always walk upright, shoulders back, chest out, with a military precision. When introduced to an adult, he would advance a few steps, then halt, stand at attention, bow slightly, and announce in a brisk staccato: "I have the honor of introducing myself. My name is Jurek Gabinet." If the adult happened to be a lady, he would bend down and gallantly kiss her hand. It was all quite impressive. I admired that elegance of his, that sophistication and savoir faire. But more than that, I secretly envied him. Why couldn't my grandmother have taught me those aristocratic manners instead of wasting my time on violin lessons and a futile struggle to master Hebrew prayers?

When the time came to say good-bye to Jurek, he behaved with his usual aplomb. He entered the living room of my grandparents' apartment briskly, looked me straight in the eye, advanced toward me, put his hands on my shoulders, faintly touched each of my cheeks with his lips, like a French general awarding the *Croix de guerre* to some war hero, and then stepped back, shook my hand, did an about-face, and stiffly marched out. That was the last time I saw him. Yet he remains among those about whom I still think from time to time. What happened to him after we left Poland? I wonder. Did his elegant manner and aristocratic bearing help him later escape the horrors of ethnic mass murder? Probably not.

My farewell to Hala, my favorite aunt, was less formal. She remained kind, affectionate, and cheerful right up to the moment of parting. There were kisses and embraces, but no tears, no sighs, only good wishes and assurances of love. She even asked a friend of hers whom I had gotten to know, a young man in his late twenties or early thirties, to join us in our good-byes. His name was something like Matthias. He and Hala held similar views regarding life and culture; they moved in the same social circles; they may even have been more than just friends, although that is merely a conjecture. I do remember, however, that he and I had become quite chummy. He told me that he too had once wanted to be a sea captain. Perhaps he still did. He too hoped to visit and explore various exotic parts of the globe. He had even read Karl May and admired Old Shatterhand, just like me. We seemed to have a great deal in common.

Now Matthias and I decided that my departure for America should not be allowed to end the friendship of two such kindred spirits. With

Hala's help we drafted a solemn agreement to remain in touch and continue exchanging experiences, achievements, hopes, and aspirations. She made copies of the document on her typewriter, drew a drop of blood from each of us to smear on the paper as evidence of the seriousness of our resolve, and witnessed our signatures at the bottom. Then we parted, a little sad, but also inspired and uplifted in spirit.

In contrast, my farewell to Jadzia, the eldest of my mother's seven sisters, was very depressing. That proud woman, always so proper, so dignified, had by then become almost a helpless cripple. A progressive disability whose exact nature was never explained to me, probably some form of arthritis, had made it difficult for her to walk and nearly impossible to use her hands. She had tried all sorts of remedies and therapies to halt the progress of her illness. On the recommendation of one of her physicians, she had even spent a year in Egypt, hoping that the hot, dry climate would help her. But nothing seemed to work. She became progressively weaker.

By the time I left Poland it had become clear to everyone, including Jadzia, that she was not likely to recover. She would probably have to spend the rest of her life dependent on the good will and financial support of her family. That cruel reality had been very hard for her to face. When we met for the last time, there were no tears, no hugs, no lingering good-byes, no declarations of undying devotion. She gave me a quick embrace, a peck on the cheek, and a book which she had helped edit years earlier while working for a publishing house. I still remember that pained expression on her face as we parted, a mixture of sorrow, bitterness, and resentment. Here I was, about to start out on an exciting new life, while her own was slowly coming to an end before she had even reached middle age. I never saw Jadzia again.

On the following day my parents and I left Gesia Street for the last time and took a taxicab to the main railroad station in Warsaw. This time, however, there was no crowd of relatives and friends to see us off, like the one which had greeted my father and mother on their arrival from America a year earlier. There were only a few members of the family and a handful of devoted well-wishers. I recall our getting into a train compartment, I recall kisses being thrown, handkerchiefs fluttering in the air, and arms waving back and forth in gestures of farewell. Then the locomotive started and we were on our way. That great adventure for which I had been waiting so long, so eagerly, so impatiently, had finally begun.

The sense of excitement I felt as we were leaving Warsaw wore off very quickly, however. Once we got beyond the limits of the city, the landscape became monotonous, nothing but fields, meadows, pine woods, and occasionally some small provincial town. Our compartment was not uncomfortable, but there was no place to take a nap, no cot or bunk, only two adjoining unoccupied seats which were not nearly as cozy as my bed in Otwock. I dozed fitfully. I remember vaguely the Polish border officials and then the German ones opening the door and asking for our papers. I have a somewhat better recollection of an hour's stopover in Berlin late in the evening, and how my father took me to the station restaurant and ordered in surprisingly good German a bowl of pea soup for my supper. Then another, even longer bumpy ride, another, mostly unsuccessful attempt to sleep, and another routine inspection by border officials, this time German and French, asking to see our passports. Finally, late the following morning we arrived in Paris, where we were to spend a few days resting, enjoying a reunion with my father's mother and three sisters, and waiting for the departure of the liner which would take us to America.

It was during this visit that I met two of my aunts for the first time. The older one was Esther, who had left Lithuania about a decade earlier. She was a little shy and retiring, I remember, but kindly and genuinely interested in getting to know the little nephew she had never seen before. I was also introduced to her husband, another emigrant from Eastern Europe, and to her son, a few years younger than I, who had been born in France. That first meeting of ours was also to be the last, however. All three of them perished in the course of the Second World War.

During our brief stay in Paris I also met my aunt Hanke, a little younger than Esther and quite different in personality and temperament. She was lively, outgoing, and jovial, though also capable of sudden outbursts of temper, as I was to discover later. Still single at the time of our meeting, she married a Frenchman shortly before the war, thereby changing her legal status from immigrant alien to French citizen. That change saved her from the fate which Esther was to suffer. I enjoyed talking to her, but she seemed less eager than her sister to spend much time with me. And who could blame her? A pretty, vivacious young woman must have found more interesting things to do in glamorous Paris than chatting with her little nephew.

In any event, to me the introduction to relatives I had never met before was not nearly as memorable as the reunion with those I had known almost from the time I was born. I must admit that the prospect of seeing Rivke again was not exactly thrilling. But the meeting with my grandmother promised to be joyful and heartwarming; I looked forward to it with great anticipation. Yet in fact our reunion was something of an anticlimax. Both she and Rivke assured me that they were so glad to see me, so happy that we were together again. They asked me how I was and how I felt. They petted me and patted me and stroked me and even embraced me from time to time. Still, I could feel that our relationship had somehow altered in the month or two since we had said good-bye in Otwock. Our lives had diverged, our prospects and expectations had changed, and now no amount of hugging or reminiscing could bring back what had been. The ties between us had become transformed, no longer uniting members of the same household, the same family, but linking mere relatives. The difference was subtle yet unmistakable and profound. Our separation became a reality for us not in Poland but in France. That was when we finally recognized that what would henceforth divide us would be much more than an ocean.

Actually, the most enjoyable part of my visit was a brief but delightful tour of Paris. My guide was my newfound aunt Esther. No one else was both able and willing to show me the sights. My grandmother knew even less about the city than I. Rivke was herself only a recent arrival, and quite apart from that, the prospect of spending a whole day with me exploring Parisian landmarks did not seem to excite her. She felt that she had already done more than enough for me during the previous ten years. And as for Hanke, she had other interests, social, cultural, and romantic, to which she preferred to devote her spare time. That left only gentle, kindly Esther, who assumed the task quite willingly. My parents did not accompany us. They had been to Paris before. Besides, they were not sightseers or explorers at heart. What interested them was the world of the theater, the cultural milieu, the artistic environment, and the cafés where actors and literati congregated. Mere buildings, monuments, statues, and boulevards left them indifferent. And so just the two of us, Esther and I, set out one morning to explore the City of Light.

The tour lasted only a few hours, but I still remember looking in fascination at the marvels of Paris. They seemed even more spectacular than the architectural splendors of Warsaw. Esther led me to the Arc de Triomphe, she showed me the obelisk in the Place de la Concorde, she pointed out the Cathedral of Notre Dame about which I had read quite a bit in Mr. Slawin's books, she guided me across the Place de l'Opéra, and she even walked with me for a block or two along the magnificent

Champs Élysées. It was all so interesting. But what I recall most vividly is the Eiffel Tower, the famous landmark which I had often heard described while still in Poland. Esther even agreed to take me up to one of the elevated platforms, from which I could get a clear view of the surrounding parts of the city. Like many foreign visitors to Paris, I was deeply impressed, probably overimpressed. I returned from our tour in a state of high excitement, eager to tell my parents all about the sights and experiences of that day. They listened politely and patiently, but I could tell that they did not share my sense of wonderment. They had already seen the Eiffel Tower.

Our stay in Paris lasted barely a week. Early on the morning of the day we were to embark for America, we took a taxi to the railroad station, where a train was waiting to carry us to Cherbourg. Our leave-taking was even shorter and simpler than the one in Warsaw a few days earlier. There were no sad relatives to see us off, no fond well-wishers like those who had accompanied us to the station when we left Poland, not even a handful. All the good-byes had been said the previous evening or earlier that morning. A few embraces, a few hurried kisses, brief assurances of lasting affection and enduring remembrance, and it was over. We went our separate ways, some to the daily routine of a job, others to the crossing of an ocean, but all of us sensing that, even if we did see each other again someday, this was a final farewell.

The train ride to Cherbourg was much shorter than the one to Paris, only about four or five hours, and our stay there was shorter still. But boarding the ship turned out to be far more complicated than I had imagined. The SS *Leviathan*, which was to take us across the Atlantic, was not sitting patiently at the dock waiting for us. Her chief port of embarkation was Southampton on the other side of the English Channel. Since only about a hundred or so additional passengers were to be picked up in Cherbourg, she remained anchored offshore, while we were all put aboard a lighter to be ferried over to the giant ocean liner.

I remember the departure quite clearly. It was evening before the lighter, packed tight with passengers, finally left the pier. And then, after a few minutes, as we rounded the long jetty guarding the inner harbor and entered the open sea, I suddenly beheld an extraordinary sight. There, about a mile in front of us, a gigantic black structure seemed to rise out of the depths of the ocean. It was enormously wide and appeared to be several stories high, almost a skyscraper. Rows upon rows of bright lights streamed out of round little windows on the side of the structure, revealing its outline and illuminating the surrounding waves.

At the top were four huge funnels emerging from what looked like a white shed. I gazed in amazement, openmouthed. As we approached the giant, a flimsy, wobbly gangplank emerged from its side, the gangplank was attached to our lighter, and we were then invited to enter the belly of the beast. The short crossing seemed quite perilous, since our pathway was swaying from side to side. But slowly and hesitantly, in twos and threes, we managed to complete the passage without a single loss. I must admit, however, that I was a little frightened, and I suspect that I was not the only one. But at last we were ready to start our journey across the Atlantic.

The *Leviathan* was at that time one of the largest passenger ships in the world, perhaps the largest. I was also told, though I cannot vouch for the accuracy of this information, that she had been built in Germany and had then been acquired by an American company. More important, once I got aboard, my stay proved on the whole quite satisfactory. Our cabin was situated deep inside, below water level, in tourist class. The Great Depression, which was to hasten the end of the Yiddish theater, had already begun, and my parents were feeling its effects. But I was not aware of that. Nor did the fact that the cabin had no porthole trouble me. Why should I care? What mattered was that it seemed very comfortable, equipped with a double bunk for my parents and a small but neat cot for me. There was even a sink with hot and cold running water and a flushing toilet. And if that was not enough, a few doors away was a large room with a bathtub as well as a shower which the passengers were free to use throughout the day. To me there was simply nothing to complain about.

The crossing itself, which lasted six days, was uneventful and, frankly, rather dull. What was a young boy to do all that time? I was exposed for the first time to American cooking, which I found nourishing though bland and a little boring. To tell the truth, I have never been entirely able to overcome that bias. I did manage to withstand the worst effects of the seasickness affecting most of our fellow passengers. The dining room, which had been full the first day after we left Cherbourg, became emptier and emptier with each succeeding meal, until by the third day not even half the tables were occupied. Then there was a slow recovery, although a return to complete normalcy was not achieved until we were just outside New York harbor. As for me, except for a single bout of nausea, I suffered no ill effects. The big problem was what to do between meals. Walking around the deck in an endless circle soon became monotonous; lying in a deck chair absorbing the sea air was not much better; and playing shuffleboard provided only a brief diversion. After a day or two on board the *Leviathan*, I was eager to get to the New World as soon as possible.

The one experience which I found interesting, almost fascinating in fact, was watching the couples dancing in the lounge every evening. I had often listened to the music emanating from the tea dances in the fancy cafés of Otwock which Rivke attended, but I had never been allowed inside to see what actually went on. That changed on board the *Leviathan*. We impecunious passengers in the tourist class did not enjoy the same elegant forms of recreation as those in the two upper classes, but we did have a small lounge, a small dance floor, and a small orchestra of four or five pieces. Some of the youngsters would gather there after dinner to watch the adults seeking a little relaxation and diversion. I was even more interested in what was taking place than most of the others. I used to watch intently the couples dancing, the men in elegant jackets, vests, white shirts, and ties, the women in flowery dresses and high-heeled shoes, gliding about romantically to the tune of a foxtrot or a tango. It seemed so pleasurable, so satisfying. And as I watched them, I wondered secretly whether I too would someday be gliding across a dance floor with some pretty young woman in my arms. It would be so much fun. I could hardly wait.

But mostly I whiled away my time thinking of how exciting it would be to arrive in New York at last. A crowd would no doubt be waiting for us at the pier; there would be cheers, shouts, laughter, and rejoicing, perhaps even a band to welcome us. Yet here again the actual experience was anticlimactic. As we sailed into the harbor, many of the passengers, I among them, gathered on the deck to see the fabled Statue of Liberty. But to me the monument was a little disappointing, not nearly as impressive as the Eiffel Tower a week earlier. What did I care about huddled masses yearning to breathe free or the wretched refuse of a teeming shore? Going through the immigration process, moreover, an experience which many newcomers to America found trying but unforgettable, was in my case quite routine. It lasted only a few minutes. After all, I had already become a citizen of the United States a year earlier, before ever seeing my new homeland, at the same time my parents were naturalized. Now the government inspectors simply waved us through.

What I remember most distinctly about my arrival in the New World is the oppressive heat of that day in September. Still dressed warmly for a Polish autumn, I sweltered and perspired. Fortunately, we were able to find a taxi without too much trouble. Soon we were crossing the East

River and then heading for the heart of Brooklyn, where we would stay for a few days with my aunt Mushel, while my parents looked for a suitable apartment near their beloved Second Avenue.

That taxi, however, was carrying me away not only from the SS *Leviathan* and Manhattan's waterfront. It was also taking me from the world in which I had grown up. There were now new challenges before me, new experiences, new expectations, new aspirations. I was turning my back, almost deliberately, on my old way of life. My parents' ties to their relatives and friends in Europe were loosening as well. All three of us would soon forget those we had left behind. We would become pre-occupied with our own needs, our own problems. The tragedy of the Second World War helped remind us of what had been. Indeed, later we were to meet again some of the survivors of the horrors of genocide. Yet even then I remembered my childhood years only fitfully and infrequently. Perhaps I preferred not to remember them.

But now, in my old age, I think more and more of those among whom I lived seventy years ago. I think of them, I remember them, I see them before me more clearly than ever. "You are always with me," I would like to say to them. "You belong to me. You are part of my innermost being." Perhaps someday we will meet again in another realm, a higher realm, where the distinctions between the Old World and the New, between the past and the present, between the living and the dead are irrelevant or nonexistent. All of them will be there: my grandmother and Rivke, Jadzia and Hala, Katia and Kazia, Mr. Slawin and Mrs. Szwagerowa, Sewus Prager and Jurek Gabinet, and many, many more. There will be embraces, greetings, tears, laughter, reflections, and reminiscences of life long ago in a vanished world. Yet could that happen? Is it really possible? I can't be sure, but I certainly I hope so. I hope so with all my heart.

Index